SIMPLY GARDENING

How to Design, Plant and Care for Your Garden

Colleen Adam

Kathy Van Vliet

Illustrations by Lea Price   Edited by Janna Ollivier

Paradise Books

P U B L I S H E R S

Published by Paradise Books, P.O. Box 18634, Delta, B.C. V4K 4V7

Copyright © 1995 by Colleen Adam & Kathy Van Vliet

Editor: Janna Ollivier

Manuscript prepared by Colleen Adam and Kathy Van Vliet

Cover photograph © by Calen Darnel – Terra Images

Inset photograph © by Colleen Adam

Interior illustrations by Lea Price

Typeset & designed by The Typeworks, Vancouver, BC

Printed and bound in Canada by Best Book Manufacturers

First edition, 1995

Canadian Cataloguing in Publication Data

    Adam, Colleen, 1958–

      Simply gardening

      Includes bibliographical references and index.

      ISBN 0-9699243-0-5

      1. Gardening. I. Van Vliet, Kathy, 1958– II. Ollivier, Janna, 1959– III. Title.

    SB453.A32 1995   635.9   C95-910424-0

Orders or inquires to:

    Paradise Books

    P.O. Box 18634

    Delta, BC

    V4K 4V7

Acknowledgements

THE IDEA FOR WRITING this book has been slowly germinating in our minds for a couple of years, but it was not until we had the good fortune to gather the following group of talented individuals (all of whom share our love of gardening) that this labour of love finally took shape.

We extend our heartfelt appreciation to our editor, Janna Ollivier, who cheerfully guided us through the thickets of publishing and smoothed out our written wrinkles with professional flare and amazing tact!

Thanks are also due to our illustrator, Lea Price, whose extraordinary artistic talent clearly reflects her love of nature, and whose graphic contributions have lifted this publication from the ordinary to the sublime; to typesetter, Susanne Gilbert, for giving us expert advice on layout; to Vic Marks, for his time and professional advice on how to best bring this book to print; and to all the staff at The Typeworks, for their care and dedication. We also wish to thank our friends and fellow gardeners, Jean Archer, Albert Duynstee, Robin Gardner, Dr. Gerald Straley and Robert Wright, for taking the time to read through our manuscript and offer their suggestions on horticultural content and accuracy.

Lastly, but certainly not least, our deepest thanks and appreciation go to our ever-patient families, who cheered us on and upon whom we relied for support and understanding throughout!

Contents

About the Authors!

"A sensitive plant in a garden grew,
And the young winds fed it with silver dew,
And it opened its fan-like leaves to the light, And closed them beneath the kisses of night."

The Sensitive Plant, Percy Shelley (1792-1822)

THE CELEBRATED 19TH century poet, Percy Shelley, possessed a love of nature, and gardens in particular. Like Shelley, Colleen Adam and Kathy Van Vliet, both experienced horticulturalists, share a deep-rooted appreciation of the beauties of nature and the delights of growing a living tapestry of colour within their garden spaces. A love of gardening translates not only into the care of living things, but also into the desire to create a soothing and beautiful environment in which one can relax. Colleen and Kathy's book conveys this inspiration and offers the reader a practical step-by-step format on how to lend form and character to a garden by using shape, colour, imagination and common sense.

The authors have concentrated on showing the reader how to assess and plan a garden from the "ground" up. These pages are full of excellent advice on the *whys* and *wherefores* of plant selection, landscape design, garden and lawn maintenance, and pest, disease and weed control. All these topics are covered to aid amateur or experienced gardeners in creating a garden setting suited to individual taste and personal time requirements.

Colleen's love of gardening can be traced to fond memories of her grandmother's vegetable patch in Saskatoon, Saskatchewan, and the fat, juicy raspberries that grew in that delightful spot. In 1981, Colleen and her husband moved westward to Delta, British Columbia, where she continues to pursue her horticultural interests with a Master Gardener certification from the highly respected VanDusen Botanical Gardens in Vancouver and a diploma in Horticulture, majoring in design, from the University of Guelph in Ontario. Today, Colleen has her own Landscape Design and Horticultural Consulting business, *Adam's Eden*, in Tsawwassen, BC. Colleen has also appeared on Kathy's television show, *Gardening Tips*.

Born in Perth, Australia to Dutch parents and raised in Richmond, BC, Kathy is a horticultural addict of longstanding. Besides her scholarship in agricultural studies at the University of British Columbia, Kathy has a diploma in Landscape Horticulture from the British Columbia Institute of Technology in Burnaby, BC. As if that were not enough, she married Len Van Vliet, owner of *Sunnyside Nurseries* in Tsawwassen, BC, and is an indispensable contributor to the management of the business. Kathy is also a Horticultural Consultant in her own right and has her own television production that has aired regularly on the Delta Cable Channel since 1987. She has travelled to Europe on gardening tours for her show, and has featured her own and other notable local gardens. Kathy has also done horticultural broadcasting for Vancouver's CKLG Radio Station.

These two talented and dedicated women jointly speak at garden clubs, libraries, church societies and garden venues, such as at VanDusen Botanical Gardens in Vancouver, BC, and have now written this invaluable homeowners guide to gardening. I predict that this copy will soon become dog-eared with use, as you find yourself pouring over its pages in search of gems of gardening wisdom.

Janna Ollivian

Editor

Introduction to the Simply Gardening concept

Many of us lead busy lives, full of intense weekday activity and very few of us enjoy unlimited bank accounts. With less time and money to devote to leisure and travel, it becomes increasingly desirable to have a retreat to which we can retire, at a moment's notice, for peace and relaxation. What could be better than vacationing in our own backyards?

Welcome to *Simply Gardening*, a book written with you, the urban gardener, in mind. Within these pages, we present gardening as a stimulating blend of science and art. But remember, the most important rule in gardening is to have fun... so, allow yourself to be creative and courageous! Be willing to attempt new things and try keeping a garden diary or journal. It will provide an excellent reference tool for you, year after year, when it comes time to plant. It will also help you to keep track of seasonal and monthly changes, how individual plants thrive in the various microclimates of your garden, and keep you abreast of the garden chores that need to be done.

There are a few basics to explore before we get started. The *Introduction* deals with fundamental gardening principles that should be clearly understood before planting the first seed... climate and soil! The chapters that follow, show how to make appropriate plant choices and how to design and maintain a garden. Common gardening problems, and how to solve them, are also discussed.

As the title suggests, gardening should be a simple and enjoyable activity. Therefore, only plants defined as low maintenance and appropriate for residential gardens will be presented here. The plants featured are suited to the climatic and geographic conditions prevailing in zones seven and eight, and specifically to the Pacific West Coast region, where we, the authors, live. However, many of the species we have listed will also grow very well in zones five and six.

In keeping with our desire to encourage an environmentally sensitive approach to gardening, only horticultural practices deemed to be environmentally safe and appropriate will be covered.

Zones and Microclimates

This section is all about choosing the right plant for the right spot! Plant requirements can vary significantly and it is therefore important to understand the conditions prevailing within different environments, or microclimates, and how individual plants will react to these. Simply put, one should always analyse a site or solve a gardening problem from the plant's point of view.

The term zone refers to a specific climatic region. Canada and Britain both use the same "one through ten" zone classification system. Under this system, each zone is defined by common minimum temperatures and other environmental conditions within a specific geographic area. One represents the coldest zone and ten, the warmest.

Regions where the coldest temperatures range from -28°C to -23°C (-20°F to -10°F) fall within zones five and six. Minimum temperatures within zones seven and eight range from

Map of Pacific Northwest

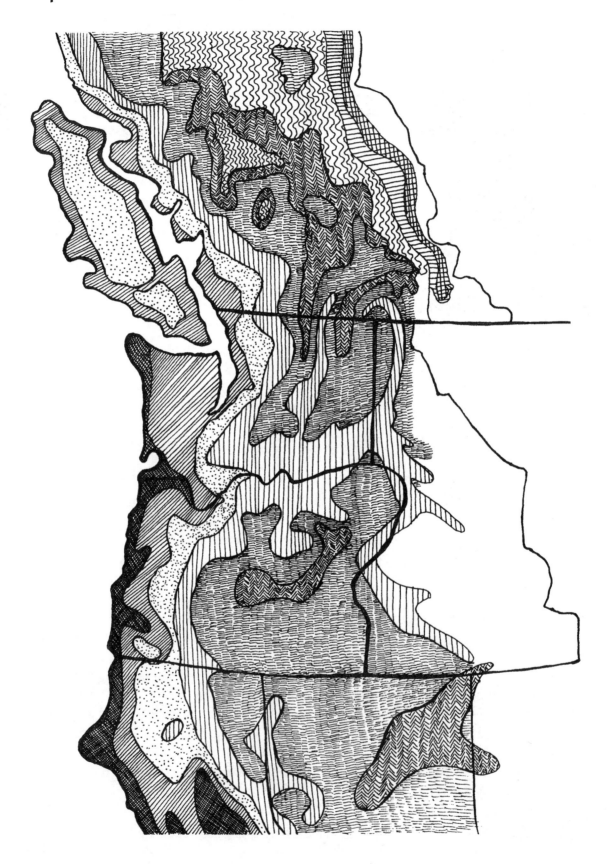

Average annual minimum temperatures

Zone 1
Below -48°C
(-50°F)

Zone 2
-46°C to -40°C
(-50°F to -40°F)

Zone 3
-40°C to -34°C
(-40°F to -30°F)

Zone 4
-34°C to -29°C
(-30°F to -20°F)

Zone 5
-29°C to -23°C
(-20°F to -10°F)

Zone 6
-23°C to -18°C
(-10°F to 0°F)

Zone 7
-18°C to -12°C
(0°F to 10°F)

Zone 8
-12°C to -7°C
(10°F to 20°F)

Zone 9
-7°C to -1°C
(20°F to 30°F)

Zone 10
-1°C to 4°C
(30°F to 40°F)

Map of North America

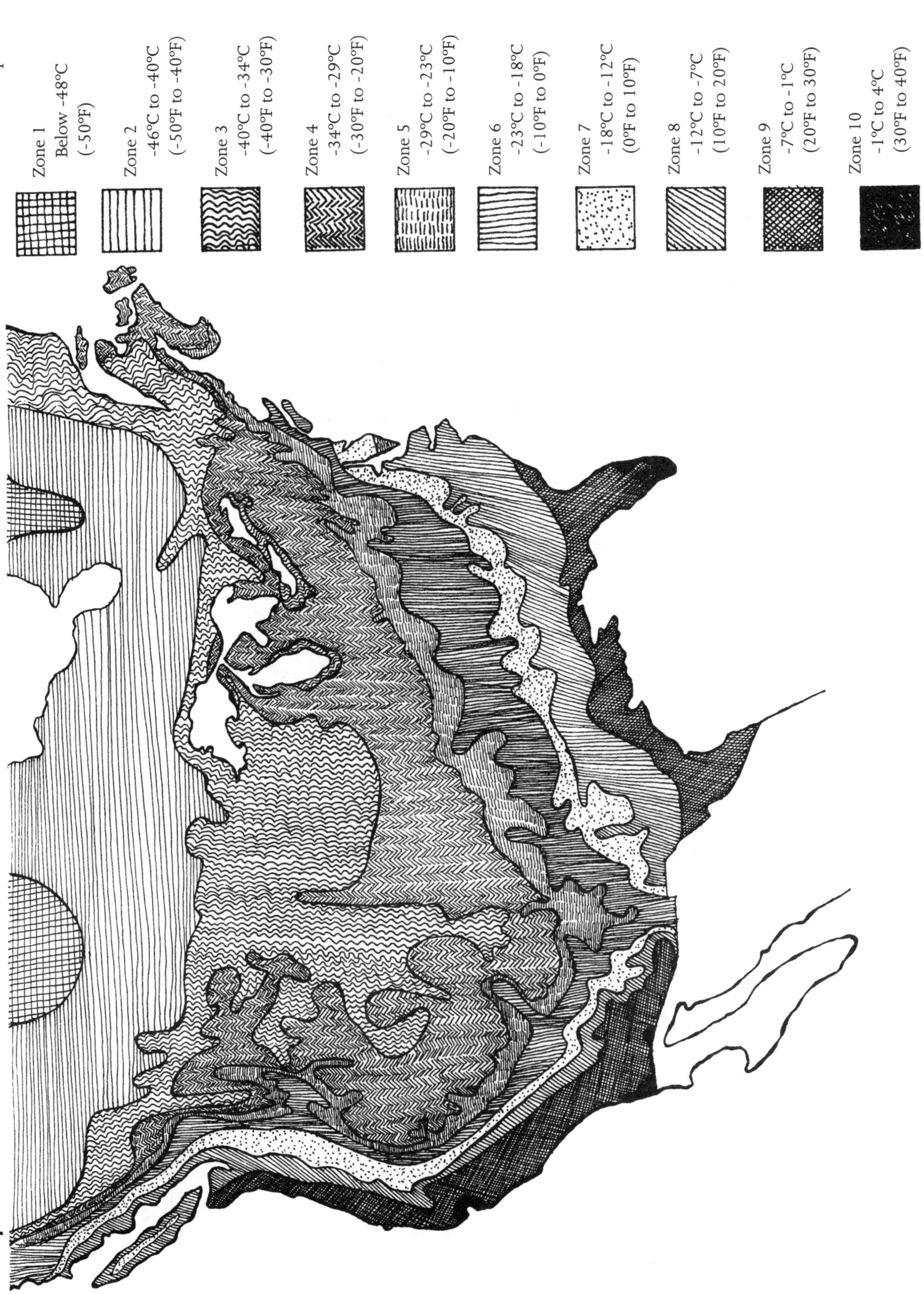

-12°C to -6°C (10°F to 20°F). This means that plants that are hardy to zone eight, or less, can be expected to survive typical winters within this zonal region. However, this does not necessarily take into consideration the type of soil or the amount of rainfall in any given area.

Although the growing zones may be the same, some plants will nevertheless grow better in some areas than in others due to a variety of factors. For example, *Rhododendron* thrives in the acidic soils and high humidity commonly found on the west coast of British Columbia, while roses (*Rosa*) grow better in the Portland area of Oregon State.

Before planting, be sure that the type of plant you choose will survive and thrive in your area. Generally, your local nursery sells plant stock that will grow in your area, but some plants will be hardier than others. For example, if you live in zone eight, in an open area where harsh winds blow all winter, you should purchase plants that are hardy in zone seven. However, if you have a sheltered spot, next to a heater or outdoor hot tub, you may be able to successfully grow a less hardy plant. For example, a windmill palm (*Trachycarpus fortunei*) or an evergreen magnolia (*Magnolia grandiflora*) could grow well under such conditions, lending your garden tropical ambience.

The limited area directly surrounding a plant, is termed a *microclimate*. All plants have a preferred microclimate and you can unintentionally or intentionally alter it by simply adding a fence, hedge or a tree. Whenever you add or take away a feature in your yard, the microclimate for the plants growing in that area will change somewhat. Therefore, it is important to understand your plants' requirements and the effect of changes to their environment.

Soil

The planting site must be properly prepared. Evaluate the grade of the land and the soil composition. Soil is the foundation of a garden and the best product will be achieved if, at the start, time is taken to ensure that the soil formation is satisfactory.

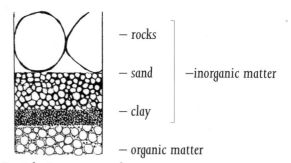

Particle sizes vary greatly.

Texture, Structure and Porosity

The three most important properties of soil are: texture; structure; and porosity.

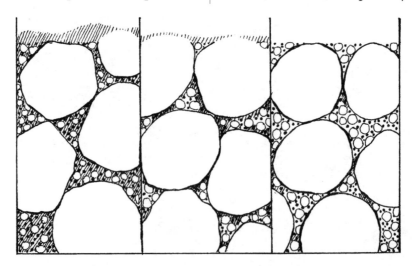

The size of the soil particles is a major factor in determining how quickly soil drains.

Texture refers to the size of inorganic minerals in the soil. These particles can range in size from rocks to sand grains to minuscule specks of clay. To find out the texture of your soil, take a moist to wet sample and roll it between your fingers. If it feels gritty, the soil is sandy. By contrast, if it feels smooth or sticky, it has a high clay content. Knowing the texture of your soil is critical because it affects important factors such as, moisture content, drainage, the supply of plant nutrients, and how easy the soil will be to work with.

Structure refers to the combined mineral and organic content of the soil. How these components are arranged, and held together, determines the size of "pores", or space, between soil particles. The size of the "pores" affects the movement of air and water through the soil, ie. its porosity.

Soil porosity affects drainage and the ability of oxygen to circulate in the soil. It also influences the ability of plant roots to penetrate the soil.

Organic Content

The organic content of soil is equally important as it provides the necessary nutrients for your plants. Sources of organic matter vary. It is formed by the decaying remains of animals, worms, insects and plants, including dead and rotting roots, leaves, stems and flowers. The level of organic matter in the soil can be augmented in a variety of ways, for example by adding compost, peat moss, well-rotted steer manure or mushroom manure. Whatever you choose to use, dig it into the soil to improve its structure. Organic matter is a natural source of nitrogen and phosphorus, and it acts as a storehouse of essential plant nutrients. It also discourages soil erosion.

A soil test is recommended as the best way to find out what sort of soil you have. Look in the Yellow Pages for a soil lab near you.

Soil Layers

If you could take a cross section of the soil, you would find the topsoil has a maximum depth of 31 cm (1 ft). The next 76 cm (30 in) is termed subsoil. Below that is the parent soil and, lastly, the bedrock.

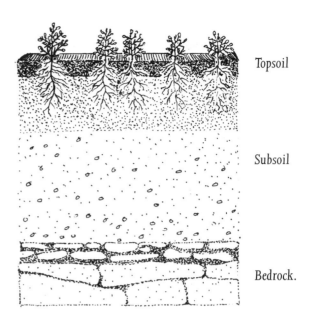

Topsoil

Subsoil

Bedrock.

A cross-section of soil layers shows that topsoil is usually no more than 30 cm (1 ft) deep.

The subsoil layer determines drainage efficiency. If it is shallow and the parent soil or bedrock is too close to the surface, good drainage will be almost impossible to achieve.

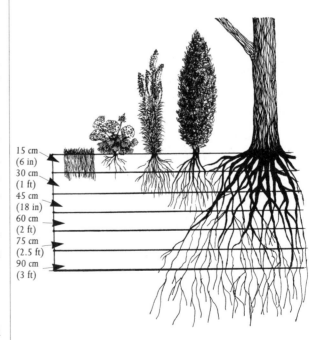

15 cm (6 in)
30 cm (1 ft)
45 cm (18 in)
60 cm (2 ft)
75 cm (2.5 ft)
90 cm (3 ft)

The roots of a plant usually take up as much area in the ground as does the visible part of the tree above the soil.

The roots of larger plants must reach down into the subsoil layer for the water and nutrients that have leached into it and it is therefore essential that they can penetrate to this depth. Remember, the roots of a large tree take up as much area in the ground as does the visible part of the tree above the soil. Conversely, most small ornamentals, including the *Rhododendron* family, have roots that remain close to the surface, making it imperative to have a good layer of topsoil.

Soil Types and Drainage

There should not be any depressions in the soil surface, where water can collect. Such areas breed disease and pests. Soil should be porous enough that water will drain into the roots of plants, pulling nutrients and oxygen along as it travels. If the soil is composed of heavy clay, the water may run off, causing erosion as it flows. If drainage is poor, the soil may become waterlogged near the roots, eventually suffocating and killing the plant.

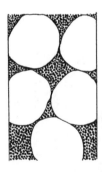

Small clay particles can fill and block pores, reducing soil drainage.

If the soil is too sandy, the water will drain through so fast that the plant will not absorb the required nutrients. The optimum soil composition lies between these two extremes. It should hold together in a moist clump when squeezed, but should also easily crumble into chunks when the clump is pinched.

A simple test to find out how quickly your soil drains, is to dig a hole 31 cm (1 ft) deep and fill it with water. If it takes fifteen to twenty minutes to drain, the soil is very sandy and you will need to add organic matter to help retain moisture. On the other hand, if it takes more than a day to soak in, then you have a very heavy clay soil. Augment it with sand and, what is more important, organic matter like peat moss. As neither amendment contains any nutrient value at all, some nutrient-rich organic matter or chemical fertilizer should also be added (having a compost pile can be an asset at a time like this when organic material is required).

Consider the time of year in which you choose to do the test. If the season is wet, the soil will drain much more slowly than usual.

New soil, manures, peat moss or anything else you may need to add to your soil, can be purchased by the bag or by the truck load. Decide what type of soil you need, in advance, and be sure to deal with a reputable distributor if you are having soil delivered to your home. It is advisable to go to the site of origin to look at the soil ahead of time, watching for weeds! If weeds are growing in the soil at the site, they will certainly sprout up again in your yard. Most dealers will have a selection of soils for you to choose from, with varying degrees of organic matter incorporated into them. If you are having it delivered, check that the dealer has brought you what you ordered before having it unloaded onto your driveway!

Once you have a clear understanding of your soil's composition, you will be ready to choose some plants. When selecting plants, consider the amount of sun that the site receives, the microclimate, the appearance of the plants (ie. whether they will complement the site), and the amount of maintenance that specific plants require. It is much easier to grow a plant in a site that satisfies its natural requirements than it is to try to force, nurture and persuade the plant to grow where it is not happy to begin with!

Composting

Composting is not only an environmentally sensitive way to lessen the amount of household garbage sent to the local landfill, but also provides

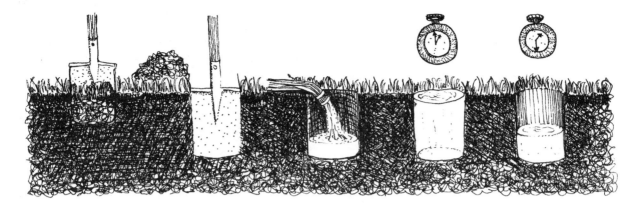

Check soil drainage:
- *Dig a hole the depth of a spade*
- *Fill it with water*
- *Time how long the water takes to soak in*

If drainage takes 15 minutes, you have a very sandy soil. If it takes more than a day to soak in, your drainage is poor.

a homemade solution for obtaining organic matter to augment the soil. Like steer and mushroom manure, compost adds structure and nutrients.

Humus is the end product of the process of decomposition. Tiny microorganisms transform garden refuse and discarded vegetable matter into humus. Compost is full of nutrients and augments the organic level of the soil. It also introduces beneficial microorganisms into the garden.

For the composting process to proceed, busy microorganisms require a proper balance of oxygen, moisture and warmth. The compost pile should be kept damp, but not soggy, and located in a sunny spot so that it will generate sufficient heat. To ensure that the compost pile receives enough oxygen, do not use tightly packed grass clippings exclusively. Add other vegetable matter and organic garden debris, and turn the pile over occasionally to keep the compost material loosened. Microorganisms will be actively converting waste material into compost during seasons of warm temperatures, such as in the spring and summer. Do not be concerned if the composting process slows markedly during winter. It will speed up again with the introduction of warmer weather.

For composting, the rule of thumb is to use only organic material, such as uncooked vegetable matter and garden clippings. Never add dairy or meat products of any kind. Also, be careful not to add grass clippings or other garden refuse that has been previously treated with an insecticide, a herbicide or a fungicide. Further, if you suspect that your compost pile or bin does not generate sufficient heat to "cook" or kill seeds, do not add weeds to it that have already gone to seed. The seeds may survive the composting process and will sprout in your garden once the compost has been spread.

Compost can be worth its weight in gold when it comes to the health of your soil.

Material placed in a compost pile or bin is best added in layers of approximately 15 cm (6 in). If you wish to add branches, cones or larger pieces to the pile, cut them down to 21 cm to 25 cm (8 in to 10 in) in length, or less. Otherwise, they will take much too long to decay. Also, adding a thin layer of high nitrogen fertilizer will encourage microorganisms to work more quickly.

Many commercially manufactured compost bins are available, but a homemade version (eg. four corner posts wrapped with chicken wire) will often do as good a job without the expense.

Add material to the compost in layers.

CHAPTER 1

Designing a Garden

W HEN YOU STAND back and look at your yard it may seem like your gardening goals are unattainable, but with some forethought almost anything is achievable. Just as one needs a recipe to bake a cake, one should have a general plan to work from when designing a garden. It will help you to produce an attractive, functional garden layout to meet your specific requirements while still being uniquely you. This does not mean, however, that the plan cannot be altered as needs and preferences change.

No two gardens are designed in the same way, but there are some general guidelines to follow to make a plan work. They will keep you on track until you attain your ultimate goal, ie. a mature garden, which is likely to take from five to seven years to reach completion. Those bitten by the gardening "bug" find that their garden is always a "work in progress"!

Setting Goals and Making Choices

Before picking up a shovel or hoe, you will need to choose a general theme or style for your yard.

The design of the house and composition of the neighbourhood should help shape your decision, to a certain extent. Do not be bound by what your neighbour has done. Then again, you do not want your yard to be so obviously different that it looks out of place.

Symmetrical beds utilise the same plants on each side, to create a mirror image.

Asymmetrical beds are arranged in a more casual fashion

One of the ways to help you visualize the result of your labours is to visit your local library and borrow as many gardening books and magazines as possible. As you look through these references, take note of the garden styles you especially like. Then review all the features that you noted and see which ones are consistent throughout. For visual inspiration, take a walk or a drive through different neighbourhoods or local parks.

By now you will know if you prefer a formal style for your yard, or a more casual look, and if you would like to include a special area such as a Japanese, water or a rock garden.

A formal yard will be very symmetrical, the shrubs and beds revealing a strict balance. For example, a formal yard may have similar plants on each side of a straight driveway, much like a mirror image. Formal beds are often arranged in linear or circular patterns and are geometrically correct. This garden style requires a great deal of maintenance in order to maintain symmetry.

In contrast, a casual style is more likely to feature beds that are asymmetrically shaped. These require less maintenance and one can be less exacting when pruning if plants appropriate for this type of garden are used (ie. some trees and shrubs are better suited to formal gardens and, consequently, will tolerate extensive shaping).

You should also think about what you want your garden to do for you... its function! Is your garden a recreational area with a pool or badminton net, or is it a passive area used more for reading and quiet contemplation? The activity level is often determined by the age and number of children in the household, if any, and the proximity of a playground or park. Do not forget to consider pets. Also, think about the amount of outdoor entertaining you expect to do. If possible, designate areas for active and passive activities, separated by shrubs or a low fence. Ideally, the function of specific areas should be agreed upon by all family members since all are likely to make use of the garden. It is also best to collectively decide what types of plants you want to have in the garden.

To aid you in your choices, and to help you to better plan your garden layout, consider the questions listed in the *Helping Hand Questionnaire* that follows, and examine the results.

Helping-Hand Questionnaire

Family Preferences:

1. Garden Maintenance:

Every family has a chief gardener (usually mom or dad!) who has a limited amount of time to devote to garden maintenance each week. Estimate the hours she/he is willing to devote to garden tasks per week and keep this number in mind when planning your garden. Remember, a garden should be a joy, not a never-ending chore, so do not allow your ambitions to run away with you.

2. Garden Style:
☐ Formal
☐ Contemporary
☐ Natural
☐ Specialized

3. Desirable Features:

Plant types:

☐ Herbs	☐ Cut flowers	☐ Roses	☐ Rhododendron bed
☐ Vegetables	☐ Fruit trees/shrubs	☐ Perennial bed	☐ Rock garden
☐ Water garden	☐ Herbaceous border	☐ Hedges	☐ Containers
☐ Shrub border	☐ Feature tree	☐ Flowering tree	☐ Other?

Functional considerations:

☐ Built-in Barbecue   ☐ Patio or deck

☐ Play area   ☐ Screen for garbage can

☐ Swing/Slides   ☐ Sand box

☐ Greenhouse   ☐ Compost

☐ Dog/pet run   ☐ Bird feeders and bath

☐ Laundry line   ☐ Storage shed

☐ Water fountain   ☐ Pond

☐ Terrace on a slope   ☐ Arbour, trellis or pergola

☐ Pathways   ☐ Hot Tub

☐ Privacy screen/fence (note: To screen out an unwanted view or maintain your own privacy, plant trees or shrubs or build a permanent structure)

☐ Wind and rain shelter for patio (note: This is important if you plan to regularly entertain outdoors)

☐ Outdoor lighting (note: Lighting adds drama and ambience when entertaining outdoors in the evening, or when viewing the garden from indoors)

☐ Other? _____

4. **Children:**

   • How many? _____

   • Ages? _____

   • Play area required? If so,   ☐ enclosed, or   ☐ open

   • Type of flooring for play area?   ☐ grass (soft)   ☐ wood   ☐ sand   ☐ gravel

   (note: Sand will be tracked into the house, and a sand box or sandy area will attract neighbourhood cats!)

5. **Adults:**

   • How many? _____

   • Ages? _____

   Life style considerations:

   ☐ Full time career   ☐ Part time career   ☐ Both have careers

   ☐ Work indoors   ☐ Work outdoors   ☐ Gardening a hobby?

   ☐ Other hobbies? _____

6. **Holiday/Business Travel:**

   • How long are you away, on average? _____

   • What time of year are you away? _____

   (note: You will probably not want to plant a lot of high maintenance annuals if you are gone for weeks at a time during the summer months)

7. **Outdoor Entertaining:**

   • Number of guests that are likely? _____

   (note: this will determine the size of your patio)

   • Frequency of daytime versus evening entertaining? _____

   (note: will you require outdoor lighting?)

   • Have you plans for a: ☐ Swimming pool   ☐ Outdoor hot tub

      ☐ Badminton court   ☐ Tennis court

      ☐ Basketball court   ☐ Other: _____

8. **Automobiles (parking requirements):**
   - Number and type of vehicles? _____
   - Need a parking area for guests?   ☐ Yes   ☐ No

9. **Lot (topography):**
   - Lot size?   ☐ small   ☐ medium   ☐ large
   - Grade?   ☐ level   ☐ sloped   ☐ combination
   - Aspect?   ☐ north   ☐ south   ☐ east   ☐ west
   - Proportion? ☐ all back yard   ☐ all front garden   ☐ 50:50   ☐ other
   - Other features (eg. dips in the land, rock outcropping, etc.):
   _____
   _____
   _____

10. **Climatic Information:**
    - Zone (note: see the Zone Map in the *Introduction*): _____
    - Microclimates? Locate shady areas, areas open to wind and driving rain, parts of the garden that are particularly sheltered, and take note of exposure (ie. north, south, east and west). Remember to take all this information into account when choosing plants.
    _____
    _____
    _____

11. **Soil Composition:**
    (note: see section on "Soil" in the *Introduction*)
    - Depth of topsoil? _____ cm
    - Drainage?   ☐ Good   ☐ Fair   ☐ Poor
    - Texture?   ☐ Sandy   ☐ Clay   ☐ Just right

12. **Views from inside the House:**
    (note: this will help you to decide where to plant trees and shrubs - and where not to do so - in order to maximize views)

    Location of windows and doors:

    Views from windows (note: some views you may wish to block out, such as that of a neighbour's window or garden shed, while other views you may wish to retain, such as a play area for children or a swimming pool):
    - Views to block out: _____
    - Views to highlight: _____

13. **Style of the House, its Inhabitants and its Surroundings:**
    - Materials used on the house (eg. wooden or vinyl siding, brick, stone?):
    _____
    - Colour of house and trim? _____
    - Location of down spouts and utilities? _____
    _____
    - Shape and location of the driveway and walkways (eg. welcoming entrance? Well lit?):
    _____
    _____

• Home security - will adding plants compromise home security by excessively reducing visibility?

_____

• Materials used for the driveway and walkways (ie. do these hard landscape materials blend with the style of the house?):

_____

• Chimney - will the heat emanating from an outdoor chimney damage nearby plants?

_____

• Style of architecture (eg. contemporary, Cape Cod, Tudor, Victorian, etc. For example, it would be unsuitable to put a Japanese garden in front of a Tudor style of home):

_____

• Floor plan (eg. if you have glass doors opening to the outside, you could place a small patio there):

_____

• Existing plants (eg. foundation plantings, existing vegetation? Can they be incorporated into your design? Will there be a problem with leaves or needles getting into gutters or a swimming pool or onto the roof?):

_____

• Size of trees (ie. there should be a balance between the size of the trees on your lot and the size of your house. The trees should not be so large that they dwarf the house, or vice versa):

_____

• Family makeup / personality (eg. does the entrance reflect your welcoming nature? If not, a couple of chairs placed on a front porch and/or a few hanging baskets may do the trick):

_____

• Notable neighbourhood characteristics: _____

_____

Note: You may find it beneficial to take photographs of your house and yard, which you can enlarge. Then lay a sheet of onion skin paper over the photo(s) and sketch in your ideas for new plants and beds, etc. This will give you a clearer idea of how the garden will look when complete.

14. Municipal Authorities:

Zoning and bylaws:
• Fencing and hedges (ie. Find out about local restrictions or you may have to make costly changes later):

_____

• Swimming pools (ie. Comply with safety codes): _____

• Street planting (ie. Include municipally planted trees in your design, as you probably will not be allowed to remove them if you wish to. Take note of the species and learn how to care for them):

_____

• Placement of utilities (ie. Never plant close to overhead wires or underground lines). Some residents have been asked to remove plants that they planted between a fire hydrant and the street, in order to keep the area clear for safety sake:

_____

_____

Now that you have an idea of the garden style you wish to adopt, you need some knowledge about gardening itself. To create the effect you want, find out how the plants you have chosen will look when mature and what they will require in order to thrive. Choosing a plant that is appropriate for the spot you have chosen for it will result in reduced maintenance and a healthier plant overall.

You also need to assess your soil composition and know how to prepare beds for planting. For more detailed information on soil, refer to the *Introduction*. In addition, there are many horticultural books available offering more detail about the scientific side of soil science and botany. Many can be found at your local library.

It is important to understand the nature of a plant's growth to determine if it is likely to outgrow its new home. Examples of overgrown plants are seen everywhere, especially trees that have grown up into the power lines. Either the trees were planted too close to the lines, or trees that grow to be too tall when mature were planted there. Trees planted under overhead wires must not attain a maximum height of more than 6.5 m (21 ft) when fully grown. Taller trees must be planted a distance of at least 5 m (16 ft) from the wires. More than 40% of all electrical interruptions are caused by tree-related problems. Your local nursery representative can be a great resource because she/he knows what species are appropriate for your area and can present you with a number of alternatives to choose from. Utility companies are also often willing to mail out specific reference material upon request.

The *Plant Encyclopaedia*, further on, provides a wealth of information about individual species, including the size that each can be expected to attain. Local parks and botanical gardens are a good "visual" source of information. There, you will be able to see the overall shape of the plants you are interested in and how well they grow in your area.

Basics of Landscape Design

Think of your yard as an extension of your home, or as an outdoor room. There should be "a ceiling", and "walls", and "a floor". These mirror the three dimensions required in a successful garden design. Each of these elements can be created through the use of hard landscape and the types of plants chosen. When planting, follow the same order that you would if building a house. First, build the frame, then construct the walls and floors, finishing with the decorative touches last of all.

Walls and screens can be made from different materials such as trees, shrubs and vines, or stone and fencing materials.

Background:Plant large trees first. Middle-ground:Add shrubs to the garden. Foreground:Finish with small plants and flowers

The Garden's Framework

The garden's framework is achieved with hard landscaping and the placement of large trees. These elements give the general shape and architectural structure to your yard. To build the "walls", add smaller trees, shrubs, fences and screens. Do not be afraid to divide the yard into smaller areas (or "rooms") with plants or structures such as these. The "flooring" or "carpeting" is represented by the lawn or ground cover, and the decorative touches consist of bedding plants, bulbs and smaller flowers.

You will also need a background, a middle-ground and a foreground to give perspective to your yard, the feeling of depth. An effective and frequently used technique is to plant larger plants in the background with middle-sized shrubs in front of these and smaller plants and flowers in the foreground. This makes sense as the smaller plants would not otherwise be seen. You may wish to locate small-flowered or delicate plants near to the area where you will be sitting outdoors, to better

appreciate them. However, do not be too rigid in following these suggestions. Be creative and be willing to make mistakes. After all, a plant can always be moved, unless it has grown too large to do so.

Repetition, Balance and Texture

The repetition of certain plants or hard landscape features is also desirable as it creates a feeling of unity and continuity in the garden. Too many different elements, all jumbled up together, will look too busy and scattered. An effective style can be achieved by using mass plantings of the same shrub or bedding plant. The result can be stunning and will also simplify the treatment of an area, allowing for easier maintenance.

It is important to have balance in your yard. Just as you would not put all of your living room furniture in one corner of the room, you should not place all of the plants in your garden in one spot. Use trees and shrubs to divide your yard into separate sections, such as an area for quiet reading and another for playing basketball.

Leaf texture adds to a garden:

A small leafed maple (Acer palmatum) has fine leaves

a Camellia has medium leaves

and a Yucca has bold, coarse-looking leaves

Different effects can be achieved, depending upon the choice of plant material.

*Cedars (Thuja) cast shade
year-round*

*Birch (Betula) allows light
to filter through it during winter*

*Bamboo (Phylostachys)
provides dappled shade all year*

The colour, size, shape and texture of a plant are important factors to consider when choosing plant material for your garden. For example, a grouping of cedars (*Thuja*) can be very weighty and will provide a much different effect than that achieved by planting a grove of birch trees (*Betula*) or a clump of bamboo (*Phyllostachys*). A dark green tree has a heavier appearance than one that is light green or yellow or has a variegated leaf.

The size and shape of leaves also influences the overall effect. For example, an Alaska fern (*Polystichum setiferum*) has a fine texture, an evergreen azalea (*Rhododendron*) has a medium-sized leaf, and a Japanese aralia (*Fatsia japonica*) has bold leaves; quite different textures that may or may not be appropriate for the style of your garden.

Acer palmatum   Fatsia japonica
A fine textured leaf creates a feeling of distance. By contrast, a large leaf makes a bold statement and seems to draw you towards it.

Try to maintain some continuity between your house, the trees, the lawn and/or the area left un-planted. Do not place all your plants around the outside of your property, bring some into the main garden area as well. Your garden should be a visually inviting and welcoming place to enjoy with friends and family, and should add interest and character to your home.

Perspective

Another thing to consider is perspective, ie. where will you be sitting or standing when viewing the garden? If you are designing a front yard, be careful that you, as the home owner, will not be seeing only the rear of the design. In the house, seat yourself at exactly the spot where you will most often be looking at your front yard and consider the scene you will be viewing. After all, if you are doing all the work, you should also enjoy the best view!

Consider "borrowing" some trees from the neighbour's yards. If you live in an area where your neighbours have large trees, plant yours in such a way as to take advantage of those already established. Create the illusion that the trees across the neighbour's fence are actually in your own yard by including them in your design.

If you have a favourite vista, you can frame it using plants, but be careful not to overdo it or you may eventually lose the view once the plants reach maturity. Conversely, if you wish to block out an unpleasant view, you can usually group your plants in such a way as to effectively hide it.

8

You can frame a view by using plantings or arbours or a combination of both.

Making a Scale Drawing

Now you are ready to get out your measuring tape and measure your lot and plot the "footprint" of your house. Locate and identify all plants that are already in existence and any other significant landmarks, like large rocks, dips in the ground, or slopes. Then, make a scale drawing of your yard. This will provide you with a workable blueprint. Make a number of copies of the final drawing, and use onion skin paper overlays, for your additions and changes.

Now, take the scale drawing and decide where in the yard you wish to locate specific areas. Where should the vegetable garden be, or the rose garden? Draw in a large egg shape or "bubble" to indicate the relative size for each featured area of your yard. This will give you a rough idea of how the yard will look and function. Putting in paths will aid in directing the flow of traffic. Try a few different arrangements to see how they look.

Before making your final decision, go outside at different times of the day and sit in the area where you intend to put the patio or deck, and assess your plan one last time while imagining the changes that will take place. At this point, you may wish to consult a professional landscape designer for advice.

When creating your design, ensure that you locate plants in the areas best suited for them. Make sure that there is sufficient sunlight and/or shade for the specific plants you have chosen. Always consider the microclimate of your planting sites. For example, one should not put a cedar hedge on the south side of a vegetable garden because it will cast too much shade. The addition or removal of a tree, or shrub will automatically alter the microclimate beneath it. Lastly, always find out how large any given tree will grow because, as it matures, the area of shade beneath it will change.

Hard Landscape

Hard landscape is the part of the garden that will not change or grow from season to season. Once it is in place, it can be depended upon to remain as it is. Materials and trends change continually, so go to various retailers and see what is available. Hard landscaping includes arbours, pergolas, gazebos, walls, fences, patios, decking, statues, birdbaths, and any other structure in the garden.

By far, the most popular element of hard landscape is a patio or deck. If you want one that will comfortably hold a table and four chairs, it should measure a minimum of 4 m by 5 m (13 ft by 16 ft). This will allow the chairs to be backed up from the table and not fall off the edge.

What you choose as hard landscape material is generally a matter of personal preference. There are a few common surfaces, however, each with their own advantages and disadvantages.

Wood is often used as a patio material and is quite easy for a home owner to install. It can also be removed or altered without too much trouble. The disadvantage of wood is that it can become very slippery, especially if it is located on the north side of a house where it is cooler and where rain freezes more quickly in cold weather. Wood also becomes slippery when algae grow on it, so be sure to keep it clean to avoid accidents. The use of salt will increase traction, but if it gets on your plants it can burn them.

Loose gravel is another option, as long as the grade of the land is not too steep. The size of the gravel will determine how comfortable it is to walk on. Stepping stones can be placed amongst loose gravel to create pathways and make walking on it more comfortable. The advantage of this type of surface is that plastic can be placed under the gravel, keeping weeds from growing up through it. It also has a softer look than cement and can be installed by the do-it-yourself home owner. Gravel can be delivered directly to your home.

Interlocking brick provides another example of a surface that is easily installed. There are many types and shapes of brick and, with some creativity, the result can be quite dramatic. But be sure to learn the proper installation technique before attempting this on your own. The disadvantage of using brick is that weeds can grow up between them, so it is best to keep a step ahead of them from the beginning.

Lastly, cement is a frequently used hard landscape alternative. However, it is not a movable surface, in that, once it has been poured, it is there to stay. There are many types of surfacing or finishing options for concrete, ranging from plain to aggregate, to imprints of blocks or bricks.

Hard landscaping choices include fences, walls, birdbaths, and all other inanimate structures.

Overview:

Getting Started:

☐   1.   Decide on a style and select your plants.
☐   2.   Grade the soil and prepare the site.
☐   3.   Install all hard landscaping.
☐   4.   Plant larger trees, then smaller ones and, finally, the shrubs.
☐   5.   Install turf and large ground cover areas.
☐   6.   Add the final touches with perennials, annuals and decorative plants.
☐   7.   Rest.

Many options are available for surfacing a patio or walkway. Hard landscape material can be used on its own or in combination with ground covers. Each alternative lends a different effect and a unique texture to the garden.

Design Examples - Scale Drawings:

The pages that follow show scale drawings of a front yard and a back yard. The first two drawings depict the lot, the house and some common hard landscaping features. "Bubbles" have also been added to illustrate the function of each designated area (eg. "active" and "passive" areas, outdoor entertainment area, flower garden, etc.).

In the second set of drawings, the yard has had all hard landscape features added, as well as new trees and shrubs and bedding plants.

The third set portrays the yard in its final stage of development, including such details as the placement of flower pots and bedding plants.

At the end of this section, extra graph paper has been provided to allow you to get started on a set of drawings for the design of your own yard. Good luck and have fun!

Back Yard

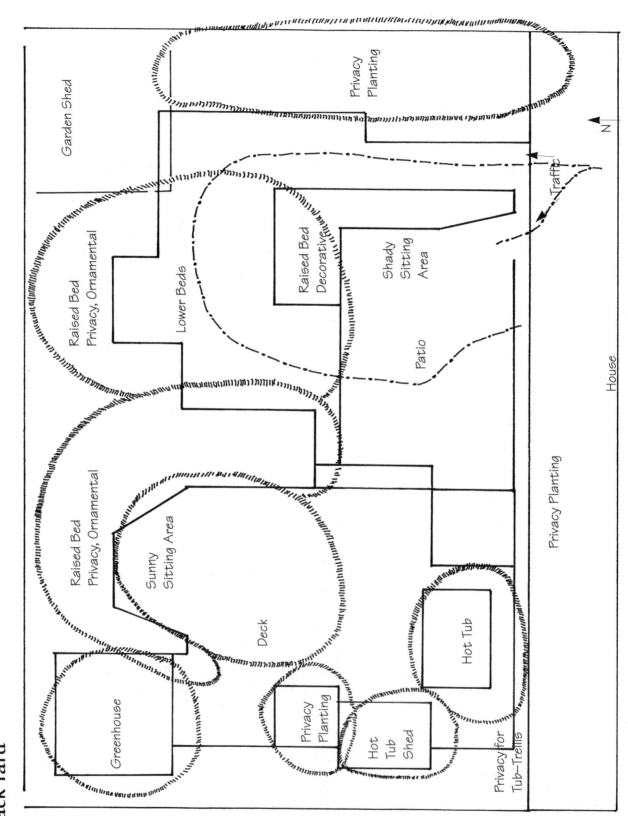

Garden Shed

Privacy Planting

N

Traffic

Raised Bed
Privacy, Ornamental

Lower Beds

Raised Bed
Decorative

Shady
Sitting
Area

Patio

House

Raised Bed
Privacy, Ornamental

Sunny
Sitting Area

Deck

Privacy Planting

Greenhouse

Privacy
Planting

Hot
Tub
Shed

Hot Tub

Privacy for
Tub-Trellis

Front Yard

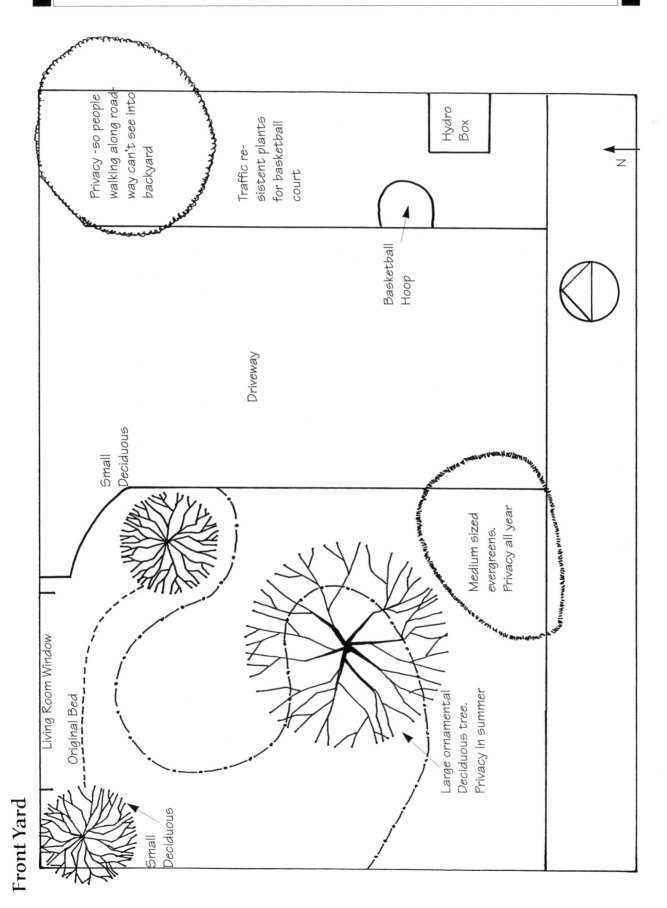

Privacy - so people walking along roadway can't see into backyard

Traffic re-sistent plants for basketball court

Hydro Box

N

Basketball Hoop

Driveway

Small Deciduous

Medium sized evergreens. Privacy all year

Living Room Window

Original Bed

Large ornamental Deciduous tree. Privacy in summer

Small Deciduous

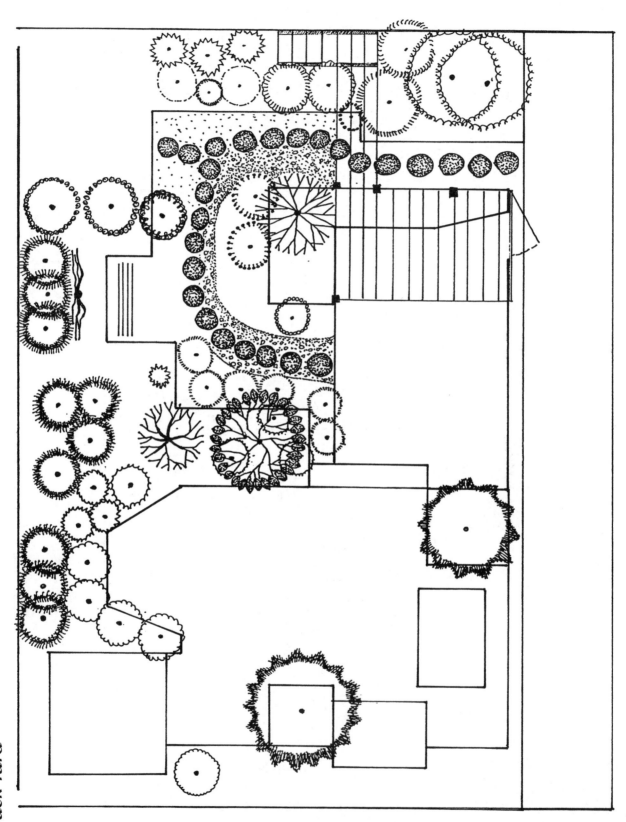

Back Yard

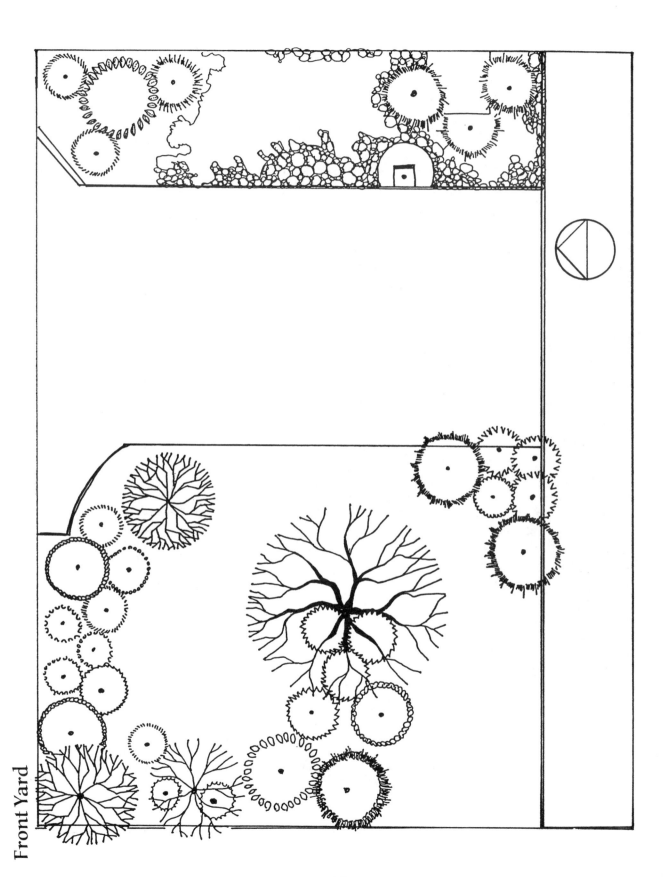

Front Yard

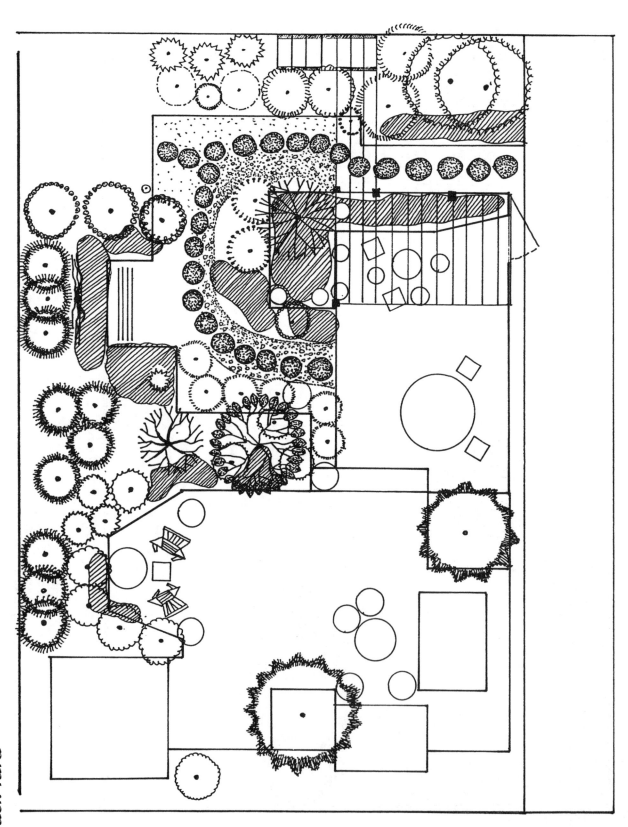

Back Yard

Front Yard

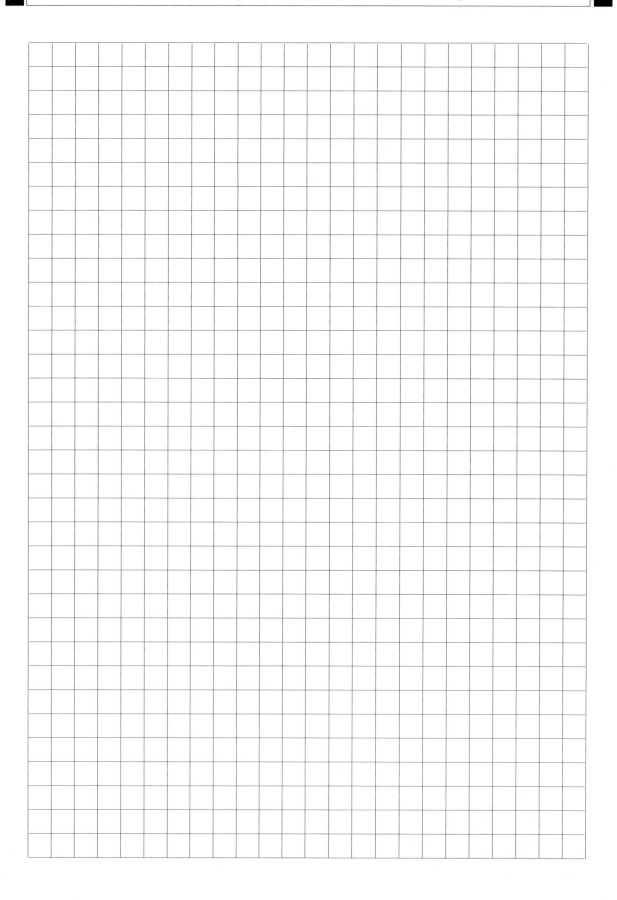

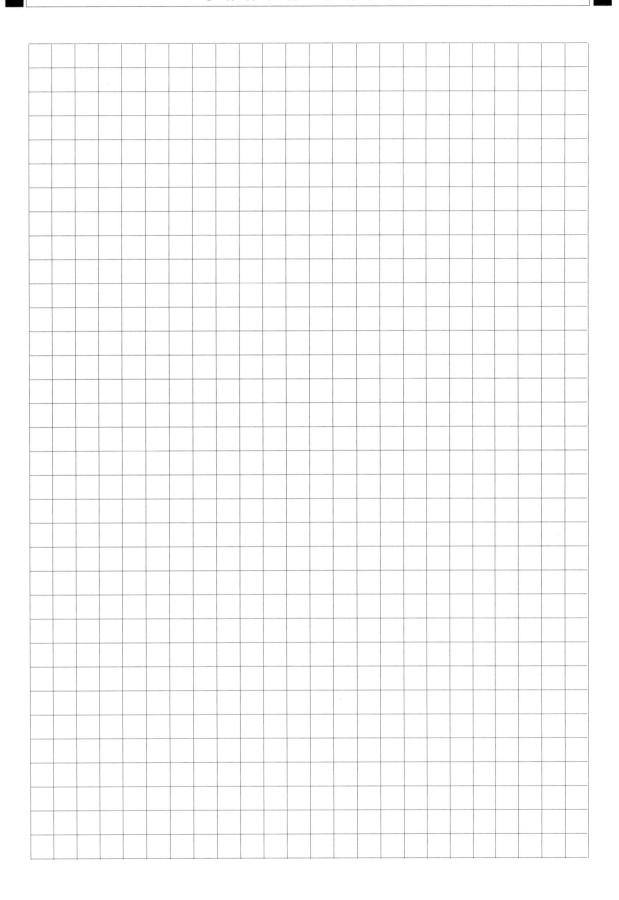

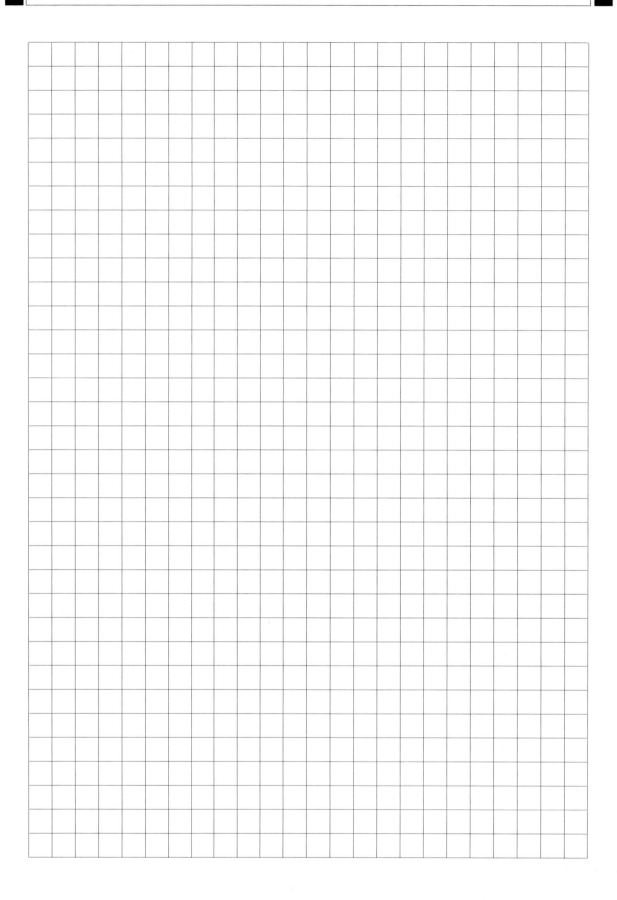

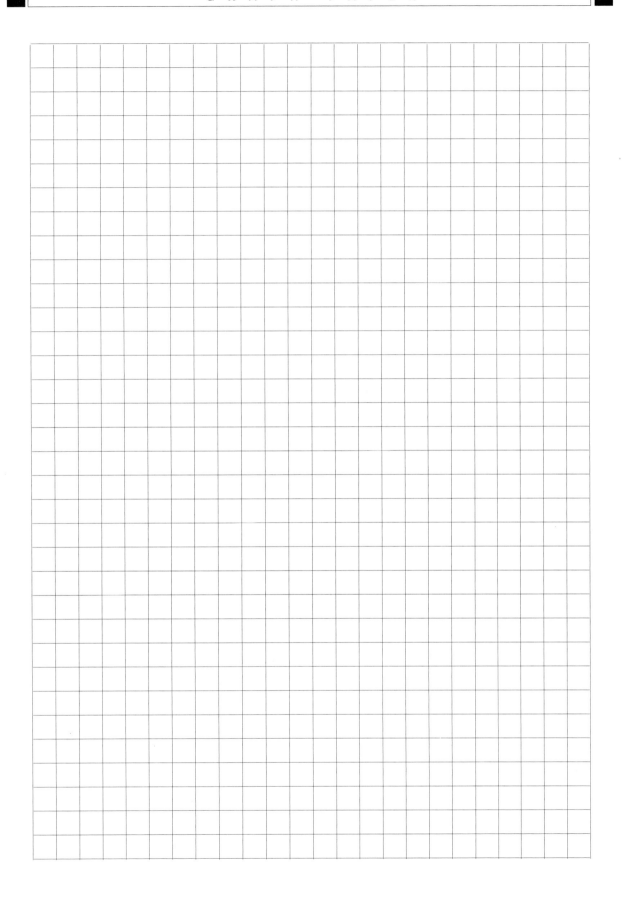

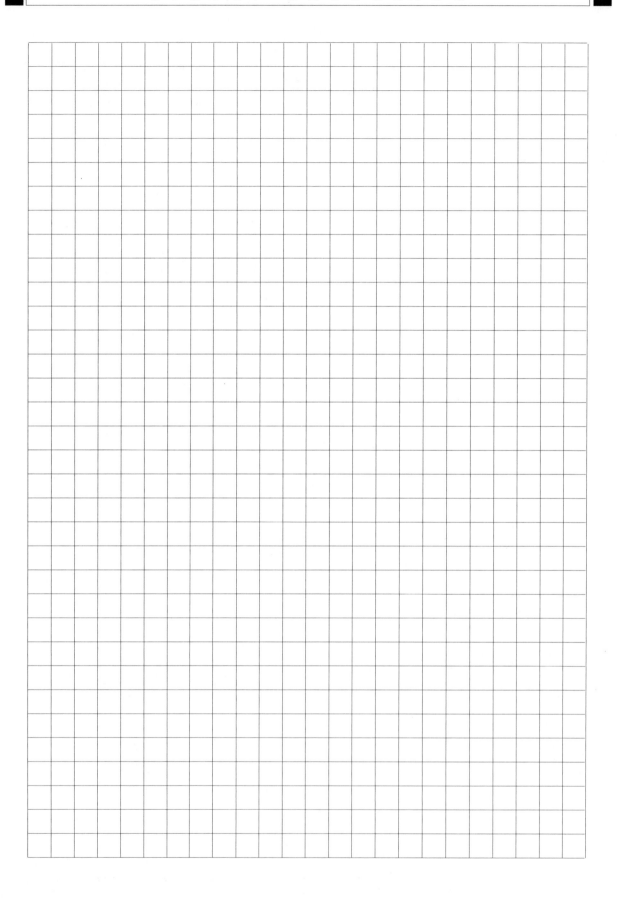

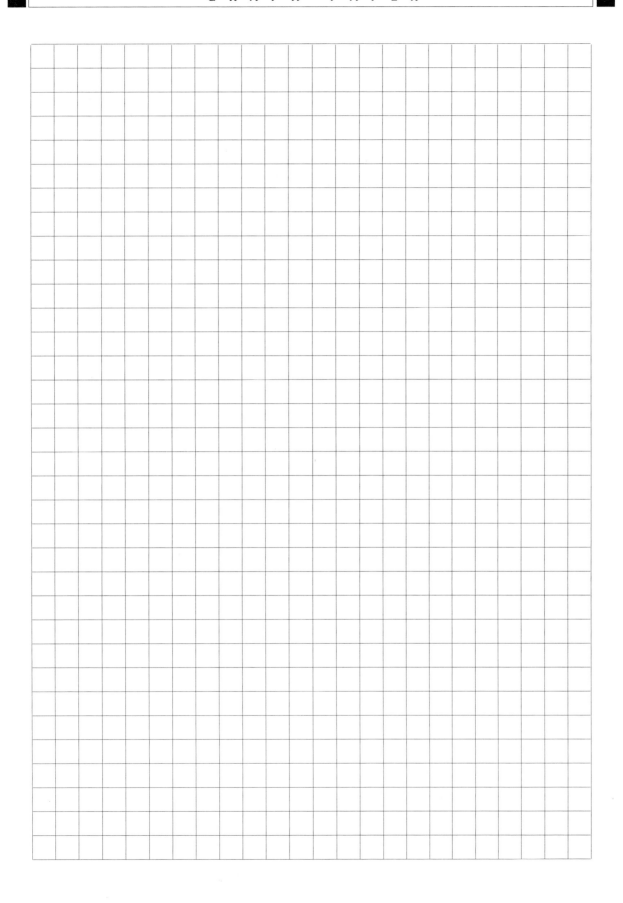

Trees and Shrubs

TREES AND SHRUBS are the backbone of every garden. Trees form the main skeleton, shrubs flesh out the area and bedding plants provide pockets of colour and finishing touches. *The Oxford American Dictionary* defines a tree as, "a perennial plant with a single stem or trunk that is usually without branches for some distance above the ground", and a shrub as, "a woody plant smaller than a tree and usually divided into separate stems from near the ground." From this description, we discover that the main difference between a tree and a shrub is size. A tree grows to be significantly larger and is therefore much more dominant in the garden.

Trees and shrubs can be divided into deciduous, semi-deciduous, evergreen and broadleaf evergreen varieties. Deciduous trees lose their leaves during the winter, leaving only their branches and trunk as elements to add character to the landscape during the cold, dormant months. Semi-deciduous plants lose some, but not all of their leaves. Evergreen and broadleaf evergreen trees and shrubs retain their leaves or needles all winter, thus maintaining the same appearance throughout the year. Broadleaf evergreens provide an interesting change from needled evergreens and can add a different texture to the garden. Leaf variegation also adds colour and interest.

There are many uses for trees and shrubs in the landscape. For example, a tree or shrub planted in the front lawn, by itself, provides a focal point as a "specimen" planting. But no matter why a tree or shrub is used in the landscape, the first step is to research choices thoroughly before purchasing and planting.

Underplanting a specimen tree in a border.

Designing with Trees and Shrubs

Larger plants, like trees and shrubs, are the prominent soft landscape features in your garden, so advance planning now will save you heartaches later. If you have chosen a formal design, then ensure that the beds are geometrically correct and distinctively placed. The trees and shrubs chosen should be able to withstand strict pruning and being continually clipped in order to maintain the desired shape. By contrast, an informal garden will be more relaxed in style.

Do not allow grass to grow right up to the trunk of a tree.

One thing to remember when planning your trees and shrubs, is that grass does not grow very well underneath them. This is because the grass does not receive sufficient sunlight. Also, grass competes with the trees and shrubs for moisture and nutrients they all require. In any case, leaving bare soil under a tree will eliminate the chance of inflicting damage caused by a lawn mower or weed whacker to the roots or trunk. An option is to add a mulch of 5 cm to 11 cm (2 in to 4 in) around the base of the tree in order to keep the area looking tidy. It will also aid in moisture retention, prevent erosion or soil compaction, and discourage weed growth. Bulbs or perennials can be safely planted beneath larger trees and shrubs, as they will not disturb their deep roots.

Site Preparation

Before digging your first hole, be sure to locate any underground hazards, such as gas and water lines, and always look up to avoid interference by overhead lines.

Stand back and look at your lot. What is the topography like, the surface of the lot? Are there dips, large rises, a rock outcropping, or steep slopes? All of these should be incorporated into your design.

If you are moving into a new area a soil test is the best way to find out exactly what your growing medium consists of (look in the *Yellow Pages* for

a soil lab near you). Also, new subdivisions are known to have soil that is very compacted from the weight of the heavy machinery used to build homes and it may be necessary to rototill. In order for the roots of trees and shrubs to properly penetrate the soil, the soil must be loosened. This will help the plants to absorb moisture and nutrients and give them a head start by encouraging strong and rapid root growth. Healthier plants will result.

It will probably be necessary to amend the soil. Some organic soil amendments to add are peat moss, compost, and well-rotted steer manure or mushroom manure. Sand may also be required in order to increase drainage, but remember that sand, like peat moss, has no nutrient value. The soil improvements need only be minor since the roots of trees will eventually grow through the topsoil and into the subsoil below, beneath the depth reached by the rototiller.

If you must make drastic changes to your soil in order to grow specific plants, then you have chosen unsuitable plants for your area. It is better and certainly easier to discover what the site offers and plant accordingly, rather than trying to manipulate the environment to suit individual plant requirements. For more details on soil and amendments, refer to the *Introduction*.

Making Choices

The first and most important thing to remember is to check the zone hardiness of the tree or shrub you plan to purchase. The *Introduction* of this book contains a map and an explanation of zones.

Do not plant something just because you like the look of it at the nursery, and especially not if you saw it growing in a zone with warmer temperatures than your own. If you plan to leave the tree or shrub in the ground all year, you must make sure that it is hardy in your area. Observe the conditions of the planting site during normal weather patterns throughout the year, taking note of wind, sun exposure, and drainage.

Always familiarize yourself with the characteristics of the tree or shrub you wish to plant. Refer to the *Plant Encyclopaedia* for information on the species that grow well in your area.

Basic Shapes

The growth patterns and natural shapes of trees and shrubs can vary significantly. Do not try to fit a wide sprawling tree in a narrow spot as the tree will not be happy there and you will not be pleased with the result or the amount of maintenance required.

There are twelve basic shapes in trees, as illustrated in the diagrams. When grouped together, a variety of trees of the same general shape will usually have the best effect. The last four shapes depicted are used for accent and should be utilized sparingly or they will overpower the garden.

Shrubs also have basic shapes that can be pleasing when used as accents or in combinations (see diagrams).

These are twelve basic tree shapes:

1. Umbrella   2. Vase   3. Horizontal Oval   4. Rounded

5. Mounding   6. Upright Oval   7. Pyramidal   8. Narrow Pyramid

9. Narrow Column   10. Columnar   11. Weeping   12. Palm

These are eight basic shrub shapes:

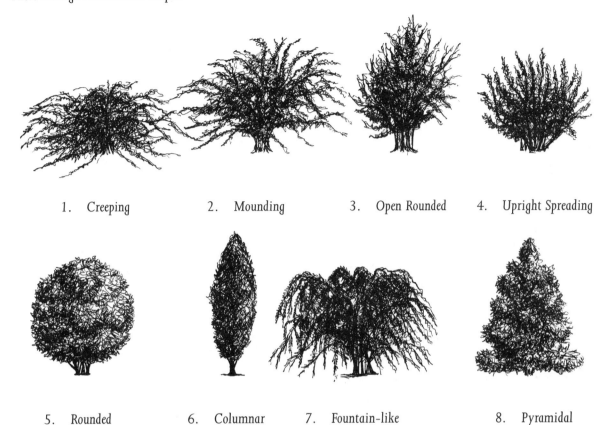

1. Creeping   2. Mounding   3. Open Rounded   4. Upright Spreading

5. Rounded   6. Columnar   7. Fountain-like   8. Pyramidal

Texture, Seasonal Interest and Size

The texture of foliage and the size of trees and shrubs should also be considered when choosing plants for the garden. For example, leaf size can be an eye-catching feature. A large leaved tree makes a bold statement and seems to draw you towards it. By contrast, a fine textured leaf creates a more subtle or delicate effect. The texture and colour of the tree trunk are other factors to consider, ie. tree trunks can be smooth, rough, peeling, white, red or even have snakelike markings such as that of the snakebark maple (*Acer capillipes*).

Bark texture can complement the landscape:

  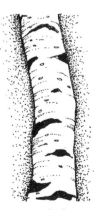  

1. *A* Magnolia has smooth bark

2. *A Sweet Gum (Liquidambar) has rough furrows*

3. Birch (Betula) has gently peeling bark

4. Paperbark maple (Acer griseum) has copper peeling bark

5. David's maple (Acer davidii) *has two colours of bark*

Include in your plan some trees and shrubs with features of seasonal year-round interest. There are many that bloom in spring and summer and some, like Rose-of-Sharon (*Hibiscus syriacus*), that bloom in late summer and into autumn. Fall colour is a necessity in the garden. For a listing of trees and shrubs, featuring their most prominent individual and seasonal characteristics, refer to the *Quick Check Chart of Trees and Shrubs* at the end of this chapter.

The ultimate or mature size of a tree is also an important factor. A tree displayed at a nursery in a five-gallon pot can look amazingly different in five to ten years. A visit to a park or botanical garden would be of great benefit to you in determining the growth pattern, size and suitability of plants for your garden.

Site Requirements

The individual needs of trees and shrubs should be understood, as some will grow best in full sun while others will prefer dappled shade. Some tolerate dry, gravelly soil while others would slowly die if forced to live in such an environment. Taking these factors into consideration when choosing plants will reduce overall maintenance. You will not have to endlessly prune damaged limbs, and healthy plants requiring less chemical applications will be the result.

Consider the specific function of the plant. Is it to be a shade tree, a hedge, a screen, a specimen or used in the middle of a border? Refer to your set of scale drawings and check that the plant you have chosen will be suited to the location.

When the site has been prepared and you have an idea of how you want it to look once planted, go to the nursery and look over the product choices. Look for a tree that is sturdy, not necessarily just tall. It will grow taller once it is planted and well maintained. Stand back, do you like the way the tree looks? Observe how the branches are arranged on the tree... you will not be able to change the plant's appearance once it comes home with you! Be sure there are no obvious cracks or wounds on the tree and, if the tree has

leaves, check them for obvious signs of disease, such as yellowing or black spots. Also check for healthy roots if you can. After purchasing your tree or shrub, be sure to protect it during the ride home, especially if it is in leaf. Do not allow the precious cargo to hang out of the back of the trunk of your car. It could result in damage from which the plant may never recover.

Planting

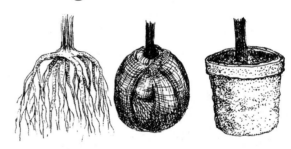

Plants can be purchased bare root, balled and burlapped or in containers. When planting, the roots should be covered by an adequate layer of soil to bring the stem back to its original depth.

An important and rarely mentioned fact is that the trunk of the tree is not the *handle!* Lift and carry the tree or shrub by the root ball, not by the trunk.

Now that you have brought your new trees and shrubs home, they are probably sitting on your driveway or front lawn as you decide how best to plant them. It is important to visualize the final result before going any further. To do this, place the trees and shrubs on top of the soil, in the spots where you want to plant them and view them from all angles - from a distance as well as close-up - to decide if you like their position. This will save you from having to move them in the future. Turn the trees until the appropriate side is facing in the direction you want, then, and only then, get your shovel.

Dig a hole that is about 15 cm to 31 cm (6 in to 12 in) wider and 11 cm to 25 cm (4 in to 10 in) deeper than the size of the pot or root ball. This will allow plenty of the rich planting mixture to surround the root ball. Remember, larger trees need larger holes!

Before planting, water the root ball thoroughly, then gently remove it from the container. If you have trouble removing it, it may be necessary to carefully cut off the pot in order to avoid damaging the roots. If the plant is balled and burlapped, place the entire root ball in the hole and then cut the twine, allowing the roots to spread out on their own. The root ball itself should be covered by a thin layer of soil. Leave the burlap in the ground - it will rot within a year or so. If the tree or shrub has been grown in a biodegradable container, it is advisable to slice down the sides of the container before putting it into the hole - these containers can take years to decompose! It is also recommended that the lip and top part of the container be removed as it can act as a wick, drawing moisture away from the plant's roots.

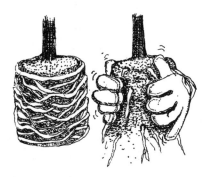

A plant grown in a container may become rootbound after a while. This can result in the roots becoming girdled, and the plant could die. Girdled roots become so constricted that nutrients cannot flow through them.

Once the plant has been removed from the container, check to see that the roots are not one solid mass. A gentle massage will encourage spreading if they are compacted. If you allow the roots to continue growing around in circles, the plant will not be properly anchored and could later become girdled or strangled, eventually dying due to a lack of nutrients! Use a clean, sharp pruner to remove any injured or damaged roots.

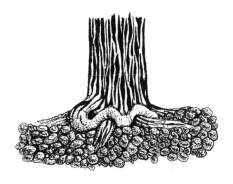

If a girdling root is not dealt with at planting time, it will continue its incorrect growth habit.

Always add bone meal to the hole to encourage root growth, then back fill the hole with good soil and firm it in. Ensure that the tree or shrub is standing straight up, not leaning. Water thoroughly with a slow hose at the base of the plant. Continue to water it faithfully when the weather is dry, especially during the first year.

If the tree needs to be staked, it is best to put the stake into the hole before you put the tree

Steps to tree planting:

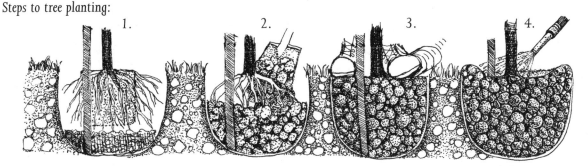

1. To avoid root damage, put the stake in the hole before planting the tree. Place bone meal and good soil in the bottom of the hole.

2. Back fill with good soil.

3. Firm soil in to avoid air pockets.

4. Water gently but thoroughly.

into it, so that you will not have to force the stake through the roots themselves. Tie the tree carefully with a soft or padded fabric. Check occasionally to be sure the tie is not too tight, it could girdle the plant and kill it.

Maintenance

Do not allow grass to grow right up to the trunk of a tree. Instead, plant a ground cover, perennials or bulbs, or just leave bare soil around the base of the tree, beyond the point to which the branch tips extend. This way the tree, and not grass, will benefit from the moisture and the nutrients in the soil. Also, a mulch spread beneath the tree can be very beneficial in reducing weeds and moisture evaporation.

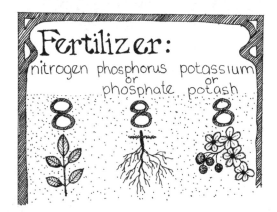

The numbers shown on a container of fertilizer represent the percentage by weight of each chemical ingredient within.

Trees and shrubs grow best if they are given fertilizer. Nitrogen (N) keeps the foliage lush and green. It is a vital nutrient that is rapidly depleted from the soil. Phosphorous (P) helps the tree to mature and encourages the production of fruits, flowers and seeds. Potassium (K) aids in the production of sugars and starches, the maturation of the tree, as well as heightening the colours of the flowers.

A combination of organic and commercially made chemical fertilizer works well. One of the easiest ways to apply nitrogen is to just sprinkle it (the fertilizer) under the tree or shrub, being careful that it does not land on the leaves, possibly burning them. Then, water it well.

In order to give a tree a thorough feeding, including phosphorous and potassium, punch holes in the ground with a screwdriver, pitchfork or specialty tool, as far out as the perimeter of the leaves. The fertilizer mixture can then be administered through these holes and watered in. Read container labels for the amounts to use and never over fertilize. More is not better! Be particularly careful with newly planted trees and shrubs. Mature plants can tolerate fertilizer but you do not want to burn young tender shoots or roots. Never fertilize after mid-July or early August because, at that time, the plants should be slowing their growth to prepare for winter. This is particularly important in areas where winter brings a drastic and sudden change in temperature.

Pruning

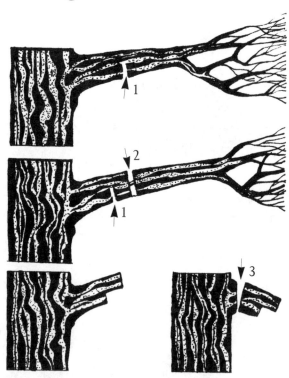

Prune large branches through a succession of three cuts:
  1. *Make the first shallow cut from below.*
  2. *The second cut is made further from the trunk, from above, leaving a stub.*
  3. *Finish with a clean cut on the outside.*
If you try to do the job with a single cut, the weight of the branch may cause it to break and tear.

The frequency, the method and the amount to prune are often points of personal preference, but there are a few guidelines to follow.

Most plants can be pruned in late winter or early spring, when trees and shrubs are dormant, usually between February and May in zones seven and eight. This way, the branch tips that died during winter can be pruned off and not left for insects and disease to infest. However, winter lasts longer in some regions, so take care that you do not prune until it is safe to do so.

Spring pruning also enhances the appearance of evergreens. For example, after pruning or cutting a hedge, there may be some unsightly branch ends and visible bare spots. If you prune it in spring, the hedge has the entire summer to grow new foliage and fill in the gaps. The only plants that should not be pruned in early spring are the shrubs that must bloom first. These are pruned right after they bloom to allow them time to set flower buds for the following spring.

When pruning, the first branches to remove are the ones that are dead, diseased, rubbing together, or crowding others near the centre of the plant.

In order to maintain the health of a tree, the first branches to prune off are the ones that are dead, diseased, rubbing against others or growing too much towards the centre of the plant. Most deciduous trees grow best if air is allowed to circulate through the branches, reducing the ability of pests and diseases to take hold. You should also leave one leader or top branch. This will result in a sturdier tree.

After the general health of the tree or shrub has been considered, the rest of the pruning is cosmetic, in that it is simply a matter of shaping the plant into the form you wish it to take. However, do not prune it against its natural shape, just accentuate it.

Helpful Hints

Some trees and shrubs, like the *Aucuba*, drop their berries, so do not plant them right beside a deck or along a drive or walkway.

If willows (*Salix*), poplars (*Populus*) and dwarf bamboo (*Arundinaria*) do not receive enough water, they have a tendency to send their roots towards the foundation of the house and towards drainage pipes. For this reason they should not be planted within 21 m (70 ft) of the foundation of a home. Given the risks involved with planting these species in urban areas, we have chosen not to include them in the *Plant Encyclopaedia*.

About the Chart of Trees and Shrubs

The pages that follow contain a *Quick Check Chart of Trees and Shrubs*. From the chart, you will discover the most striking features of specific species of trees and shrubs. For more detailed information about the species or varieties that most interest you, refer to the *Plant Encyclopaedia*.

The chart does not include every tree or shrub grown in zones five through eight, but rather those that are consistent performers and are therefore good, dependable choices for your garden. Neither in the chart nor in the *Plant Encyclopaedia* will you find high maintenance plants that require a lot of spraying with chemicals in order to thrive. As we wish to encourage an environmentally sensitive approach to gardening, plants that require excessive applications of chemicals, due to a susceptibility to disease and/or insect infestation, will not be covered.

The columns of the chart list various categories of information pertaining to each species, and are defined as follows:

Common name:

This is the name that a plant is commonly known by. Plants can have several common names that will differ depending on the region that you live in. The chart lists the trees and shrubs alphabetically by their most "commonly" known common names.

Botanical name:

This is the "scientific" name of a plant (note: the *Plant Encyclopaedia* lists all species alphabetically by their scientific names).

Location:

Location refers to the site requirements of a plant, specifically, how much sunlight is needed. Full sun ①, part shade ②, shade ③.

Size:

The trees and shrubs mentioned fall into one of the five following height categories, when they have reached ten years of age:

```
Creeper  = under 31 cm (1 ft)
Dwarf    = under 1 m (3 ft)
Small    = 1 m to 1.5 m (3 ft to 5 ft)
Medium   = 1.5 m to 3 m (6 ft to 10 ft)
Large    = over 3 m (10 ft)
```

Deciduous/Semi-Deciduous/Evergreen/Broadleaf Evergreen:

This category indicates whether a tree or shrub is deciduous (D), semi-deciduous (SD), an evergreen with needled or scaled leaves (E), or a broadleaf evergreen (BE).

Berry/Flower:

This column identifies whether a plant has fruit (fr) or flowers (fl) as well as the season in which these will be at their peak: Spring (Sp); Summer (S); Fall (F); and Winter (W). These times may vary slightly from year to year, depending on seasonal temperatures and the geographic area in which you live.

Special Feature:

If the tree or shrub has a special feature, such as exceptional autumn colour or fragrance, or is attractive to birds, it is identified in this column.

Note:

Also included in the chapters that follow, are *Quick Check Charts* relating to common ground covers, vines, annuals, perennials, ferns, ornamental grasses, and bulbs. For quick reference, all of the charts are listed in the *Table of Contents* under their relevant chapter headings.

*Back yard photographs
of scale drawing in
Chapter 1*

LEFT: Wisteria on arbour roof

ABOVE: Espalier apple on trellis

LEFT: 'Winning Edge' hydrangea beside
rock path

Hard landscape materials

RIGHT: Marble ends

MIDDLE: Interlocking bricks

BOTTOM: Flagstone and bricks

Specimen trees can be underplanted with a variety of plant material

LEFT: Japanese maple

MIDDLE: Sweet gum

BOTTOM: 'Crimson King' maple

Plant textures vary

UPPER LEFT: Bold texture: Gunnera in background, lavatera in foreground

LEFT: Medium texture: Variegated euonymus, weeping blue atlas cedar

MIDDLE: Fine texture: Blue oat grass and Japanese blood grass in the foreground

QUICK CHECK CHART OF TREES AND SHRUBS

COMMON NAME/ *Botanical Name*	LOCATION (SUN ①, PART SUN ② OR SHADE ③)	PLANT TYPE (D, E, SD, BE)	SIZE (AT 5 TO 10 YEARS)	FLOWER (fl) AND/ OR FRUIT (fr) AND THE SEASON		COMMENTS
Abelia 'Edward Goucher' *Abelia 'Edward Goucher'*	①②	SD	small	fl	S	Fragrant lilac-pink flowers Showy bronze bracts in autumn
Aralia, Japanese *Fatsia japonica*	②③	BE	medium			Large-leaved tropical-looking plant
Arbutus, Strawberry *Arbutus unedo 'Compacta'*	①②	BE	medium	fl fr	F F	White flowers and red strawberry-like edible fruit
Aucuba Japanese 'Gold Dust' *Aucuba japonica 'Gold Dust'*	②③	BE	small	fr	F,W	Red berries on female plants Varieties have variegated leaves
Azalea, Rockery *Rhododendron*	①②	BE	dwarf	fl	Sp	White, pink, red and purple flowers
Bamboo, Golden or Goldstem *Phyllostachys aurea*	①②	BE	medium			Tropical-looking foliage A good screen plant
Bamboo, Heavenly or Sacred Bamboo *Nandina domestica*	①②③	BE	small			Interesting fall colour, especially if planted in a sunny location
Barberry Darwin Barberry *Berberis darwinii*	①②	BE	small	fl fr	Sp S	Orange-yellow flowers Bluish-black berries attract birds
Warty Barberry *Berberis verruculosa*	①②	BE	dwarf	fl fr	Sp S	Yellow blooms, reddish fall colour. Bluish-black berries attract birds
Wintergreen Barberry *Berberis julianae*	①②	BE	small	fl fr	Sp S	Yellow flowers, good fall colour. Bluish-black berries attract birds
Beautyberry *Callicarpa bodinieri*	①②	D	small/ medium	fr	F,W	Neon purple berries Attractive autumn foliage

COMMON NAME/ Botanical Name	LOCATION (SUN ①, PART SUN ② OR SHADE ③)	PLANT TYPE (D, E, SD, BE)	SIZE (AT 5 TO 10 YEARS)	FLOWER (fl) AND/ OR FRUIT (fr) AND THE SEASON		COMMENTS
Beech						
Copper Beech *Fagus sylvatica 'Purpurea'*	①	D	large			Reddish or purple foliage
Weeping Copper Beech *Fagus sylvatica 'Purpurea Pendula'*	①	D	small/ large			Unusual weeping form Purple leaves
Birch						
Himalayan White Birch *Betula jacquemontii*	①	D	large			White bark
Young's Weeping Birch *Betula pendula 'Youngii'*	①	D	medium			Weeping form White bark
Black Locust, Honeylocust *Robinia pseudoacacia 'Frisia'*	①	D	large	fl fr	Sp F	White flowers and yellow leaves. Dark bean-like pods
Blueberry *Vaccinium corymbosum*	①	D	small	fl fr	Sp S	Vibrant fall colour Edible blueberries
Bog Rosemary *Andromeda polifolia*	①②	BE	dwarf	fl	Sp	Small pink flowers and narrow blue-grey leaves
Boxwood, English or Common *Buxus sempervirens*	①②③	BE	dwarf			Excellent for shearing and training for a formal garden
Broom						
Lydia Broom *Genista lydia*	①	D	dwarf	fl	Sp	Masses of golden yellow blooms
Moonlight or Warminster Broom *Cytisus praecox*	①	D	small	fl	Sp	Profusion of creamy yellow blooms
'Vancouver Gold' Broom *Genista pilosa 'Vancouver Gold'*	①	D	creeping	fl	Sp	Golden-yellow flowers cover the plant
Butterfly Bush *Buddleia davidii*	①②	D	small	fl	S	Attracts butterflies Prune hard in early spring
California Lilac *Ceanothus thyrsiflorus 'Victoria'*	①	BE	small	fl	Sp	Blue flowers in late spring Prune lightly after flowering

COMMON NAME/ Botanical Name	LOCATION (SUN ①) PART SUN ② OR SHADE ③)	PLANT TYPE (D, E, SD, BE)	SIZE (AT 5 TO 10 YEARS)	FLOWER (fl) AND/ OR FRUIT (fr) AND THE SEASON		COMMENTS
Camellia *Camellia japonica*	①	BE	medium	fl	Sp	Various colours, from white to shades of pink and red, some bicoloured
Cedar						
Blue Atlas Cedar *Cedrus atlantica* 'Glauca'	①	E	large			Tall tree with blue-grey needles
Danish, Emerald, 'Smaragd' *Thuya occidentalis* 'Smaragd'	①②	E	medium			Narrow screen or hedge
Excelsa Cedar *Thuja plicata* 'Excelsa'	①②	E	large			Fast growing hedge plant
Weeping Blue Atlas Cedar *Cedrus atlantica* 'Glauca Pendula'	①	E	medium			Weeping form with blue-grey needles
Cherry						
'Amanogawa' Flowering Cherry *Prunus serrulata* 'Amanogawa'	①	D	large	fl	Sp	Extremely narrow tree
Autumn Flowering Cherry *Prunus subhirtella* 'Autumnalis'	①②	D	large	fl	F,W	Sporadic, semi-double, white to pink flowers
Cinquefoil, 'Yellow Gem' *Potentilla fruticosa* 'Yellow Gem'	①②	D	dwarf	fl	S	Yellow flowers last all summer and into fall
Cotoneaster						
'Coral Beauty' Cotoneaster *Cotoneaster dammeri* 'Coral Beauty'	①②	BE	dwarf	fl	S,F	White flowers followed by coral-red fruit
Rock Spray or Fishbone Cotoneaster,) *Cotoneaster horizontalis*	①②	D	small	fl fr	Sp S,F	Herring-bone pattern made by the branches
Willowleaf Cotoneaster *Cotoneaster salicifolius floccosus*	①②	BE	medium	fl fr	Sp F	Tree-like shrub with long narrow leaves
Cypress						
Dwarf Hinoki Cypress *Chamaecyparis obtusa* 'Nana'	①②	E	dwarf			Tidy, easy-care shrub suitable for small spaces

COMMON NAME/ Botanical Name	LOCATION (SUN ①, PART SUN ②, OR SHADE ③)	PLANT TYPE (D, E, SD, BE)	SIZE (AT 5 TO 10 YEARS)	FLOWER (fl) AND/ OR FRUIT (fr)	AND THE SEASON	COMMENTS
Golden Thread Cypress *Chamaecyparis pisifera* 'Filifera Aurea Nana'	①	E	small			Wide golden mop-like plant Good as a filler plant
Weeping Nootka Cypress *Chamaecyparis nootkatensis* 'Pendula'	①	E	medium			Narrow graceful weeping form
Daphne Rock or Garland *Daphne cneorum*	①	BE	dwarf	fl	Sp	Extremely fragrant pink flowers. Low spreading shrub
Dogwood Korean *Cornus kousa*	①②	D	medium	fl	S	White bracts in late spring to early summer, and outstaning fall colour
Enkianthus, Redvein *Enkianthus campanulatus*	①②	D	small	fl	S	Creamy bell-shaped flowers with red veins; outstanding fall colour
Escallonia, Frades *Escallonia x exoniensis* 'Frades'	①②	BE	small	fl	Sp, S,F	Long lasting blooms; glossy green leaves
Euonymus 'Emerald Gaiety' Euonymus *Euonymus fortunei* 'Emerald Gaiety'	①②	BE	dwarf			Variegated foliage in cream and green
Evergreen Euonymus *Euonymus japonicus* 'Aureovariegatus'	①	BE	small			Variegated foliage in yellow and green
Firethorn *Pyracantha coccinea*	①	BE	medium	fl fr	Sp S,F	Thorny plant; has an interesting look when espaliered along a fence
Forsythia, 'Lynwood Gold' *Forsythia intermedia* 'Lynwood Gold'	①	D	medium	fl	Sp	Early yellow blooms
Goldenchain Tree *Laburnum watereri* 'Vossii'	①②	D	large	fl	Sp	Golden blooms in late spring, followed by brown, poisonous seed-pods
Harry Lauder's Walking Stick *Corylus avellana* 'Contorta'	①	D	medium			Graceful catkins in fall and winter. Extremely twisted branches

COMMON NAME/ *Botanical Name*	LOCATION (SUN ① PART SUN ② OR SHADE ③)	PLANT TYPE (D, E, SD, BE)	SIZE (AT 5 TO 10 YEARS)	FLOWER (fl) AND/ OR FRUIT (fr) AND THE SEASON	COMMENTS
Heather					
Scotch Heather *Calluna vulgaris* 'H.E. Beale'	①②	BE	dwarf	fl S	Long spires of lavender blooms
Winter Heather *Erica carnea* 'King George'	①②	BE	dwarf	fl F,W	Long lasting light mauve blooms.
Hemlock					
Mountain Hemlock *Tsuga mertensiana*	①②	E	large		Unusual evergreen for a small garden
Sargent Weeping Hemlock *Tsuga canadensis* 'Pendula'	①②	E	small		Weeping shrub, used to cascade over walls, rocks, etc.
Holly, Convex Leaf Japanese *Ilex crenata* 'Convexa'	①②③	BE	small		Easy to clip and maintain Often is mistaken for boxwood
Honeylocust, Sunburst *Gleditsia triacanthos* 'Sunburst'	①	D	large		Golden leaflets make a showy display
Hydrangea					
Bigleaf Hydrangea *Hydrangea macrophylla*	②	D	small	fl S	Usually, the flowers are blue
Peegee or P.G. Hydrangea *Hydrangea paniculata*	①②	D	medium	fl S	Flowers are white, then turn pink. Tree-like shrub
'Winning Edge' Hydrangea *Hydrangea macrophylla 'Winning Edge'*	②	D	dwarf	fl S	Deep pinkish blooms
Japanese Umbrella Pine *Sciadopitys verticillata*	②	E	medium		Long, thick, needle-like foliage, arranged like umbrella spokes
Jasmine, Winter *Jasminum nudiflorum*	①②	D	small	fl W	Yellow tubular flowers bloom in late winter on vine-like arching branches
Juniper					
'Blue Star' Juniper *Juniperus squamata* 'Blue Star'	①②	E	dwarf		Blue-grey needles on a compact shrub

COMMON NAME/ Botanical Name	LOCATION (SUN ①) PART SUN ② OR SHADE ③)	PLANT TYPE (D, E, SD, BE)	SIZE (AT 5 TO 10 YEARS)	FLOWER (fl) AND/ OR FRUIT (fr) AND THE SEASON		COMMENTS
Hollywood Juniper *Juniperus chinensis 'Torulosa'*	①②	E	medium	fr		Interesting twisted shape Blue fruit is favoured by robins
'Old Gold' Juniper *Juniperus chinensis 'Pfitzeriana Old Gold'*	①	E	dwarf			Popular low growing filler plant. The tips of the foliage are golden coloured
'Skyrocket' Juniper *Juniperus virginiana 'Skyrocket'*	①	E	medium			A narrow, blue-grey shrub Imparts a dramatic effect
Katsura Tree *Cercidiphyllum japonicum*	①②	D	large			A relatively pest-free tree Fall colour is pink to yellow
Leucothoe, Drooping 'Rainbow' *Leucothoe fontanesiana 'Rainbow'*	①②	BE	dwarf	fl	Sp	Variegated foliage White bell-shaped flowers
Lilac, 'Miss Kim' or Korean *Syringa patula 'Miss Kim'*	①②	D	small	fl	Sp	Lavender-blue fragrant flowers bloom in late spring
Lily-of-the-valley Shrub, or 'Mountain Fire' Andromeda *Pieris japonica 'Mountain Fire'*	①②	BE	small	fl	Sp	White flowers, with bronze new leaves in spring, turning green in summer
Lingonberry or Mountain-cranberry *Vaccinium vitis-idaea minus*	①②	BE	dwarf	fl fr	Sp S	Urn-shaped pink-white blooms. Edible red berries in summer
Little Leaf Linden *Tilia cordata*	①	D	large	fl	S	Heart-shaped leaves White blooms
Longleaf or Cascading Mahonia *Mahonia nervosa*	②	BE	dwarf	fl fr	Sp S	Fragrant yellow flowers Blue-black berries
Magnolia Evergreen Magnolia *Magnolia grandiflora*	①	BE	large	fl	S	Fragrant creamy-white flowers Medium sized cultivars are available
Saucer Magnolia *Magnolia x soulangiana*	①②	D	large	fl	S	Fragrant white flowers with crimson centres

COMMON NAME/ Botanical Name	LOCATION (SUN ①) PART SUN ② OR SHADE ③)	PLANT TYPE (D, E, SD, BE)	SIZE (AT 5 TO 10 YEARS)	FLOWER (fl) AND/ OR FRUIT (fr) AND THE SEASON		COMMENTS
Siebold's or Oyama Magnolia *Magnolia sieboldii*	①②	D	large	fl	S	Fragrant white flowers in early spring
Star Magnolia *Magnolia stellata*	①②	D	medium	fl	S	White flowers, rose-purple at the base
Maidenhair Tree *Ginkgo biloba*	①	D	large			Fan-shaped leaves that turn from light green to golden in autumn
Maple 'Bloodgood' Maple *Acer palmatum* 'Bloodgood'	①②	D	large			Leaves are purple-red in spring and summer, then turn scarlet in autumn
'Burgundy Lace' Japanese Maple *Acer palmatum* 'Burgundy Lace'	①②	D	medium			Deeply cut leaves with purple-red summer colour
Coral Bark or 'Senkaki' Maple *Acer palmatum* 'Sango Kaku'	①②	D	large			Bright coral bark year-round Yellow leaves in autumn
Crimson Queen Laceleaf Maple *Acer palmatum* 'Dissectum Crimson Queen'	①	D	small			Finely-cut leaves emerge in spring, turning scarlet in autumn
Green Laceleaf Japanese Maple *Acer palmatum* 'Dissectum Viridis'	①	D	small			Finely-cut, light green leaves that turn yellow in autumn
Red Japanese Maple *Acer palmatum* 'Atropurpureum'	①②	D	large			Red-purple leaf colour all summer
'Red Sunset' Maple *Acer rubrum* 'Red Sunset'	①	D	large			Brilliant scarlet fall colour
'Shindeshojo' Japanese Maple *Acer palmatum* 'Shindeshojo'	①	D	medium			Pink-crimson new spring growth
Snakebark Maple *Acer capillipes*	①	D	large			White, vertical, snake-like markings on the trunk

COMMON NAME/ Botanical Name	LOCATION (SUN ①, PART SUN ② OR SHADE ③)	PLANT TYPE (D, E, SD, BE)	SIZE (AT 5 TO 10 YEARS)	FLOWER (fl) AND/ OR FRUIT (fr) AND THE SEASON		COMMENTS
Vine Maple *Acer circinatum*	①②	D	large			Orange, red and yellow autumn leaves
Mexican Mock Orange *Choisya ternata*	①②	BE	small	fl	Sp	Fragrant white flowers sporadically bloom through-out the year
Mimosa Tree or Silk Tree *Albizia julibrissin*	①	D	medium	fl	S	Finely textured, light green foliage and fluffy pink flowers
Mock Orange *Philadelphus virginalis*	①	D	medium	fl	Sp	Aromatic white flowers bloom in late spring
Mountain Laurel *Kalmia latifolia*	②	BE	small	fl	Sp	Red, pink or white flowers Dwarf varieties are available
Mulberry, Weeping *Morus alba 'Pendula'*	①	D	medium			Tree has a weeping form
Oregon Grape *Mahonia aquifolium*	①②	BE	small	fl fr	Sp S	Fragrant yellow flowers Blue-black berries attract birds
Pernettya *Pernettya mucronata*	①②	BE	dwarf	fl fr	Sp F,W	White flowers Large berries
Photinia, Fraser's *Photinia x fraseri*	①	BE	medium			New foliage is bright scarlet year-round
Pine Austrian Black Pine *Pinus nigra*	①	E	large			A handsome background plant
Dwarf Pumilio Mugho Pine *Pinus mugo pumilio*	①②	E	small			Long dark green needles
Weeping Japanese Red Pine *Pinus densiflora 'Pendula'*	①	E	small			Drooping branches Suitable for Oriental gardens
Portugal Laurel *Prunus lusitanica*	①②	BE	medium	fl fr	Sp S	White fragrant flowers Dark red-purple berries Dark green foliage year-round

COMMON NAME/ Botanical Name	LOCATION (SUN ①) PART SUN ② OR SHADE ③)	PLANT TYPE (D, E, SD, BE)	SIZE (AT 5 TO 10 YEARS)	FLOWER (fl) AND/ OR FRUIT (fr) AND THE SEASON		COMMENTS
Quince, Flowering *Chaenomeles japonica*	①	D	medium	fl fr	Sp S	Flowers are pink, peach or white, followed by quince fruit
Rhododendron *Rhododendron*	①②③	BE	small/ medium	fl	Sp	Wide range of colours and sizes. Tolerance of light conditions depends on the variety chosen
Rock Rose or Sun Rose *Helianthemum nummularium*	①	BE	dwarf	fl	Sp	Small blooms in shades of pink, white, yellow or orange
Rose or Shrub Rose *Rosa*	①	D	small	fl fr	S F	Many colours and varieties are available. Hips appear in fall and winter
Rose-of-Sharon *Hibiscus syriacus*	①②	D	medium	fl	S,F	Blooms from July until fall, with large blue, pink or white flowers
Salal *Gaultheria shallon*	①②	BE	small	fl fr	S F	White flowers bloom in early summer, followed by blue-black berries in late summer
Sarcococca						
Fragrant Sarcococca *Sarcococca ruscifolia*	②③	BE	small	fl fr	W Sp	Fragrant white flowers Dark red berries
Himalayan Sweet Box *Sarcococca hookeriana humilis*	②③	BE	dwarf	fl fr	W Sp	Fragrant flowers bloom in late winter. Blue-black berries
Sequoia, Weeping *Sequoiadendron giganteum* 'Pendulum'	①②	E	large			Narrow weeping form
Skimmia, Japanese *Skimmia japonica*	②③	BE	small	fl fr	Sp F,W	Fragrant white flower clusters Bright red berries
Smoke Bush or Purple Smoke Tree *Cotinus coggygria* 'Royal Purple'	①	D	medium	fl	S	Flowers resemble smoke-like puffs. Leaves are purple in summer and turn orange, yellow and red in fall

COMMON NAME/ Botanical Name	LOCATION (SUN ①, PART SUN ②, OR SHADE ③)	PLANT TYPE (D, E, SD, BE)	SIZE (AT 5 TO 10 YEARS)	FLOWER (fl) AND/ OR FRUIT (fr)	AND THE SEASON	COMMENTS
Snowdrop, or Japanese Snowbell Tree *Styrax japonica*	①②	D	large	fl	Sp	Scented white flowers bloom in late spring or early summer
Sourwood, Sorrel Tree *Oxydendrum arboreum*	①②③	D	large	fl	S	White flowers Narrow leaves that turn orange-red in autumn
Spruce Serbian Spruce *Picea omorika*	①	E	large			Narrow evergreen. Blue-grey underside of branches
Sumac, Stag Horn Sumac *Rhus typhina*	①②	D	large	fl fr	Sp F,W	Most noted for its yellow-orange, scarlet and red fall colours. Tiny blooms followed by reddish fruit
Sweet Gum *Liquidambar styraciflua*	①	D	large			Wrinkled bark Excellent autumn leaf colour
Viburnum David's Viburnum *Viburnum davidii*	①②	BE	small	fl fr	Sp F,W	White flowers bloom in late spring. Colbalt-blue berries
'Spring Bouquet' Viburnum *Viburnum tinus* 'Spring Bouquet' 'Summer	①②	BE	small	fl fr	W,Sp S	White flowers Metallic blue berries
'Summer Snowflake' Viburnum *Viburnum plicatum* Snowflake'	①②	D	medium	fl	S	White flowers bloom from May until frost. Purple to red leaf colour in autumn
Weigela 'Bristol Ruby' *Weigela* 'Bristol Ruby'	①②	D	small	fl	Sp,S	Ruby-red flowers bloom in late spring and into the summer
Windmill Palm *Trachycarpus fortunei*	①②	BE	medium			Large fan-shaped leaves Trunk is covered with hairy fibres
Wintergreen *Gaultheria procumbens*	①②	BE	dwarf	fl fr	S F,W	White flowers bloom in early summer. Hot pink to red berries

COMMON NAME/ Botanical Name	LOCATION (SUN ①, PART SUN ②, OR SHADE ③)	PLANT TYPE (D, E, SD, BE)	SIZE (AT 5 TO 10 YEARS)	FLOWER (fl) AND/ OR FRUIT (fr) AND THE SEASON		COMMENTS
Witch Hazel, Chinese *Hamamelis mollis*	①②	D	medium	fl	W	Fragrant thin yellow flowers bloom in late winter
Yew Hick's Yew *Taxus x media 'Hicksii'*	①②③	E	medium	fr	S,F	Poisonous reddish berries
Melford Yew *Taxus baccata 'Melford'*	①②	E	small	fr	S,F	A narrow evergreen
Yucca, Weeping *Yucca recurvifolia or pendula*	①②	E	small	fl	S	Bold, sword-shaped foliage White flowers bloom in early summer

Ground Covers and Vines

IN SMALLER URBAN gardens, ground covers and vines play an important role by producing a living wall or carpet of colour and texture. These plants create a vertical or horizontal plane that takes up less space, overall, than many other plant species. You can choose from evergreen, deciduous, annual or perennial varieties. The choices are as varied as are the results.

Ground Covers

Ground covers assume an important function in design, as they provide a smooth transition from a flat surface to vertical structures, such as shrubs or trees. The most commonly used ground cover is grass (refer to *Chapter 4: Installing a New Lawn and Maintaining an Old One*, for more information on turf). The term *ground cover* refers to the use of a plant, not to a specific category or generic classification. It is simply a plant that is used in a mass planting and is usually low growing.

The variety to choose from is immense, from strawberries (*Fragaria*) to periwinkle (*Vinca minor*) to low growing junipers (*Juniperus species*). As mentioned above, ground covers can be perennial, annual, evergreen or deciduous. A simple mass of *Impatiens* provides an example of an annual ground cover that is replaced from year to year. However, when we speak of ground covers, we usually mean the perennial type that will grow for years, covering more and more area if it is not pruned back.

Each species of ground cover is unique and can lend a totally different look to your garden. Whatever types you choose, be sure to find out how widely they will spread so that you can plant them at an appropriate distance from each other. Refer to the *Plant Encyclopaedia* for the information you require.

See the *Quick Check Chart of Common Ground Covers* at the end of this chapter for a listing of popular varieties.

A ground cover can be any plant that is planted in mass and remains relatively low growing.

Strawberries (Fragaria)   Periwinkle (Vinca)   Juniper (low growing Juniperus)

Vines

Today, one of the most frequent uses of vines in gardens is as a screen, an alternative to a hedge. A shrub hedge provides privacy, but it usually takes up a lot of room, 1 m to 1.5 m (4 ft to 5 ft) in depth, significantly reducing the size of the garden.

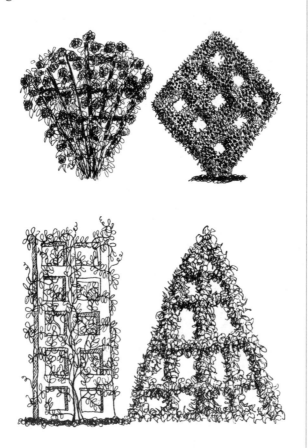

A well-placed trellis with vines growing over it ensures privacy and produces an ever-changing tapestry of colour.

By contrast, a well-placed trellis with vines growing over it will produce an ever-changing tapestry of colour without compromising the limited available space.

When choosing a vine to grow in your yard, ensure you have provided proper support for its potential growth. *Wisteria* needs strong support for its branches and trunk, while a lighter weight vine, like *Clematis*, is quite happy on a lattice.

A Clematis flower

Wisteria *vine*

As with any plant, understand the requirements of the vine in terms of sun exposure, soil preference, moisture, etc. Some vines need to be tied onto a support while others are able to climb on their own. When tying a vine, do not use twist ties. They have a wire in them that will eventually girdle the branch and kill it. Use a soft fabric and do not tie it too tightly. Periodically check the ties to ensure they are not too taut.

To help you to decide which vine(s) to plant in your own garden, refer to the *Quick Check Chart of Common Vines* in the pages that follow. Descriptions of their distinctive characteristics have been included to make the task of choosing plants easier for you. Refer to the *Plant Encyclopaedia* for more information pertaining to the individual species you are interested in.

Helpful Hints

- Ensure that supports have sufficient strength to bear the weight of the plant.
- *Clematis* roots must be shaded.
- When feeding *Wisteria*, use a fertilizer with a lower nitrogen content or it will produce more greenery and fewer flowers.
- For colour and interest year-round, grow a variety of vines together.

Some vines need to be tied while others support themselves and climb by tendrils, suckers, aerial roots, or by twining.

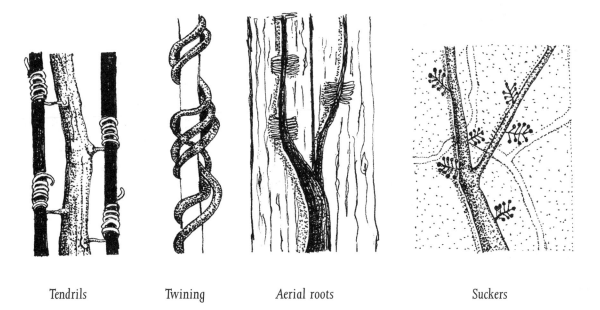

Tendrils   Twining   Aerial roots   Suckers

QUICK CHECK CHART OF COMMON GROUND COVERS

COMMON NAME/
Botanical Name

	LOCATION (SUN ①, PART SUN ②, OR SHADE ③)	PLANT TYPE (D, E, SD, BE)	HEIGHT	SPREAD	FLOWER AND/OR FRUIT AND THE SEASON		COMMENTS
Bugleweed *Ajuga reptans* 'Bronze Beauty'	①②③	BE	15 cm (6 in)	30 cm (12 in)	fl	Sp	Violet-blue flowers and dark bronze leaves
Bunchberry *Cornus canadensis*	①②	SD	15 cm (6 in)	30 cm (12 in)	fl fr	Sp S	White flowers in late spring. Red fruit in late summer
Chameleon Plant *Houttuynia cordata* 'Variegata'	①②③	D	30 cm (12 in)	30 cm (12 in)			Multi-coloured, heart-shaped leaves
Cinquefoil, 'Yellow Gem' *Potentilla fruticosa* 'Yellow Gem'	①②	D	30 cm (12 in)	60 cm (2 ft)			Yellow flowers bloom from May into October
Cotoneaster 'Coral Beauty' Cotoneaster *Cotoneaster dammeri* 'Coral Beauty'	①②	BE	45 cm (18 in)	60 cm (2 ft)	fl fr	Sp S,F	White flowers Coral-red berries
Fish-bone Cotoneaster *Cotoneaster horizontalis*	①②	D	1 m (3 ft)	2 m (6 ft)	fl fr	Sp S,F	White flowers Red berries
English Ivy *Hedera helix*	①②③	BE	3m (10 ft)	60 cm (2 ft)			A vine, it will cling to surfaces. Good erosion control
'Grace Ward', Lithodora *Lithospermum diffusa* 'Grace Ward'	①②	BE	15 cm (6 in)	45 cm (18 in)	fl	S,F	Royal blue flowers
Heather Scotch Heather *Calluna vulgaris* 'H.E. Beale'	①②	BE	45 cm (18 in)	45 cm (18 in)	fl	S	Spires of lavender blooms
Winter Heather *Erica carnea*	①②	BE	30 cm (12 in)	90 cm (3 ft)	fl	F,W	Long lasting flowers in white, mauve and carmine
Japanese Spurge *Pachysandra terminalis*	②③	BE	25 cm (10 in)	30 cm (12 in)			Interesting foliage for shady areas

COMMON NAME/ Botanical Name	LOCATION (SUN ①, PART SUN ②, OR SHADE ③)	PLANT TYPE (D, E, SD, BE)	HEIGHT	SPREAD	FLOWER AND/ OR FRUIT AND THE SEASON		COMMENTS
Juniper 'Old Gold' Juniper *Juniperus chinensis* 'Pfitzeriana Old Gold'	①	E	60 cm (2 ft)	1.5 m (5 ft)			Low, wide growing habit. Golden tipped foliage year-round
Kinnikinnick *Arctostaphylos uva-ursi* 'Vancouver Jade'	①②	BE	10 cm (4 in)	1 m (3 ft)	fl fr	Sp F	Pink-white flowers Red berries in autumn
Mother of Thyme *Thymus serpyllum* 'Coccineus'	①	BE	7 cm (3 in)	30 cm (12 in)	fl	Sp	Tiny rose-red fragrant flowers
Periwinkle *Vinca minor*	②③	BE	15 cm (6 in)	45 cm (18 in)	fl	Sp	Lavender-blue flowers bloom sporadically until autumn
Phlox, Creeping *Phlox subulata*	①	BE	10 cm (4 in)	60 cm (2 ft)	fl	Sp	White, pink, mauve or blue flowers
St. John's Wort *Hypericum calycinum*	①②	BE	30 cm (12 in)	45 cm (18 in)	fl	S	Golden flowers bloom all summer
Viburnum David's Viburnum *Viburnum davidii*	①②	BE	60 cm (2 ft)	1.5 m (5 ft)	fl fr	Sp F,W	White flowers bloom in late summer Colbalt-blue berries
Wormwood *Artemisia stelleriana* 'Silver Brocade'	①②	D	20 cm (8 in)	60 cm (2 ft)			Silver-grey foliage

QUICK CHECK CHART OF COMMON VINES

COMMON NAME/ Botanical Name	LOCATION (SUN ①, PART SUN ②, OR SHADE ③)	PLANT TYPE (D, E, SD, BE)	SPREAD	FLOWER AND/ OR FRUIT	AND THE SEASON	COMMENTS
Akebia, Fiveleaf *Akebia quinata*	①②	SD	4.5 m (15 ft)	fl fr	Sp S	Fragrant rose-purple flowers and fruit in the summer
Clematis *Clematis "Jackmanii"*	①②③	D	6 m (20 ft)	fl	S	Violet-purple flowers
Clematis montana rubens	①②③	D	4.5 m (15 ft)	fl	Sp	Fragrant pink flowers
Clematis 'Nelly Moser'	①②③	D	3 m (10 ft)	fl	Sp,S	Large, mauve-pink flowers
Evergreen Clematis *Clematis armandii*	①②	BE	6 m (20 ft)	fl	Sp	Fragrant white flowers
English Ivy *Hedera helix*	①②③	BE	3 m (10 ft)			Self-clinging vine Aerial roots
Honeysuckle 'Gold Flame' Honeysuckle *Lonicera 'Gold Flame'*	①②	D	3.7 m (12 ft)	fl	S	Gold and red flowers bloom in summer until first frost
Hall's Honeysuckle *Lonicera japonica 'Halliana'*	①②	SD	4.6 m (15 ft)	fl	S	Fragrant white and yellow flowers bloom all summer
Hydrangea, Climbing *Hydrangea anomala petiolaris*	②	D	3 m (10 ft)	fl	S	White flowers bloom all summer
Trumpet Vine *Campsis radicans*	①	D	3 m (10 ft)	fl	S	Dark trumpet-like flowers Aerial roots
Virginia Creeper *Parthenocissus quinquefolia*	①②③	D	6 m (20 ft)			Self-clinging vine Leaves have five leafets
Winter Jasmine *Jasminum nudiflorum*	①②	D	2 m (6 ft)	fl	W	Yellow flowers bloom in late winter
Wisteria Chinese Wisteria *Wisteria sinensis*	①	D	8 m (25 ft)	fl	Sp	Fragrant violet-blue flowers
Japanese Wisteria *Wisteria floribunda*	①	D	7 m (23 ft)	fl	Sp	Fragrant lilac-blue flowers

Installing a New Lawn and Maintaining an Old One

How to Seed and Feed

Preparing the Bed

The first and ultimately the most important element in seeding a lawn, or laying sod, is the preparation of the soil. The lawn will be there for a very long time and is a high demand crop, so preparation is essential.

First, level the subgrade or contour it closely to the desired final grade. Be sure that the drainage is good, and that the grade (if any) slopes away from the house and other buildings. Sticks, debris, and large stones should be removed.

Well-drained loam is the best soil for a lawn. Sandy soils dry too quickly and clay soils are hard to work with and may become compacted. Add a uniform layer of topsoil, at least 5 cm (2 in), but no more than 15 cm (6 in), deep. If the depth is insufficient, the lawn will not be healthy as it will develop shallow roots and have low resistance to stress (ie. drought). For more information on soil, refer to the Introduction.

Before sowing grass seed, ensure that the seedbed is properly prepared. The entire area should be hand weeded. Ideally, seedbed preparation should begin six weeks before sowing the seed. The area should be thoroughly weeded every two weeks during this time. This ensures that any weed seeds left in the soil will have had time to germinate and grow to a height where they can be easily pulled up, before the grass seed is spread.

It is always advisable to have a soil analysis done before sowing grass seed. If you send a soil sample to a lab, be sure to mention the type of crop (turf) to be sown in it. The analysis you receive will include a readout of exactly what is needed to augment the soil, what elements are lacking or are excessive, as well as identifying your pH level (ie. level of acidity).

Phosphorus is the prime element to consider at this time because it is needed to encourage strong root growth. It is represented by the second of the three fertilizer numbers. Use a fertilizer with a ratio of 1:2:1 or 1:3:1. Ideally, a fertilizer numbered "16-32-6" or "10-30-10" is best to use, in the case of turf. To apply fertilizer, spread it evenly over the bed and work it into the soil, with a rake, to a depth of 7 cm to 11 cm (3 in to 4 in). Once again, read all instructions before doing so.

The key to good germination is a firm seedbed, so roll the bed before spreading the seed. The seedbed should be firm enough that a person can walk on it without leaving a footprint.

Seeding a New Lawn

After the soil is rolled and firm, it should be lightly raked, or scuffled, to a depth of .5 cm

Always use top quality grass seed.

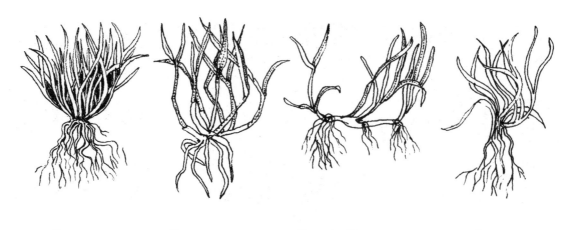

| Fescue | Bent grass | Kentucky blue grass | Rye |

(¼in). The seed can then be evenly distributed and the area rolled once more. This will ensure that the seed has firm contact with the soil and that germination will be more successful as a result. Another option would be to seed the area, then gently rake, and roll. The method to use is up to you.

The best time for seeding in zones seven and eight, is in early September to the middle of October, if the autumn is not particularly cold. Spring seeding, done in March and April, is second best, and still allows the turf to be well established before the hot days of July and August arrive. In cooler zones, the best time for seeding is from mid-August to the end of September. This allows the seedlings sufficient time to grow before the temperature drops too drastically. Alternatively, the seed can be sown in spring, but you must ensure that the new grass has enough time to become well established before the heat of summer arrives.

The type of seed to use depends upon the intended use of the area as well as the climate and the amount of maintenance you are willing to expend on it. Use only certified, top quality grass seed. Blends of seed are continually changing, depending on the area where you live and the type of conditions present.

Be sure to read the instructions and spread the seed at the correct rate. For an even distribution it is best to cover the area once with half of the seed while walking in one direction, eg. east to west. Spread the other half of the seed while walking at a 90-degree angle, eg. north to south.

Watering a New Lawn

Too much watering can result in puddles and patchy lawn growth

Once the seed is spread, the soil must be kept moist. Frequent, light watering will be necessary. If you water too heavily, the seed will be washed into puddles, resulting in a lawn that is not at all uniform in appearance. If the weather is not overly hot and your soil is not too sandy, watering the seedbed for twenty minutes, three times a day will bring the desired results. After the seed has sprouted, watering may be less frequent, but the soil will still need to be kept moist, otherwise the seedlings will die.

Steps for turf preparation:

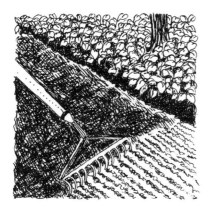

1. Rake   2. Roll   3. Seed

Fertilizing a New Lawn

The first application of fertilizer for your newly seeded lawn should be done when the grass blades are 7.5 cm (3 in) long. Use a fertilizer at only half of the usual strength. If you are seeding in autumn, use a 16-20-0 or 11-48-0 ratio, and if you seed in spring, use one with a higher nitrogen level (ie. the first number listed).

Mowing a New Lawn

When the grass is 7.5 cm (3 in) long, and has had its first application of fertilizer, it can then be cut back to 5 cm (2 in) long. However, if more than one third of the leaf blade is cut off, the lawn will suffer from shock. Be sure the blade of your mower is sharp or you will rip the tops off of each leaf blade, leaving a ratty looking lawn. Also ensure that the soil is dry when mowing or the soil will become too compacted.

Herbicides

Do not use herbicides on a lawn for six to eight weeks after new growth is apparent.

How to Lay Sod or Instant-Turf

When sodding your lawn, the technique and preparations are the same as for seeding except that the sod is unrolled and laid down rather than spreading seed. Rolling the sod is very important even though you may think it unnecessary. The roots must have firm contact with the new soil bed. Ensure that the seams alternate in order to achieve a more finished look.

When unrolling sod, alternate the seams, like masonry in a brick wall.

Seeding and Sodding – a Summary

1. Prepare the soil
2. Pull weeds
3. Fertilize and rake the soil
4. Roll the soil
5. Gently rake, or scuffle, the top of the soil
6. Spread the seed or lay the sod
7. Roll once again
8. Water
9. Provide regular maintenance

Maintaining a Mature Lawn

Mowing

The height at which you maintain your lawn is one of the most important factors in lawn care as it determines all other management practices. The correct height to mow your lawn will depend upon the type or the cultivar of grass you are growing. For example, bentgrass, generally used for golf greens, will tolerate being mowed quite short, 1 cm (½ in) or less, while Kentucky bluegrass should be no less than 3 cm (1¼ in) high. The lawn must be mowed often enough that not more than one third of the blade is removed at any one time. The average home lawn seed mixture will result in a lawn that should be kept at a height range of 2.5 cm to 5 cm (1 in to 2 in) in length. This will mean mowing twice a week during times of rapid growth.

When it is hot and dry outside, be sure to raise the height of the cutting blade on your mower. This will give the grass more resistance to severe weather. Remember, the shorter you mow, the more shallow the roots will be, causing the grass to dry out quickly. Grass also benefits from extra length in autumn, helping it cope with the stresses of winter temperatures.

Always keep the blade of your lawn mower sharp. A dull blade will tear off the tops of the blades of grass rather than slicing them off.

If the lawn is properly maintained, you can leave the grass clippings on the lawn when you mow, and allow them to decompose naturally. If, however, the clippings are too long, be sure to remove them in order to prevent thatch buildup.

For the first mowing in spring, the grass should be left a little longer than for subsequent mowings.

Never mow the lawn when it is wet. The cut will be poor because the blades of grass may be torn rather than sliced off. Not only will the lawn be less healthy, as a result, but it is also much more difficult to mow when wet.

Keep tools clean and in good working order.

Fertilizing

Fertilizing a lawn is necessary! Heavy rain quickly leaches out many of the nutrients in the soil. Regardless of what region you live in, nutrients will be depleted from one year to the next, and should therefore be replenished.

With regard to lawn fertilization, it is very important to achieve an even distribution. One way to do this is to take half of the fertilizer and apply it in one direction on the lawn, north to south, and then take the other half and apply it in an east to west direction. By using a throw spreader rather than a drop spreader, you will be less likely to miss strips of lawn and will thereby avoid a "checker board" effect.

Do not fertilize the lawn when the grass is wet. The chemicals will stick to the wet blades instead of working down to the soil, and the grass may be burned as a result.

Do not use more fertilizer than necessary. If you do, you will be mowing your lawn every other day, and the lawn will be much more susceptible to stress. Ideally, you should split your fertilizing schedule into at least three, or four applications during the year. For example:

- Mid-May, early September, and November

or

- Early May, mid-June, early September, and November

In spring, use a fertilizer with a higher nitrogen level (ie. the first number in the ratio). The autumn application should not be attempted until the lawn is dormant (ie. the lawn has stopped growing for the winter) and the fertilizer should have a lower nitrogen level. Some fertilizers are specifically identified as "Winterizing" and are appropriate for the last application in November.

Fertilizer nutrients are better absorbed if the pH level of the soil is close to the 6.5 mark. For this reason, if you have an acidic soil, lime should be applied to the lawn first. Ideally, the lawn should be limed two weeks before fertilizer is applied, to allow time for the pH of the soil to alter. An application once per year is usually sufficient for lime. If you are unsure as to whether lime is required, it is recommended that you have your soil tested at a lab.

Watering

The average lawn needs no more than 3 cm to 5 cm (1 in to 2 in) of water per week. Infrequent, heavier watering brings about stronger lawn growth than frequent, light watering. Correct watering encourages deeper root growth and results in a lawn that is more resistant to natural stresses. A healthy lawn also grows more vigorously and weeds have a harder time taking hold.

In order to gauge the amount of water to apply, place containers (tins or ice cream buckets) on your lawn at various distances from the sprinkler. Turn the sprinkler on and measure how much water your sprinkler puts out within an hour. If you have accumulated 1.5 cm (½ in) of water during that time, then you know that you will need to water for two to three hours, in total, for the week. This measuring need only be done once, but it is necessary in order for you to correctly gauge your specific watering needs.

Early morning is the best time of the day to water your lawn. Evening watering will leave your lawn cool and damp at night, which will encourage the growth of diseases. Watering in the heat of the day only results in water being quickly evaporated and wasted.

Thatch

Thatch is made up of partially decomposed lawn clippings that have been left on the lawn, forming a layer between the grass and the soil. When this layer gets too deep, it can cause problems in your lawn. The turf may actually root in the thatch rather than in the soil, causing the grass, when stressed, to quickly die back. Thick thatch may also restrict the amount of water that gets to the roots of the grass. Finally, excessive thatch

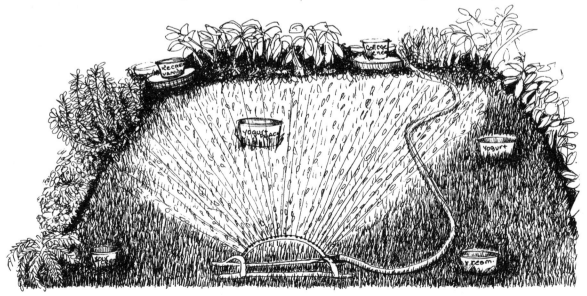

A mature lawn needs 3 cm - 5 cm (1 in - 2 in) of water each week. Each year in spring, when you first sprinkle, use containers to measure your water output.

If thatch is too deep, the grass will root in it rather than the soil. As a result, the roots will not be firmly established. They could be pulled out with only a gentle tug.

buildup provides a great place in which disease and insects can thrive and overwinter.

A small layer of thatch, 1 cm (¼ in) deep, is beneficial for the lawn because, as it decomposes, its nutrients are returned to the soil and, ultimately, to the grass. A thin layer also prevents rapid water evaporation.

If the thatch layer is more than 2.5 cm (1 in) deep, remove it. Power raking or vertical mowing should be done in spring or early autumn to allow the lawn to recover and rejuvenate quickly. To prevent thatch buildup, follow these steps:

- Do not over fertilize or over water, as doing so only encourages excessive growth, resulting in excessive cutting and allowing for a buildup of excessive thatch.
- Never cut off more than one third of the leaf blade at one time. This allows the cuttings to decompose between mowings. If the grass is particularly long, it is advisable to remove the clippings after or while mowing.

Moss

Moss is found in the lawn when conditions favour moss more than they favour turf. Moss cannot invade a healthy, vigorous turf. If your lawn is prone to moss growth, you must change the existing conditions in order to encourage the grass and discourage the moss. By following the instructions below, you should be able to get your moss problem under control:

- Remove as much moss as you can with a steel hand rake.
- Treat the area with moss killer (copper or aluminum sulphate), making sure to read the label for application instructions. The lawn should be wet when the chemical is applied to make it stick to the moss. Do not water the area for forty eight hours following the application. The chemical should settle on the moss itself, not leach into the soil.
- Let the moss die. Your lawn will probably look really awful right about now! But, do not despair, just take a steel hand rake and remove all the dead moss that you can.
- Reseed the area, if necessary.
- Proper maintenance and regular fertilization will keep your lawn in good condition thereafter.

Conditions in Which Moss Thrives

1. *Drainage:*

Moss likes to be damp, therefore good drainage for the lawn is essential. If the soil becomes compacted over time, you may need to aerate the lawn. This is done by punching holes in the soil. An aerator should remove twelve holes in every square foot. The plugs can be left lying on top where they will decompose and break down. Aeration can be done twice during the year, spring and autumn. Aeration machines can be rented when needed. It may be necessary to apply 1 cm to 2.5 cm (½ in to 1 in) of sand, followed by lime, in order to sufficiently improve drainage, raise the pH level and reduce the recurrence of moss.

2. *Shade:*

Moss likes the shade. If you are trying to grow grass in a shady area, be sure that the seed mix contains red fescue. Most nurseries have seed that has been specifically developed for shady conditions.

3. *Soil pH:*

Moss likes acidic soil. That is why it is necessary to lime the lawn, it "sweetens" the soil. Lime itself does not kill the moss, it simply alters the pH level of the soil. If you are treating your lawn for moss, you will need to apply lime twice a year for two years and then once a year after that. As previously mentioned, a soil test is the most accurate way to find out the pH level of your soil.

4. *Poor fertility:*

Moss grows well if soil fertility is poor. Ensure good fertility by following a regular schedule for applying lawn fertilizer. A spring application of a fertilizer, such as 28-4-8, will increase the vigour of the lawn, giving the moss less of a chance to thrive.

Summary of Moss Removal:

1. Use shade tolerant seed if the area to be seeded is in the shade
2. Improve drainage conditions
3. Kill moss by:
   - wetting it
   - using moss killer
   - raking up and throwing away the dead moss
4. Lime your lawn regularly
5. Fertilize your lawn on schedule
6. Ensure proper lawn maintenance

Note

For a description of the common weeds found in lawns, as well as instructions on how to eradicate them, refer to the section entitled *Woe to Weeds… identification, treatment and prevention*, in Chapter 6.

CHAPTER 5

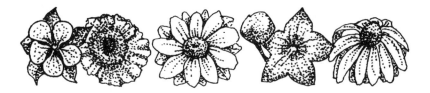

Flowers in the Garden

IN THE GARDEN, flowers provide the finishing touch, or the icing on the cake. They offer bright aesthetic appeal and play a decorative role in garden design. The variety of colours, forms and textures is limitless. The choices you make will reflect your own taste and style, so experiment with combinations and enjoy yourself!

Choosing Flowering Plants

First of all, assess the site (ie. soil composition and microclimate) where the plant is to be placed. Ensure that the plant's requirements match the site or you will be doing more maintenance than necessary and the plant will not be as healthy as it could be.

Imagine the plant when fully grown. Take into account the size, colour, blooming time, leaf texture and whether it will complement other plants within its immediate vicinity, before making your final choice.

Bed Design and Combinations

Use plants of various heights to produce a three-dimensional effect. If planting in a container or a bed, to be viewed from all sides, place the tallest plants in the centre. However, if the bed is only visible from three sides or fewer, the tallest plants should be placed at the rear of the bed to maximize their impact and so as not to obscure smaller plants.

If planting in a container or basket, think of the design as if it were a bouquet of flowers. Be creative! It is always advisable to add some height to the arrangement with some taller plants. Next, add plants of medium height. These can be one species, or be a mix of different plants with varied textures. Finally, add some low or spreading annuals around the border, arranging them so that they cascade over the edge of the pot.

Another option is to use only one plant species in a bed or container, such as a mass planting of

Plant your containers to resemble a bouquet of flowers, with taller plants in the centre

58

Impatiens. The bed could consist of plants, all one colour, or a variety of colours. You may prefer to use an assortment of different plant species, all the same colour, resulting in a monochromatic colour scheme with differing shapes and textures to please the eye. For example, a garden of only white-flowering plants can be very stunning, especially at dusk.

Lastly, always remember that gardening is a blend of science and art. Be willing to experiment and to make changes when necessary.

Plant Types

Flowers are divided into groups, depending on how they grow. Annuals are plants that start as seed, then bloom and produce seed again, all in one growing season. Annuals will not survive winter unless brought inside, although some may seed themselves in the garden and sprout as new plants the following spring. An annual that freely seeds itself is *Cosmos*.

Cosmos

The original plant dies at the end of its season, but the seeds hibernate in the ground until the springtime sun warms up the soil, causing the seeds to "wake up" and germinate.

Biennials are plants that take two years to complete a life cycle. In the first year, only foliage is produced. Flowers and seeds are manufactured in the second year.

Perennials, are plants that survive winter by becoming dormant. In spring, part of the original plant, usually the root system, sends out new shoots. Three popular shade-loving perennials are *Astilbe*, ferns and *Hosta*.

Another group of flowers are those produced by bulbs, corms and/or rhizomes. This group of plants includes familiar spring-flowering bulbs, such as the daffodil (*Narcissus*) and the tulip (*Tulipa*), as well as summer-flowering bulbs like *Begonia* and *Dahlia*.

All About Annuals

Preparing the Bed

The annual bed can be planted with different flowering plants, changing the theme or colour scheme from year to year, but the preparation remains the same! In spring, you can prepare the bed for planting annuals once the soil is dry enough to be worked and once the spring-flowering bulbs have been either dug up or the tops taken off. Turn the soil and add organic matter such as compost, peat moss or well-rotted steer or mushroom manure. In the first year, a soil test may be required. Let the lab technician know that annuals are to be planted in the soil.

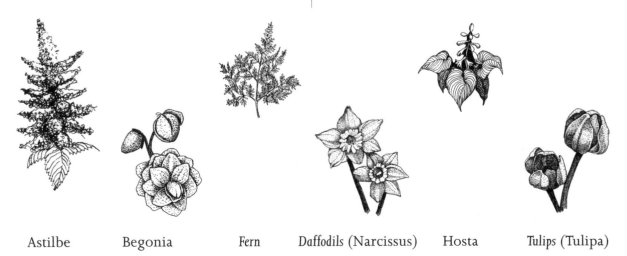

Astilbe   Begonia   Fern   Daffodils (Narcissus)   Hosta   Tulips (Tulipa)

Chemical fertilizers should also be added and dug into the soil. Use a fertilizer with a ratio of 5-20-20 or 5-10-15, at this stage. Be aware that a high nitrogen level (the first number in the ratio) will encourage growth of foliage to the detriment of flower production. Therefore, the first number listed should not be the highest of the three.

If planting a container, it is best to use a planter soil mix. These mixes are usually available in bags and can be purchased at your local nursery. Planter mixes are developed specifically for container gardening and have the correct drainage and nutrient levels for growing annuals.

When to Plant

Be sure there is no danger of frost when planting out your transplants. Planting times vary from region to region, so if you are unsure as to whether it is safe to plant, ask your local nursery representative. It is usually safe to set out annuals around the middle of May, although some gardeners prefer to wait until the end of the month. Each year, the weather is a little bit different, so take temperatures and climatic conditions into consideration.

For the widest variety of choice, annuals should be purchased early and kept in a sheltered area, such as a cold frame or carport. They can even be placed underneath a picnic table that has had a sheet of clear plastic draped over it, simulating a greenhouse. Be sure to water and care for your plants during this time. You may find that you need to repot some of your new annuals, like geraniums (Pelargonium), into larger containers to ensure proper air circulation. Doing so will result in a stronger plant.

How to Plant

Water and then drain the flats of annuals before planting them outside. If possible, plant them on a cool or cloudy day. This will generally keep the transplant from wilting. Dig a hole large enough for the root, place the plant in the hole and then firm down the soil around it. Finally, water the newly planted annuals thoroughly to give them a boost and reduce stress. If you wish to stimulate rapid growth, use a transplanting fluid. This will encourage root growth and result in a healthier, stronger plant. Be sure to read and follow all directions on the container.

Most flats contain many plants and are usually less expensive.

Maintenance

The first two weeks after planting are the most critical. The root systems of annuals are very shallow and can easily dry out. Hot, dry winds or bright sunny days will quickly deplete all moisture in the top 5 cm to 8 cm (2 in to 3 in) of soil, which could prove fatal to your new plants. At first, most bedding plants must be watered daily. Be sure to water in the morning, and do not water the plants from above. A soaker hose or weeping hose laid on the soil is more effective than overhead sprinkling. If water is left on the leaves, disease could become rampant.

If the annuals are planted in the ground, in a good soil, a single weekly watering may be sufficient, once they are well established. If the plants are in containers, the amount of water required will vary depending on the size of the container and the exposure it receives. For example, a small basket exposed to sun and wind all day long could easily need watering twice a day, whereas a large clay pot placed in the shade may only require water every couple of days. Take note of the weather and the state of your plants and you will quickly come to understand how to best tend to their individual needs and how frequently to water them. Remember, a plant that is under stress is more susceptible to insects and disease, so do not allow your annuals to dry out.

Once per week, cultivate or weed your annual beds to reduce the weed population. Your annuals do not need competition for the nutrients and moisture stored in the soil. Applying a mulch will also help with weed prevention and moisture retention. Also, a thin layer of organic matter, about 2 cm (¾ in), of compost or well-rotted steer or mushroom manure will reduce the need for commercial fertilizers, preventing a buildup of salt in the soil.

Bedding plants need to be fed in order to produce their best show of flowers. A weak solution of a 20-20-20 fertilizer mix or fish fertilizer, used twice a week, should be sufficient. Alternating between organic and chemical fertilizers is best for the soil. Also available are slow release fertilizers that can be added to containers or sprinkled around the base of annuals. These will supply your plants with all the nutrients they need for about six weeks. Prepared planter mixes often contain all the nutrients required for the first few weeks after planting.

One other important task in maintaining annuals is the ongoing removal of finished flowers. This is called dead-heading and is necessary in order to encourage annuals to produce more blossoms. If dead flowers are left on the stems, the energy of the plant will go into making seed rather than producing more flowers.

Overview:

1. Design bed.
2. Prepare soil.
3. Purchase bedding plants - If starting annuals from seed, plant the seeds shortly after Christmas in order to have mature transplants by the middle of May. However, be aware that some seeds take longer than others to germinate and grow.
4. Plant out the annuals when there is no longer a fear of frost and temperatures are warm enough:
   Hardy bedding plants - Late April to early May in zones seven and eight.
   Tender bedding plants - Mid May to early June in zones seven and eight
5. Maintain a regular schedule of watering, weeding and dead-heading.

See the *Quick Check Chart of Annuals*, at the end of this chapter, for a listing of popular annual bedding plants that grow well in most regions. For more detailed information regarding specific varieties, refer to the *Plant Encyclopaedia*.

All About Perennials

One of the primary differences between preparing a bed for perennials, as opposed to annuals, is that you will not have the opportunity to dig amendments into the soil each spring. To do so, would, of course, disturb the existing perennial plants. The perennials you plant this year will be established for quite awhile, making proper soil preparation from the very beginning paramount. Make sure your site is well-drained. Add the soil amendments that are necessary (based on your soil test) and then decide upon which perennials to plant. For a more detailed look at soil composition, refer to the *Introduction*.

Designing a Perennial Bed

When planning a perennial bed, choose plants of various heights, colours and textures, the same as you would for a bed of annuals. One main difference to consider when designing a perennial bed, as opposed to an annual bed, is that perennial plants bloom for a much shorter period of time than annuals. Many perennials bloom in spring, followed by beautiful foliage all summer. A mixture of perennials and annuals often provides a pleasing alternative if you like to have nonstop colour in your garden throughout the seasons.

Maintenance

In spring, it is recommended to add a mulch of compost or well-rotted manure to the perennial bed to improve soil structure and fertility.

Summer maintenance for perennials, as for annuals, largely consists of ensuring that plants receive sufficient water and nutrition. Remember to regularly dead-head spent flowers, as well.

Perennials also require autumn cleanup and winter preparation. Some gardeners prefer to remove the tops of the plants in the fall to provide fewer havens in which pests can overwinter. Also, topping them at this time ensures that there is no new growth to be accidentally cut off in the spring. However, other gardeners prefer to leave the tops on until spring in case of significant winter damage. The choice is yours and you may want to try doing it one way this year and the other way next year, then decide which method works best for you.

Since perennials stay in the ground all winter, they may need to be mulched with something like peat moss or compost, or covered with evergreen boughs, to protect them from harsh winter conditions. This will also keep the soil at a more consistent temperature throughout the cold season. The freeze and thaw that can recur all winter long can cause roots to break and perennials to die. Ensure the soil is well drained because, if water is allowed to sit on the top of perennials, the plants may rot over the winter and have to be replaced in the spring.

In case of a dry autumn or spring, remember to water plants regularly so that they do not dry out.

Dividing Perennials

Dividing perennials can be done in spring or autumn. It is generally only necessary when a plant spreads over too great an area, or when the centre of it has died out. Perhaps, you just want to put the same type of plant in another part of the garden or share it with your neighbour.

If the centre has died out, you will have to dig the entire plant out of the soil. Then, cut sections off from around the outer healthy part of the plant. If free of disease and pests, these sections can immediately be replanted.

On the other hand, if the plant is whole and healthy, it will not be necessary to completely dig it up. Simply take a sharp spade and cut off a section of the plant, including the attached root area. The part removed can then be replanted.

Digging up perennials to make new transplants provides an excellent opportunity to amend the soil before filling in the area with new plants. If a perennial has been in one spot for years, the soil will likely require some additional organic matter and some bone meal to replenish its nutrients.

See the *Quick Check Charts*, at the end of this chapter, for a listing of popular perennial bedding plants, ferns and ornamental grasses. For more detailed information regarding specific varieties, refer to the *Plant Encyclopaedia*.

Propagation and Seed Sowing

Many gardeners propagate bedding plants by taking cuttings or by starting new plants from seed. There are several books devoted entirely to this

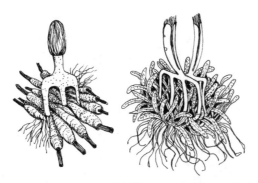

Dividing perennials can be done with a fork, spade or knife.

topic and to the specific needs of specialty plants. Given the availability of these excellent references, this section will cover only the general aspects of propagation and seed sowing.

Some plants are much easier to propagate than others and, subsequently, are more rewarding to grow. If using seed, understand the growth requirements of the type of seed you plan to sow, ie. the temperature required for germination to take place and how many weeks must pass before mature seedlings can be planted outdoors.

Taking cuttings of some of the more popular bedding plants, like *Fuchsia* and geranium (*Pelargonium*) is really quite simple. It can be done in one of two ways. Either take the cuttings in autumn, or bring the plant indoors, let it grow and take the cuttings in early spring. Whenever you decide to do this, be sure to use a rooting hormone that is #1 strength (for soft cuttings). This will encourage root growth and produce better results. The other strengths of rooting hormone are for hard wood cuttings of shrubs and trees.

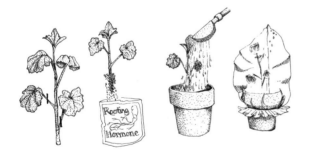

When taking cuttings:

1. *Remove a healthy growing tip, and strip off the lower leaves*
2. *Dip in a planting hormone*
3. *Plant and water well*
4. *Cover with clear plastic for two weeks, simulating a greenhouse, and place in a warm spot, on top of the fridge, perhaps.*
5. *Check periodically to maintain moisture levels and ensure plant health.*

Remove a section, about 11 cm (4 in) long, from a healthy growing plant. Strip off the lower leaves, dip it in the rooting hormone and plant it in a lightweight growing medium, such as sand or a mixture of equal amounts of sand and peat moss. Water and then cover with a clear plastic bag, fastening down the edges securely. This simulates a small greenhouse. Place the planted cutting in a warm spot, such as on top of the fridge, for two weeks, checking intermittently to see if water is required. After this time, remove the plastic and place the cutting near a natural light source or a growing lamp.

Spring Bulbs

There are few sights more satisfying and uplifting than the appearance of bulbs in the cool, rainy days of early spring. Hope is once again renewed as the growing year shifts into gear. In mild coastal areas, bulbs generally emerge earlier than in many other parts of North America. There has even been a few years in which some regions have had bulbs blooming in January, while others are still experiencing snowstorms and bitter cold.

The bulbs most often found in these gardens are the tulip (*Tulipa*), the daffodil (*Narcissus*), and the *Crocus*. There are many other minor bulbs that can also add to a spectacular spring display. Not all of these plants are members of the family of "true" bulbs, but for ease of reference we will call them bulbs. They all have a storage unit under the soil that produces a plant.

To complement the appearance of a bulb bed, you can underplant the bulbs with pansies (*Viola*), primrose (*Primula*) or any other small spring-flowering plants. The colour contrast of a yellow daffodil and a blue forget-me-not can be very attractive. Forget-me-nots, however, tend to become weedy-looking and/or show spots of mildew. Therefore, once they go to seed, just gather up and sprinkle the seed on the ground. Pull out the damaged or unruly plants to make room for summer-flowering annuals, such as fibrous begonia (*Begonia* x *semperflorens* - *cultorum*) or marigolds (*Tagetes patula*).

Tulips

Tulips are much more showy if they are planted in masses of the same colour. It is also important to plant varieties that will bloom in a sequence of colour. Different varieties bloom at different times within a season. Since 1969, tulips have been categorized by their period of bloom and assigned a division number. Listed below are the blooming categories of tulips, their corresponding division numbers and the highlights of each variety.

Early Blooming Tulips:

SINGLE EARLY (DIVISION #1):
Begins to bloom in early May
- Many colours available
- 25 cm to 61 cm (10 in to 24 in) tall
- Rounded petal tips
- Rounded flower base
- Good for planter pots
- An excellent bedding plant that can be lifted from the bed early enough for replacement by annuals

DOUBLE EARLY (DIVISION #2):
Blooms at the same time as the Single Early
- Larger flower than that of the Single Early, up to 11 cm (4 in) across
- Flowers last longer than those of the Single Early
- 25 cm to 61 cm (10 in to 24 in) tall
- Flowers can become top heavy

T. KAUFMANNIANA (DIVISION #12):
Also known as the water lily tulip
- Blooms early
- Flower is cone-shaped when closed
- Many colours available (often bicoloured)
- 11 cm to 25 cm (4 in to 10 in) tall
- Pointed petals often turn backwards when open
- Leaves hug the ground and are mottled in appearance

T. FOSTERIANA (DIVISION #13):
Very early
- Hybrids have warm colours
- Very large flowers
- 31 cm to 45 cm (12 in to 18 in) tall
- Striped or mottled leaves
- Used widely in park bedding

T. GREIGII (DIVISION #14):
Early spring
- Brilliant array of colours available
- 21 cm to 41 cm (8 in to 16 in) tall
- Striped or mottled leaves

TULIPA SPECIES (DIVISION #15):
Originally wild
- Flowers early
- Small plant
- Spreads by seed, making it ideal for naturalizing
- Excellent choice for rock gardens

Mid-Season Blooming Tulips:

MENDELAND (DIVISION #3) AND TRIUMPH (DIVISION #4):
Blooms midway through spring

Single Early

Double Early

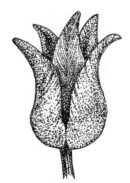

Tulipa greigii

- 51 cm to 61 cm (20 in to 24 in) tall
- Conical flowers on sturdy stems
- Triumph is similar to Darwin, but blooms earlier

DARWIN HYBRIDS (DIVISION #5):

Some of the most spectacular and the largest of tulips

- 61 cm to 71 cm (24 in to 28 in) tall
- Very large flowers
- Brilliant reds and yellows
- Blooms earlier than Darwins
- Excellent as a bedding plant

Late Blooming Tulips:

DARWIN (DIVISION #6):

Most widely known and used tulip

- 61 cm to 71 cm (24 in to 28 in) tall
- Large flowers with flat or square bases
- Wide range of colours available
- Stems are long and strong
- Makes an excellent bedding plant

LILY-FLOWERED (DIVISION #7):

Graceful, long, narrow, reflexing petals

- 51 cm to 66 cm (20 in to 26 in) tall
- Late flowering
- Suitable for beds

COTTAGE (DIVISION #8):

May-blooming

- Slender flower shape
- Wide colour range
- Different varieties vary in height

REMBRANDTS (DIVISION #9):

Same blooming time as Darwins

- Striped or streaked flowers (broken colour)

PARROT (DIVISION #10):

Deeply fringed and wavy petals

- Brilliant colours
- 45 cm to 61 cm (18 in to 24 in) tall
- Newer varieties are stronger

DOUBLE LATE OR PEONY-FLOWERED (DIVISION #11)

Same blooming time as Darwins

- 45 cm to 55 cm (18 in to 22 in) tall
- large, top-heavy flowers sometimes cause them to fall over
- Newer varieties are being bred for stronger stems

Other:

MULTIFLORA HYBRIDS:

Carry several flower heads to one stem

- 45 cm to 51 cm (18 in to 20 in) tall
- Blooms in May
- Various colours

Narcissi

The name *Narcissus* is the botanical name for the entire category of related bulbs, while "daffodil" is a common name that often refers to the larger species of the *Narcissus* family. They are graded by bulb size and by the expected size of the flowers. "Double Nose I", or DNI, is indicative of the highest quality rating, while DNII is considered to

Darwin

Lily flowered

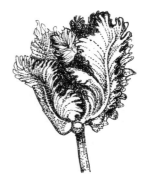

Fantasy parrot

be secondary. There is also "jumbo", which represents the largest flower. DNIII denotes the lowest grade. DNII-rated bulbs are quite sufficient for the home gardener, but if you wish to force bulbs for indoor blooms, use those rated as DNI. DNIII-rated bulbs are usually less expensive, but they normally do not flower until the second year.

Narcissi are also divided into groups, or "divisions", according to their appearance. The corona refers to the trumpet or the part of the flower that sticks out, face forward, while the perianth segments are the petals or the flat parts of the flower. We will refer to these parts as "trumpet" and "petals" for ease of reference.

Description of Narcissi by Division Number:

DIVISION #1:
TRUMPETS
- The trumpet is as long as or longer than the petals
- Trumpet colours range from yellow to white as well as bicolour varieties
- There are some dwarf varieties

DIVISION #2:
LONG-CUPPED
- The trumpet measures one third, or more, but less than the total length of the petals themselves
- The trumpet is usually brightly coloured

DIVISION #3:
SHORT-CUPPED
- The trumpet measures not more than one third the length of the petals
- Trumpets are often brightly coloured
- They can be very fragrant

DIVISION #4:
DOUBLES
- These have many petals

DIVISION #5:
TRIANDRUS
- The flowers in this group are generally smaller than those in the divisions mentioned above
- These are hardy bulbs that will bloom in the shade
- Especially well suited for rock garden use
- Triandrus has a small trumpet and petals that arch backwards
- Many varieties are available in this division

DIVISION #6:
CYCLAMINEUS
- Drooping clusters of very small flowers
- The petals arch backwards and stand on a stem, 15 cm to 21 cm (6 in to 8 in) tall

DIVISION #7:
JONQUIL AND JONQUIL HYBRID
- Has a flower resembling a trumpet, and narrow leaves
- Flowers remain for quite a while and require little care
- Often fragrant

Trumpet

Double

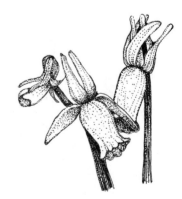

Cyclamineus

DIVISION #8:
TAZETTA
- Four to eight fragrant flowers on each stem
- The trumpet is much shorter than the petals
- Quite hardy

DIVISION #9:
POETICUS
- Trumpet is yellow and often fringed

DIVISION #10:
SPECIES AND WILD
- Miniatures
- Often used in rock gardens

DIVISION #11:
SPLIT-CORONA
- The trumpet is split for at least one third of its length

DIVISION #12
MISCELLANEOUS
- All others

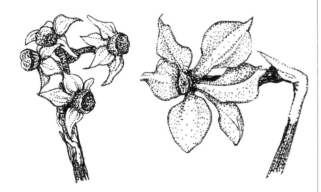

Tazetta   Poeticus

Hyacinth

As one of the most fragrant spring flowers, the hyacinth (*Hyacinthus*) is a favourite ingredient in most gardens. Hyacinths are available in a variety of colours, including white, pink, rose, purple, blue, lilac and yellow. Dwarf varieties are also available.

Most hyacinths purchased at nurseries fall into the hybrid category. This means that different types have been hybridized or cross-pollinated to produce the large flowered varieties you see in the garden. The only disadvantage is that, within a few years, the hyacinth may slowly revert to be-

ing more like one of its original parents and will no longer produce such large flowers. If this occurs, it is time to remove the old bulbs and replace them with new ones.

After a few years, Hyacinth reverts back to being more like one of its parent species and no longer produces such large flowers.

After handling hyacinth bulbs, be sure to wash your hands with soap and water. Some people react to the dust or to the invisible barbs on the bulbs. If you suffer from allergies, you should consider using gloves when handling them.

Close to Christmas time you may be able to purchase forced hyacinths at your local nursery.

Crocus

Crocuses come in many different colours and sizes. It can be a great addition to any garden, but is a small bloomer and therefore shows best if planted in large masses, so that the small, but beautifully tinted flowers can be properly appreciated.

Crocus

The crocus is a low maintenance bulb and can be left in the ground from year to year. These bulbs provide good value for money as they continue to multiply on their own from year to year.

Bulbous Iris

The bulbous iris is gaining popularity and makes a graceful addition to the colours of spring. Dwarf varieties are lovely in the rock garden, *Iris reticulata* being a particular favourite. It emerges just before the crocus and lasts a little longer. This little beauty also forces well for indoor planting.

Bulbous Iris
(Iris reticulata)

Summer Bulbs

The final group of bulbs are those that bloom in the summer. Most of these bulbs are very tender and must be removed each autumn or they will die. *Begonia* and *Dahlia* are the most common summer-blooming bulbs.

There are many other plants that bloom in summer that you may not realize are bulbs! The *Anemone* provides a case in point. At the nursery, you will more than likely buy the plant as a potted perennial, but it is, technically, a summer bulb.

Windflowers
(Anemone ranuculoides)

Planting Bulbs

Planning your early-spring flower bed can be a bit of a challenge when having to keep in mind such details as blooming times, colour varieties and differences in the heights of plants.

Bulbs planted in a bed receiving full sun will emerge and bloom before all others, and will generally produce better results.

Think about from where you will be observing the bed, your vantage point. Perhaps you will be viewing it primarily from indoors because of cool weather. If this is the case, try to place the bed where it can be easily viewed from inside the house. Decide on the design of the bed and figure out how many bulbs you will need. The distance between the bulbs is gauged by the size of the bulb itself.

When it is time to plant the bulbs (in autumn for spring-flowering bulbs), make sure the soil composition is appropriate for them. If required, add soil amendments before planting the bulbs. The soil should be deep and well-drained, a sandy-loam with a moderate amount of organic matter. It would be best to rototill compost, peat moss or well-rotted manure and sand, if it is needed, into the bed before planting. An addition of a fertilizer with a ratio of 9-8-6, raked or dug into the soil, will encourage a better display of flowers in the spring.

Soil preparation should be done in early autumn as soon as your annuals have finished blooming, usually around mid-October (or earlier, if you live in a colder region). The soil should be loose, so do not walk about in the bed when it is raining or you will compact the soil. Arrange the bulbs in place using a trowel or bulb planter and add a little bone meal and bulb dust to each hole. If planting a large area, shovel off the topsoil to the necessary depth and arrange the bulbs with their pointed ends up (to ensure that the stems grow upwards and the roots grow downwards). Cover them over with topsoil.

	5 cm (2 in)
	10 cm (4 in)
	15 cm (6 in)
	20 cm (8 in)

Plant bulbs at the correct depth.

Always plant bulbs at the appropriate depth. In general, six times the diameter of the bulb will equal the correct planting depth. Plant similar bulbs at the same depth so that they will bloom at the same time.

After the bed is planted, rake the top to smooth it out and plant some complementary early spring plants like pansies (*Viola*) or primrose (*Primula*).

Maintenance

After the bulbs have bloomed, remove the flower heads while leaving the bulbs intact in the bed until the foliage dries up and turns brown. This is not the prettiest sight to see in the garden, but allowing the green foliage to completely wilt and die is worthwhile if you plan to leave the bulbs in the bed for a few years. As the foliage turns brown, nutrients are being gathered into the bulb to ensure strong future growth. Once the foliage has completely withered, remove and destroy it in order to reduce the potential for transmitted disease.

Spring-flowering bulbs can be left in the bed year round. However, if you plan to dig up the bulbs, it is best to do it after the leaves have wilted. After digging them up, allow them to dry in the sun for a couple of hours. Then remove all excess soil and check for disease and/or insects. Destroy diseased bulbs immediately and store healthy ones in a cool, dry, well-ventilated spot away from sunlight, until planting time rolls around again.

Forcing Bulbs

It is such a joy to see spring bulbs blooming in the house during the dark days of winter, long before outdoor bulbs have a chance to poke their heads through the soil. It is definitely worth the little extra effort it takes to force bulbs to bloom indoors.

Some bulbs are specifically prepared for forcing, but if you know how the process works, almost any bulb can be used. All you need to do is to convince the bulbs that they have passed through winter so that they will bloom in what they think is spring. By controlling temperature and light conditions, you can force the bulbs to bloom much sooner than they would in nature.

Plant bulbs in sandy-loam soil in pots. Be sure to choose bulbs that are large and healthy. Cover them with soil, water them well and place in a cool, dark spot for twelve to fifteen weeks. A temperature of 5°C to 10°C (42°F to 50°F) is best, but do not let them freeze. Cover the pots with boxes, newspaper or blankets, and remember to regularly check them for water. The roots must have moisture in order to grow to a certain size, otherwise the bulbs will not sprout.

Another method is to dig a trench outside, place the pots in it and cover them with soil. You could even place them in an old fridge (if you have one) in the garage for the twelve to fifteen week period. A dark cold frame can also be used, but it should be closely watched and, if frost is expected, the pots must be brought under cover, into the garage, for example.

Once the simulated "wintertime" has passed and the sprouts have emerged, place the pots in a slightly warmer, sunny area. Once the bulbs are ready to bloom, you can bring them into any part of the home that you choose. When the bulbs have finished blooming and the foliage has wilted they can be dried and planted in the garden, come autumn, for blooms the following year.

See the *Quick Check Chart of Bulbs*, at the end of this chapter, for a listing of some popular bulbs. For more detailed information regarding specific varieties, refer to the *Plant Encyclopaedia*.

Note:

Once again, we stress that the *Quick Check Charts* and the *Plant Encyclopaedia* do not contain an exhaustive listing of plants, but include only those plants that can be considered consistent performers and that have been shown to be fairly resistant to pests and disease. We prefer to take an environmentally sensitive approach to gardening and it would be inconsistent and, indeed, imprudent to include plant species that generally require excessive chemical controls in order to thrive and survive.

QUICK CHECK CHART OF ANNUALS

COMMON NAME/ Botanical Name	LOCATION (SUN ①, PART SUN ②, OR SHADE ③)	HEIGHT	SPREAD	COMMENTS
Alyssum *Lobularia maritima*	①②	10 cm (4 in)	25 cm (10 in)	Fragrant white flowers Pink and dark mauve also available
Begonia, fibrous *Begonia x semperflorens-cultorum*	①②	25 cm (10 in)	25 cm (10 in)	Green or bronze foliage, and pink, white or red flowers
Cigar Flower *Cuphea ignea*	①②	25 cm (10 in)	25 cm (10 in)	Orange-red flowers with a grey tip, giving them a "cigar-like" appearance
Coleus *Coleus hybridus*	②③	30 cm (12 in)	25 cm (10 in)	Vibrant variegated foliage in mixtures of cream, pink yellow and maroon
Cosmos *Cosmos bipinnatus*	①	1 m (3 ft)	45 cm (18 in)	Fast growing, with pink, purple, white or mauve-red blooms
Dracaena Palm, Blue *Cordyline indivisa*	①②	1.5 m (5 ft)	60 cm (2 ft)	Excellent plant to use with other annuals or with small plants grouped beneath it
Dusty Miller *Senecio cineraria*	①	45 cm (18 in)	30 cm (12 in)	Grey foliage lasts year-round, hence the plant has fall and winter interest Tiny yellow flowers bloom during the summer
Fuchsia *Fuchsia x hybrida*	②	25 cm (10 in)	45 cm (18 in)	Trailing plant that blooms in the shade White, pink, coral, mauve or scarlet colour combinations
Geraniums Common Garden Geranium *Pelargonium x hortorum*	①②	30 cm (12 in)	30 cm (12 in)	Continuous blooms of white, pink, mauve or red
Ivy Geranium *Pelargonium peltatum*	①②	30 cm (12 in)	20 cm (8 in)	Flowers in shades of clear pink, mauve, white, dark red, and white with red stripes

COMMON NAME/ Botanical Name	LOCATION (SUN ①, PART SUN ②, OR SHADE ③)	HEIGHT	SPREAD	COMMENTS
Iceplant *Lampranthus multiradiatus*	①	20 cm (8 in)	20 cm (8 in)	Florescent pink, daisy-like flowers bloom all summer until first frost. Easy-care plant that grows well in containers and is drought-tolerant
Impatiens, Busy Lizzy *Impatiens wallerana*	②	25 cm (10 in)	20 cm (8 in)	It quickly fills a garden bed with blooms, in white, light and dark pink, coral, mauve and red.
Johnny-jump-up, European Wild Pansy *Viola tricolor*	①②	15 cm (6 in)	15 cm (6 in)	Bicolour flowers of white, yellow and purple bloom during the summer
Lavatera *Malva trimestris*	①	45 cm (18 in)	30 cm (12 in)	Large, silky, clear pink flowers bloom from late spring into the summer
Lobelia *Lobelia erinus*	①②	20 cm (8 in)	20 cm (8 in)	Flowers are white, rose, light blue, royal blue, and blue with a white centre
Marguerite Daisy *Chrysanthemum frutescens*	①②	90 cm (3 ft)	90 cm (3 ft)	Daisy-like flowers are white, yellow and pale mauve. Good cut flowers
Marigold *Tagetes patula*	①	25 cm (10 in)	25 cm (10 in)	Dazzling bright flowers in yellows and oranges. Dwarf varieties are available
Pansy *Viola hortensis*	①②	20 cm (8 in)	20 cm (8 in)	Many colours and sizes are available Some flowers reach 5 cm (2 in) across. Self-seeds freely
Petunia *Petunia x hybrida*	①	18-30 cm (7-12 in)	18-30 cm (7-12 in)	Large flowers in white, pink lilac, dark mauve, red and bicolours of white and dark mauve or red
Salvia Victoria Blue Salvia *Salvia farinacea*	①	60 cm (2 ft)	25 cm (10 in)	Violet-blue flower spikes stand high above the grey-green foliage
Swan River Daisy *Brachycome iberidifolia*	①②	25 cm (10 in)	25 cm (10 in)	Petite daisy-like flowers of light-mauve with finely textured foliage

QUICK CHECK CHART OF PERENNIALS

COMMON NAME/ Botanical Name	LOCATION (SUN ①) PART SUN ② OR SHADE ③)	HEIGHT	SPREAD	FLOWER (fl) AND/ OR FRUIT (fr) AND THE SEASON		COMMENTS
Alyssum, 'Gold Dust' or Basket of Gold *Alyssum saxatile 'Gold Dust'*	①	30 cm (12 in)	30 cm (12 in)	fl	S	Fragrant golden flowers and grey foliage
Anemone Japanese Anemone *Anemone x hybrida*	①②	60 cm (2 ft)	60cm (2 ft)	fl	S F	Pink, semi-double flowers bloom in late summer and into fall
Arabis 'Snow Cap' *Arabis caucasica 'Snow Cap'*	①②	20 cm (8 in)	30 cm (12 in)	fl	Sp	Fragrant white flowers appear in early spring
Aubrieta *Aubrieta deltoidea 'Cascade Blue'*	①	20 in (8 in)	30 in (12 in)	fl	Sp	Bluish-mauve flowers bloom in mid to late spring Shear lightly after flowering
Baby's Breath *Gypsophila paniculata 'Bristol Fairy'*	①	90 cm (3 ft)	90 cm (3 ft)	fl	S	The double white flowers are often used in arrangements. Best grown from cuttings
Bergenia, Heartleaf *Bergenia cordifolia*	①②	30 cm (12 in)	45 cm (18 in)	fl	Sp	Mauve-pink, pendulous, clustered blooms and large glossy leaves
Bugleweed *Ajuga reptans 'Bronze Beauty'*	①②③	15 cm (6 in)	30 cm (12 in)	fl	Sp	Dark bronze leaves and violet-blue flowers
Bunchberry *Cornus canadensis*	①②	15 cm (6 in)	30 cm (12 in)	fl fr	Sp S	White flowers in late spring Red fruit in late summer
Candytuft, 'Little Gem' *Iberis sempervirens 'Little Gem'*	①②	20 cm (8 in)	30 cm (12 in)	fl	Sp	White luminescent blooms Compact evergreen with narrow foliage
Carnation, 'Tiny Rubies' *Dianthus gratianopolitanus 'Tiny Rubies'*	①②	20 cm (8 in)	30 cm (12 in)	fl	Sp	Fragrant pink flowers bloom above tufts of narrow grey leaves

COMMON NAME/ Botanical Name	LOCATION (SUN ①) PART SUN ② OR SHADE ③	HEIGHT	SPREAD	FLOWER (fl) AND/ OR FRUIT (fr) AND THE SEASON		COMMENTS
Chameleon Plant *Houttuynia cordata* 'Variegata'	①②③	30 cm (12 in)	30 cm (12 in)	fl	S	Multi-coloured heart-shaped foliage in shades of cream, green, bronze, red and yellow
Columbine *Aquilegia x hybrida*	①②	15-90 cm (6-36 in)	30-60 cm (12-24 in)	fl	Sp	Flower colours can be mixtures of blue, crimson, yellow, pink, red, or white
Coral Bells *Heuchera sanguinea*	①②	45 cm (18 in)	30 cm (12 in)	fl	Sp	Coral bell-shaped flowers appear in late spring. Purple leaved varieties are also available
Cranesbill *Geranium cinereum* 'Dwarf Ballerina'	①②	20 cm (10 in)	45 cm (18 in)	fl	S	Pink flowers with dark veins
Elephant Ear Plant *Gunnera manicata*	①②	over 2 m (6½ ft)	2 m (6½ ft)			Giant rhubarb-like leaves. Dies down completely in winter
False Spiraea or Meadow Sweet *Astilbe arendsii* 'Deutschland'	①②	45 cm (18 in)	60 cm (24 in)	fl	Sp	Fragrant white plume-like flowers
Fuchsia *Fuchsia magellanica* 'Riccartonii'	①②③	60-90 cm (2-3 ft)	60-90 cm (2-3 ft)	fl	S	Scarlet flowers all summer
'Grace Ward', Lithodora *Lithodora diffusa* 'Grace Ward'	①②	15 cm (6 in)	45 cm (18 in)	fl	S	Royal blue flowers bloom from late spring into autumn. Broadleaf evergreen
Heron's Bill or Storksbill *Erodium chamaedryoides*	①②	8 cm (3 in)	30 cm (12 in)	fl	S	White and light pink flowers with darker veins. Cultivars of other colours are available
Irish moss *Sagina subulata*	①②	5 cm (2 in)	30 cm (12 in)	fl	Sp	Tiny white blooms cover a carpet of rich emerald green
Japanese Spurge *Pachysandra terminalis*	②③	25 cm (10 in)	30 cm (12 in)			A broadleaf evergreen that spreads underground

COMMON NAME/ Botanical Name	LOCATION (SUN ①, PART SUN ②, OR SHADE ③)	HEIGHT	SPREAD	FLOWER (fl) AND/ OR FRUIT (fr) AND THE SEASON		COMMENTS
Lavender, English *Lavandula angustifolia*	①	30-60 cm (1-2 ft)	45 cm (18 in)	fl	S, F	Grey foliage and scented lavender spikes of flowers Cultivars of different colours are available
Lenten Rose *Helleborus orientalis*	②③	45 cm (18 in)	45 cm (18 in)	fl	W, Sp	Evergreen plant with greenish, purple, or rose coloured flowers that bloom in late winter into spring
Leopard's Bane *Doronicum cordatum*	②	45 cm (18 in)	60 cm (2 ft)	fl	Sp	Yellow daisy-like flowers Dies down completely in winter
Michaelmas Daisy *Aster novae-angliae* 'September Ruby'	①	90 cm (3 ft)	45 cm (18 in)	fl	S	Ruby red flowers bloom in late summer A good cut flower
Mother of Thyme, Red *Thymus serpyllum* 'Coccineus'	①	7.5 cm (3 in)	30 cm (12 in)	fl	Sp	Small fragrant rose-red flowers bloom in late spring Aromatic foliage
Periwinkle *Vinca minor*	②③	15 cm (6 in)	45 cm (18 in)	fl	Sp	Lavender-blue flowers bloom sporadically from spring to fall
Phlox, Creeping or Moss *Phlox subulata*	①	10 cm (4 in)	60 cm (2 ft)	fl	Sp	Profusion of white, pink, mauve or bluish blooms
Plantain Lily *Hosta undulata*	②③	20 cm (8 in)	60 cm (2 ft)	fl	Sp	Heart-shaped, bold foliage and stalks of lily-like mauve or white flowers.
Primula English Primrose *Primula vulgaris*	①②	15-60 cm (6-24 in)	20-30 cm (8-12 in)	fl	S	Wide range of coloured flowers. Many varieties and sizes. Watch for slugs
'Wanda' Primula *Primula juliae* 'Wanda'	②③	25 cm (6 in)	30 cm (12 in)	fl	W, Sp	Magenta-purple flowers bloom from late winter into spring. Cultivars of other colours are available

COMMON NAME/ Botanical Name	LOCATION (SUN ①, PART SUN ②, OR SHADE ③)	HEIGHT	SPREAD	FLOWER (fl) AND/ OR FRUIT (fr) AND THE SEASON		COMMENTS
Sedum						
'Autumn Joy' Sedum *Sedum telephium 'Autumn Joy'*	①②	30 cm (12 in)	45 cm (18 in)	fl	S, F	Succulent green leaves, and clusters of pink to rose coloured flowers that bloom from late summer until frost
'Dragon's Blood' Sedum *Sedum spurium 'Dragon's Blood'*	①②	5 cm (2 in)	30 cm (12 in)	fl	S, F	Rosy red flowers bloom from mid-summer into autumn. Bronze-red fleshy leaves
Shasta Daisy *Chrysanthemum x superbum*	①②	90 cm (3 ft)	90 cm (3 ft)	fl	S	White flowers bloom in late spring until first frost
St. John's Wort *Hypericum calycinum*	①②	30 cm (12 in)	45 cm (18 in)	fl	S	Golden flowers Vigorous underground roots
Strawberry, 'Pink Panda' *Fragaria x 'Pink Panda'*	①②	15 cm (6 in)	30 cm (12 in)	fl	Sp	Pink flowers followed by edible fruit
Thrift, Sea *Armeria maritima 'Dusseldorf Pride'*	①	20 cm (8 in)	25 cm (10 in)	fl	Sp	Pink flower clusters bloom in late spring and into summer. Grass-like foliage
Woolly Yarrow *Achillea tomentosa 'Aurea'*	①	20 cm (8 in)	30 cm (12 in)	fl	S	Yellow clusters of flowers
Wormwood *Artemisia stelleriana 'Silver Brocade'*	①②	20 cm (8 in)	60 cm (24 in)			Lacy grey foliage Frequently used in container gardening

QUICK CHECK CHART OF FERNS

COMMON NAME/
Botanical Name

COMMON NAME/ Botanical Name	LOCATION (SUN ①, PART SUN ②, OR SHADE ③)	HEIGHT	SPREAD	COMMENTS
Alaska Fern *Polystichum setiferum*	②③	30-45 cm (12-18 in)	45 cm (18 in)	A very finely textured fern
Deer Fern *Blechnum spicant*	③	90 cm (3 ft)	30-91 cm (1-3 ft)	Two types of fronds, one evergreen, the other deciduous
Hart's Tongue Fern *Phyllitis scolopendrium*	②③	30 cm (12 in)	30 cm (12 in)	Shiny, wide, blade-like fronds
Lady Fern *Athyrium filix-femina*	②	90 cm (3 ft)	91 cm (3 ft)	Large fronds of triangular shape. Native to coastal British Columbia
Maidenhair Fern *Adiantum pedantum*	②③	60 cm (2 ft)	60 cm (2 ft)	Finely textured "airy" foliage. Dies down completely in winter
Painted Fern, Japanese *Athyrium niponicum 'Pictum'*	②③	30 cm (12 in)	30 cm (12 in)	Unusual silver-grey fronds Dies down in the winter
Sword Fern or Autumn Fern *Dryopteris erythrosora*	③	60 cm (2 ft)	60 cm (2 ft)	New rusty-brown fronds contrast with the dark glossy mature evergreen fronds
Western Sword Fern *Polystichum munitum*	②③	0.6-1.2 m (2-4 ft)	1.2 m (4 ft)	Glossy, leathery, sword-like fronds

QUICK CHECK CHART OF ORNAMENTAL GRASSES

COMMON NAME/
Botanical Name

COMMON NAME/ Botanical Name	LOCATION (SUN ①, PART SUN ②, OR SHADE ③)	HEIGHT	SPREAD	COMMENTS
Blue Fescue or Sheep Fescue *Festuca ovina* 'Glauca'	①②	30 cm (12 in)	30 cm (12 in)	Silver-blue needle-fine blades year-round
Blue Oat Grass *Helictotrichon sempervirens*	①	60 cm (2 ft)	60 cm (2 ft)	Coarse silver-blue arching blades
Dwarf Fountain Grass *Pennisetum alopecuroides* 'Hameln'	①	60 cm (2 ft)	60 cm (2 ft)	Attractive colour in late summer and autumn
Eulalia Grass *Miscanthus sinensis*	①②③	1.8 m (6 ft)	1.5 m (5 ft)	Bold arching leaves with loose panicles
Feather Grass *Stipa tenuissima*	①	45 cm (18 in)	45 cm (18 in)	Wispy seed heads from mid-summer into fall
Japanese Blood Grass *Imperata cylindrica* 'Rubra'	①②	60 cm (2 ft)	30 cm (12 in)	Upper half of blades are bright red Dies down completely in winter For a special effect, place it so that sunlight filters through the foliage
Pampas Grass *Cortaderia selloana*	①②	1.8 m (6 ft)	1.8 m (6 ft)	White plumes in late summer into fall

QUICK CHECK CHART OF BULBS

COMMON NAME/ Botanical Name	LOCATION (SUN ①, PART SUN ②, OR SHADE ③)	HEIGHT	SPREAD	FLOWER SEASON	COMMENTS
Anemone, Windflower *Anemone coronaria*	①②	25 cm (10 in)	8 cm (3 in)	S	Soak overnight before planting. Flowers white, red, or mauve. Plant in spring for blooms in summer
Begonia, Tuberous *Begonia x tuberhybrida*	②③	30 cm (12 in)	25 cm (10 in)	Sp, S	Large double flowers in white yellow, pink, red, coral, orange, and some bi-coloured varieties. Blooms from late spring until frost
Crocus *Crocus*	①②	10 cm (4 in)	8 cm (3 in)	Sp	Flowers are white, yellow, blue, mauve, and striped with mauve. Cultivars of different sizes are available
Daffodils *Narcissus hybrids*	①②	15-40 cm (6-16 in)	15 cm (6 in)	Sp	Fragrant yellow, orange or white flowers. Cultivars of different colours, sizes and blooming periods are available
Dahlia *Dahlia hybrids*	①	0.3-1.2 m (12-48 in)	30-45 cm (12-18 in)	S	Numerous types and colours
Hyacinth *Hyacinthus orientalis*	①②	25 cm (10 in)	15 cm (6 in)	Sp	Fragrant white, pink, blue and purple flowers
Iris, Dwarf *Iris danfordiae*	①②	15-20 cm (6-8 in)	8 cm (3 in)	W, Sp	Blooms in late winter Flowers are yellow with dark speckled throats
Snowdrop *Galanthus nivalis*	②	15 cm (6 in)	8 cm (3 in)	W	Double or single white flowers bloom in late winter
Tulip *Tulipa hybrids*	①②	15-20 cm (6-24 in)	15 cm (6 in)	Sp	Many colours, sizes and bloom periods. Dwarf varieties bloom earlier than most taller varieties

Dealing with Garden Pests – Insects, Disease and Weeds

Infamous Insects... friends and foes!

Once the garden is established, you will need to protect it from marauding insects, coming to devour or damage your favourite plants. In this section, we will steer you towards a better understanding of the common insects you will be likely to encounter in your garden. Through descriptions and illustrations, we will help you to identify these insects and provide you with sound advice on how to eliminate them from your garden or, at the least, reduce their damaging effects.

Integrated Pest Management

As gardeners, we must be realistic in our expectations. Insects will always exist and it is absurd to bring out the sprayer every time we see something moving in the garden. It is far better, for plants and the environment in general, to take a more sensitive and strategic approach to pest control. The concept of *Integrated Pest Management* (IPM), which we endorse, involves the coordinated use of a variety of methods to control garden pests. Gardeners that use the IPM approach view pest control in an all encompassing fashion, ie. each species of pest is dealt with individually, its main point of vulnerability is identified and a method of control is developed to exploit it without major disruption to the environment.

While many different methods of control can be used, it is familiarity with the characteristics of individual pests that is of vital importance. For example, in a greenhouse, the use of yellow sticky traps may be all that is required to control whitefly. In such a case, toxic chemicals are not necessary, so why use them? Such traps are easily made by cutting out squares of yellow plastic or heavy yellow paper and rubbing a sticky household substance on them. The whitefly is attracted to the yellow colour, lands, and becomes permanently stuck. Some home gardeners use empty yellow dish soap bottles smeared with heavy motor oil. You can also purchase commercially manufactured traps for the same purpose, from your local nursery. Tie a string to the trap in order to hang it up in the greenhouse. You can also use sticky traps in the garden itself, as a monitor to find out what species of insects are living there.

IPM also employs biological controls, whenever appropriate, such as the use of lady bugs to kill aphids. In an enclosed greenhouse, this method of control works very well. However, it is not so effective outdoors as the lady bugs tend to fly away. It is suggested that a clear, sweet liquid, like soda pop, be sprayed on the plant(s) before releasing the lady bugs. This will encourage them to stay close to home and consume your aphids.

This leads to another aspect of IPM, which involves learning to differentiate between beneficial insects and harmful insects in your area. Beneficial insects should be welcomed with open arms and encouraged to take up residence! Therefore, please take care not to spray them with an insecticide or they will be destroyed.

Various means of insect control are described below. In IPM, a number of methods may be combined in order to gain control with the least amount of negative environmental impact.

Methods of Insect Control

1. Making Sensible Plant Choices (cultural control):

A factor of great importance in reducing potential infestation is to choose garden plants that have a higher resistance to the pests commonly found in your area. A case in point is provided by the *Rhododendron* and its pest, the weevil. The adult weevil chews the edges of leaves while weevil larvae feed on the roots. This eventually results in an unhealthy plant with ragged leaves and, if enough root damage is done, the plant itself will die. It has been discovered that weevils do not like the *Rhododendron* varieties that display a "hairy" or a "fuzzy" underside to the leaves, such as those of 'Snow Lady'. Weevils will usually not eat them. By choosing to use such varieties, you discourage pests from establishing themselves and multiplying in your garden.

2. Manual Methods:

Another method of control is mechanical, or manual. This means that pests are removed by hand or by machine. For example, weevils feed on *Rhododendron* at night and, if you are willing to go out after dark, you can manually remove them from the host plant. Place a white sheet on the ground under the shrub in question, shake the branches and the weevils will fall onto the sheet and be clearly visible. As they are slow moving, you will be able to scoop them up easily and dispose of them.

3. Traps and Barriers:

Traps or physical barriers can be strategically placed in the garden to catch or thwart pests. For example, make a slug trap from an old yogurt container by punching holes in it. Put slug bait or

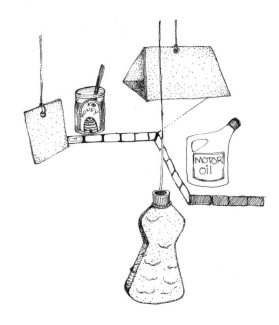

Traps can be made at home or purchased at your local garden centre.

beer in the container, leave it outside, close to the damaged plants, and remove it after a few days. As slugs like to hide in damp, cool areas during the day, a rolled newspaper also makes an effective trap. Place the rolled paper underneath a shrub, beneath which the slugs regularly congregate. Then remove and destroy the paper after a couple of days.

4. Chemical Control:

Chemical control involves the use of a chemical that is purposely introduced into the garden environment to kill pests. Chemicals can be administered in the form of liquid sprays, liquid drenches, dusts, etc. The goal, depending on the formulation used, is to ensure that the chemical either comes in direct contact with the insect and destroys it, or that the insect consumes the chemical and dies as a result.

There are a wide variety of chemicals to choose from. Some chemicals are extremely toxic, while others, like insecticidal soaps, are comparatively gentle and less harmful to the environment. Strong chemicals are often very effective, but it has become apparent that some insects are developing a tolerance to the more widely used chemical compounds. Also, soil in the areas where large quantities of toxic chemicals have been used in the past continue to be toxic for years. Ground water and run off water can also harbour these chemicals, so understand exactly what you are using and be careful of how you use it! Remember, all chemicals impact on the environment, not just on a specific pest.

When choosing a chemical, always *read the label* and do not increase the amount recommended for use, more is not always better! The importance of handling chemicals in a safe and careful manner cannot be stressed enough. For guidelines on handling pesticides, refer to the *Pesticide Safety Code* produced by the Ministry of Agriculture and Fisheries, Province of British Columbia, at the end of this chapter.

5. Biological Control:

Biological control involves the use of a beneficial living organism in order to control a harmful pest. Biological controls can take one of three forms: predators, ie. insects that eat other insects; parasites, ie. insects that lay eggs inside other insects; or fungi, bacteria or viruses that weaken or kill the harmful insect. Biological control proves most effective in an enclosed greenhouse environment. Again, an excellent example is provided by lady bugs, which are often used to control aphid populations. However, due to their short life span, lady bugs are available for only a limited time, at most retail nurseries.

6. Control Combinations:

Biological and chemical controls can be used individually or together. If an infestation is particularly severe, you may at first have to use a chemical form of control to arrest the problem temporarily, and then introduce a biological control at a later date in order to manage the level of the pest population. However, ensure the chemical administered is no longer toxic before introducing a biological control, otherwise it may also be destroyed, defeating the purpose of the exercise.

There is more than one way to deal with most of the pests encountered in the garden. Some controls, however, have been found to be more effective on certain insects than on others.

To help you to decide which method of control can be effectively used in your own situation, follow these steps:

How to Choose a Control Method

1. Identification:

Understand the pest and its weaknesses. Less control can be used if the insect is attacked when it is in its most vulnerable state. A knowledge of an insect's life cycle will help you to control the pest more effectively.

2. Monitor the Pest:

Becoming familiar with how your garden functions and its seasonal changes will enable you to select the best time for introducing pest controls. Monitor which pests are in your garden by using a yellow sticky trap. Traps can be purchased commercially or you can make your own, as previously described.

3. Determine Injury Level:

Has there truly been enough damage done to warrant using a control, whether biological or chemical?

4. Action Level:

You have decided that a control is necessary, but when should you use it? If employing a biological method of control, you will need to obtain the controlling insect at its correct phase of development, corresponding with the most vulnerable stage in the pest's life cycle.

5. Treatment:

Decide whether to use a biological, or physical (ie. manual), or chemical, or cultural (ie. choosing plant species that are resistant to pests and disease) method of control. Carry out the control and closely monitor its results.

6. Evaluate the Results:

Was the method of control effective? Keep a garden journal to help you remember, from year to year, which methods worked and which did not, and the time of year you can expect to receive your unwanted *guests*.

Three R's of Pest Management for a Healthier Environment:

1. Reduce the amount of pesticide used, by properly timing the application.
2. Replace pesticides with non-toxic control methods whenever possible.
3. Redesign your garden management system to promote a healthier environment.

Beneficial Insects

A beneficial insect is one that is advantageous to have in the garden. Be careful when spraying pesticides, that you do not destroy these little helpers.

Beneficial insects fall into three main groups, pollinators, predators and parasites. Pollinators are insects that perform the pollination function in the garden. Without them, the harvest in the garden would be considerably reduced. The most common garden pollinator is the bee.

Predators are insects that eat other insects. Perhaps the most well-known predator is the lady bug, with its voracious appetite for aphids.

Parasites are insects that live on or within other insects. Parasites, such as certain types of wasps, often lay their eggs in a host, where they hatch and proceed to feed on and kill the host.

Some Common Beneficial Insects:

Beetles:

- Lady bugs or lady-birds are beetles. There are hundreds of related beetles that prey on aphids, spider mites, and other insects.
- Ground beetles are also friendly insects, welcome in the garden. They can be recognized by their iridescent black colour. You have probably seen these beetles in your garden - they are the ones that always seem to scurry away when you lift up a rock. It would be a shame to inadvertently kill them because they love to dine on slug eggs, grubs and insect pupae.

Lady beetle larva and adults

- Another beetle is the rove beetle, which is distinguished by its similarity to an earwig, except that the rove beetle does not have tail pincers. This beetle preys on grubs and other pests in the soil.

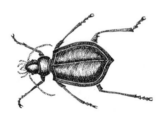

Ground beetle

Flies:

There are many fly species and some of them are very useful in the garden. The beneficial flies are:

Aphid midge larva

- Aphid midge: Larvae are 2 mm to 3 mm ($1/5$ in) in length and bright orange in colour. They consume great quantities of aphids. The adults are characterized by their long legs.
- Tachinid flies: Adults are large, bristly and grey. These flies are parasites to tent caterpillars.

Syrphid fly

- Syrphid flies: Adults display yellow and black, or white and black, stripes. Greyish larvae eat copious amounts of aphids.
- Dragonflies and Damselflies: These harmless garden helpers dispose of many mosquitoes, midges and gnats. The nymphs live in water and prey on mosquito larvae.

Dragonfly / Damselfy

Lacewings:

Lacewings are very delicate in appearance with large, finely veined wings. There are many kinds of lacewings and they all prey on aphids, spider mites, thrips, leafhoppers, small caterpillars and insect eggs. The larva has an especially large appetite.

Lacewing

True Bugs:

Distinguishing characteristics include the triangular shape, located just behind the head, as well as wings that lay flat on the back of each insect. Different varieties of true bugs vary greatly in size, but they all share an appetite for aphids, leafhopper nymphs, beetle larvae, caterpillars, thrips, spi-

der mites and moth eggs. They use their needle shaped beaks to suck the fluids from their prey.

Wasps:

There are many wasps that do not sting people, but are parasitic to pests. These wasps lay their eggs in the larvae of pests, such as tent caterpillar larvae.

Ichneumonid wasp

- The ichneumonid wasp is slim with long antennae and ranges from 5 mm to 3 cm (¼-1¼ in) in size.
- The bracconid wasp is smaller than the ichneumonid.
- Chalcid wasps are the smallest, with many measuring less than 1 mm in length.

Spiders:

Spiders are wonderful predators to have in the garden.

Spiders are just about the best predators you can have in your garden! All of them are beneficial.

Harmful Insects

Now, let us look at some of the most common garden pests! The type of damage done by pests will vary. Some insects suck the juice from plants while others chew pieces out of the leaves. Sucking insects include aphids, spider mites, thrips and white flies. Chewing insects include snails and slugs, weevils, caterpillars, loopers, and cutworms. Insects that cause damage inside plant tissue are borers and miners .

Types of Chemical Controls for Insects

Control methods vary according to the specific type of damage done and the pest doing it. Some pests, like slugs and weevils, can be picked off of plants by hand... that is, if one is not overly squeamish and is willing to go out at night with a flashlight and a pail!

Different chemicals work in different ways depending on the type of insect damage discovered. Therefore, before deciding on a method of control, you must fully understand the nature of the damage, what caused it and how to best reverse the problem with as little environmental impact as possible.

Most chemicals come in a spray. A systemic insecticide is a chemical that is absorbed by a plant by being translocated, or carried, into every part of the plant. It can be compared to taking medicine that travels through the entire body. These systemics are generally used for pests that suck the juice from plants, such as aphids. While feeding, they automatically consume the chemical along with the plant's fluids.

Non-systemic insecticides are used for insects that chew on plant parts. The poisonous chemical is applied to cover the surface of the damaged area and the insects consume it as they feed on the plant.

Oils, such as dormant oil, are deadly to over-wintering pests. Dormant oil is often mixed with lime sulphur and sprayed onto dormant deciduous trees and shrubs to suffocate insects and egg masses. Do not use it when a tree or shrub is in leaf because the leaves will suffocate. There is, however, a lighter type of oil available for summer usage on some plants.

Some pesticides work best at a specific temperature. It is always necessary to carefully read the label on all containers before using garden chemical products.

Pesticides come in different forms and the following abbreviations are used to indicate the formulation of the chemical:

E	=	Emulsion
EC	=	Emulsifiable Concentrate
D	=	Dust
WP	=	Wettable Powder
G	=	Granules
S	=	Suspensions

Listed below are some of the most popular (or should we say unpopular?) pests to be found in local gardens. Included are descriptions of the type of damage they cause, as well as suggested methods of control.

Before reaching for a chemical control, consider whether the area to be treated is frequented by children, pets, wild animals or birds, or even fish in a pond. Remember that most chemicals are toxic and extremely hazardous to health.

For each active ingredient or chemical mentioned, various brand-name products are available and can be purchased at local nurseries. It is your responsibility to carefully read the labels of the products you purchase to find out the correct measurements and rates of application. If after reading all directions and specifications you are still not sure how to properly and safely use a product, ask your local nursery representative. Every nursery that is licensed to carry pesticides must have a person on staff who is certified to sell them. Do not hesitate to speak with the experts!

The timings mentioned below, regarding applications of physical and chemical controls, apply mainly to zones seven and eight. Gardeners in other zones may find that slightly different timings apply in their area.

Most pests are not overly picky as to which plants they feast on, so keep an eye open for them in every corner of your garden!

Common Garden Pests:
Aphid:

Identification:

Aphids are tiny, only 2 mm to 3 mm ($\frac{1}{10}$ in) long, with a soft, pear-shaped body. They can be winged or wingless and can be black, brown, green or yellow. They are often found in clusters called colonies, clinging to the underside of leaves.

Aphid and
Aphid colony

Damage:

Aphids suck sap from the leaves of plants. The leaves affected may wilt, turn yellow, twist and eventually fall off. If an infestation is severe enough, the growth of the plant will be stunted and new growth will be malformed. While aphids suck the juice from plants, they secrete a substance called honeydew. This honeydew provides a perfect environment in which sooty mould can grow. Also, aphids can carry a virus from one plant to another, resulting in worse problems!

Plants:

Aphids are attracted to a wide variety of plants. Shade trees, ornamental shrubs, birch (*Betula*), chrysanthemums, flowering cherry (*Prunus*), honeysuckle (*Lonicera*), roses (*Rosa*), flowering annuals, vegetables and almost anything else you can think of, will be tasty to an aphid.

Controls:

With aphids, as well as other pests, the sooner you notice them and implement a control, the better off you will be. Aphids are able to reproduce quickly and their offspring are ready to suck juice from your plants almost immediately, even when they are so small that they are difficult to detect with the naked eye.

Physical:
• Use the garden hose and spray the aphids off of the leaves. Use a strong stream of water, being sure to reach underneath the leaves. This should be repeated every three or four days and then weekly, as required.

Chemical:
Many chemicals are used to control aphids.

Find one containing:
• Pyrethrum, or rotenone, or malathion, or diazinon… and be sure to read the label each time you use it!
• A dormant spray used in February or March will kill aphids and eggs that are overwintering on deciduous trees and shrubs.
• Insecticidal soap.

Natural enemies:
• Beetles
• Flies
• Lacewings
• Midges

Cutworm:

Identification:

Cutworms are soft-bodied, fleshy caterpillars that can grow up to 4 cm (1½ in) in length and do most of their feeding at night. During the night they climb and feed from plant to plant. In daytime, they hide in the soil around the plants that they feed on. When cutworms are disturbed they curl up and form a C shape.

Cutworm feeding

Damage:

Young, tender plants may be completely chewed off at or just below the ground level. Pieces may also be eaten out of the leaves, or most of the leaf could be missing with only the centre vein left intact.

Plants:

Anything with tender stems, both ornamental and vegetable.

Controls:
Physical:
• Collars can be placed around particularly susceptible plants. Effective deterrents can be

made out of tin cans, milk cartons or tar paper. Use collars around tender and favourite plants and vegetables, such as tomato or cabbage.

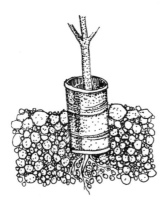

Collars can be used as barriers against cutworms.

- Also be sure to clean up the garden area in August. Leftover debris will only serve to shelter the cutworm population.

Chemical:

- If collars are inappropriate, you can sprinkle granular insecticide containing diazinon, around the base of the plants and work it into the soil. Read the label to find out the correct amount to use and which plants are appropriate for this treatment.
- For climbing cutworms, spray the plant with insecticide containing carbaryl. Read the label before using this product.
- You can also make a bait that will effectively protect young transplants and seedlings. Sprinkle it around the base of the plants:
  - 1.8 kg of bran, plus
  - 1.7 L of water, plus
  - a powdered form of insecticide containing carbaryl (read the label for suggested amounts to use).

Cypress Tip Moth:

Identification:

The cypress tip moth can usually only be identified by the damage it does. You may be able to find the tiny (4 mm, [⅙ in], long) white or greyish cocoons in the branches. Watch for these cocoons in June and July. The underside of the brown tip of a branch will have a pin-hole sized opening where the larva has emerged after having sucked the tip dry.

Damage:

The tips of evergreen tree branches turn brown and drop off.

Plants:

Cypress (*Chamaecyparis*), junipers (*Juniperus*) and cedars (*Thuja*), especially the emerald cedar (*Thuja occidentalis* 'Smaragd'), are affected.

Controls:

Chemical only:

- Spray in late April, mid-June and early July with an insecticide containing diazinon. Read the label to determine dilution rates and which plants to safely use it on.

Earwigs:

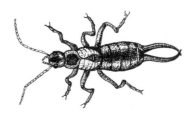

Earwig

Identification:

Earwigs are dark brown insects that have pinchers instead of a tail. They are about 1.6 cm (½ in) long. They do most of their damage at night and hide during the day.

Damage:

Earwigs chew holes in leaves.

Damage done by an earwig

Plants:

Many plants, flowers and vegetables are vulnerable, especially *Dahlia*.

Controls:

When the first signs of damage become evident in May and June, initiate the chosen method of control immediately to keep the number of earwigs from getting out of hand.

Physical:
- Earwigs can be trapped in a folded newspaper that has been set out overnight. A pot turned upside down with tissue paper inside it will also trap these night feeders. To dispose of earwigs it is best to burn them.

Chemical:
- Dust or spray the soil around infested plants with insecticide containing carbaryl (at label dosage), or scatter bait pellets about.
- Additional control can be achieved by spraying with insecticidal soap, used as directed on the label.

Leafminer:

Identification:

Small whitefly larvae.

Leafminer tunnels within a leaf

Damage:

Leafminers are so-named because they are small maggots that tunnel or mine their way inside the layers of a leaf or stem. Affected plant tissue takes on a blotchy look. You may be able to detect the actual tunnels, which resemble wiggly lines on a leaf. A leaf that has been infested with this insect becomes disfigured. If you break open the leaf, you will see the small maggot itself, or its eggs.

Plants:

The most vulnerable plants are birch (*Betula*), mock orange (*Philadelphus*), spruce (*Picea*), perennials like columbine (*Aquilegia*), and other orna-

mentals. In the vegetable patch, beets, swiss chard and spinach are attractive to leafminers. The following weeds also make fine hosts for the insect: pigweed, sheep sorrel and lambsquarters.

Controls:

Physical:
- Remove all leaves showing evidence of leafminer infestation. Place the leaves into a plastic bag, seal it tightly and throw it into the garbage.
- Remove all weeds that qualify as alternate hosts for the leafminer.
- Yellow sticky traps, previously discussed, are also effective.
- Use a light-weight material, available at nurseries, to form a barrier in the vegetable patch.

Chemical:
- When damage first becomes evident, spray the plant with insecticide containing malathion, at label dosage.

Leatherjackets or Marsh Crane Fly:

Identification:

Worm-like maggots that lurk just below the soil surface. They measure approximately 3.8 cm (1½ in) long.

Damage:

The larvae can do considerable damage to the roots of plants and to the root system of your lawn. They seem to be a problem only in coastal areas.

Leatherjacket larva

Plants:

The larvae are usually found in the lawn.

Controls:

There are always some leatherjackets around, so evaluate whether there are really enough larvae in your soil to warrant chemical treatment. If you are unable to find more than twenty maggots per 900 cm² (144 in²) of turf, then do nothing.

Chemical only:

• Spray once when the ground is not frozen, between the first of October and the end of May, with insecticide containing diazinon. Read the label to find out the strength required for your lawn.

Scale:

Scale

Identification:

What resembles scale is actually the egg covering on a tree branch. The covering is round or oval-shaped, with a shell-like appearance. Its diameter measures up to 4 mm (1/6 in), and it has a waxy covering. The insects are not often seen, as they hatch from the covering and quickly scurry away. There are many different types of scale, each with a plant of preference upon which it feeds.

Damage:

One of the symptoms of a bad scale infestation is the appearance of sooty mould. However, if the scale is eliminated, the sooty mould should not return. Scale insects also suck the sap from plants, leaving them weakened.

Plants:

Scale prefers tough, leathery-leaved plants like *Camellia japonica*. Some scale insects are attracted to dogwood (*Cornus*), cedar (*Thuja*), honeylocust (*Gleditsia*), maple (*Acer*), juniper (*Juniperus*), pine (*Pinus*) and yew (*Taxus*).

Controls:

Physical and Chemical Combination:

• Scale can be scrubbed off of a plant with a wet toothbrush, followed by a spraying of an insecticide containing malathion, which helps to prevent further infestation. Spraying alone, will most likely not be effective, as the chemicals may not penetrate the scale coverings.

• In early June, when the scale insects are crawling, you can spray with insecticidal soap.

• Use a dormant oil in late winter or early spring (on deciduous plants only) as a preventive form of control. This can be applied only *before* the buds (leaves) of a tree or shrub break open. The oil will suffocate the insect and any of the eggs that are overwintering on your deciduous trees and shrubs. Read the label for dilution strengths.

Slugs and Snails:

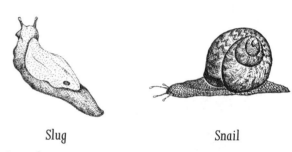

Slug   Snail

Identification:

Slugs are slimy, soft bodied pests that look like snails without their shells. They measure from 3 cm up to 11 cm (1 in to 4 in) in length and can be orange, green, brown, grey or black. Slugs and snails are more active at night and prefer damp, cool areas. Look for the silvery, slimy trails they invariably leave behind, for proof that damage was caused by a slug.

Slugs leave a shiny trail behind them as they feast on plants.

Damage:

Slugs and snails chew holes into the foliage of plants. They can even devour entire soft stemmed plants like annuals or perennials.

Plants:

Almost anything tender is vulnerable.

Controls:

It helps to understand the preferred living conditions of slugs and snails so that you can eliminate those conditions or at least control the situation sufficiently to reduce the slug and snail population. These pests like to hide in shaded, damp areas during the day. It is therefore advantageous to remove any debris or excess vegetation that could shelter them. Keep an eye out for them and begin your chosen method of control as soon as the first slugs and snails emerge in the spring. They stick around during mild winters, so do not assume that you can ignore them until spring, if this is the case.

Physical and Chemical Combination:

You can make a slug trap from an old plastic container.

• Traps are a useful way to help reduce the population without spreading chemicals throughout the garden. A trap can be made by taking an old coffee tin or yogurt container and punching a few holes in the bottom of it. Place some slug bait in the container, replace the lid and place the trap in the area where slugs have been detected. Slugs will be able to access the bait, which will destroy them, whereas pets, birds and other small animals will be less likely to be poisoned. As the bait is attractive and deadly to dogs and cats, it should not be sprinkled about in the open unless you are absolutely certain that no pets, or other animals or birds, will have access to it. Check the trap every couple of days and, when necessary, dump out the pests and replace the bait.

• A product shown to be effective is a slug and snail killer containing "diatomaceous earth". This is an all natural ingredient that is becoming increasingly available at garden shops, nurseries and bird stores. It is a bit more expensive than other products, but is completely natural and harmless to pets and visiting birds. Carefully read all instructions before using it.

• If you are willing to do so, you can simply go outside in the evening or after a heavy rain and scoop up or pick up the slugs by hand. This is a great job for kids, or for less squeamish adults!

Natural Enemies:
• Ducks eat slugs!

Spider Mites:

Identification:

Mites are very small and usually cannot be seen with the naked eye. They are commonly found on the underside of plant leaves. While you may not be able to see the spider mites themselves, you may notice the fine webs they spin beneath the leaves. As they prefer hot, dry conditions, they are often a problem with regard to indoor plants.

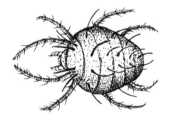

Red spider mite

Damage:

Mites suck the juice from the plants, which eventually causes the leaves to have a yellow, speckled or freckled appearance. Ultimately, the leaves will turn brown, new growth will be stunted and the entire plant may become deformed.

Plants:

Juniper (*Juniperus*), roses (*Rosa*), spruce (*Picea*), cedar (*Thuja*), and many flowers and indoor plants are vulnerable to spider mites.

Controls:

Physical:

- Mites like conditions to be hot and dry, so try to keep your plants well watered. Mites multiply rapidly, making timely control a necessity. The first thing to do when spotting evidence of mites is to give your plants a good, thorough shower.

Chemical:

If the above method is not effective, then you may need to spray your plants with:

- insecticidal soap, or
- insecticide containing malathion or dicofol, according to label instructions.

Tent caterpillars:

Identification:

Tent caterpillars
in tent

Tent caterpillars are so named because they form tents in the branches of trees during spring or early summer. Their colours vary and their bodies are usually hairy. They are similar to the fall webworm in terms of their tent building ability.

Damage:

These caterpillars can quickly defoliate a tree, weakening it considerably. An infested tree will be less tolerant of disease and increasingly vulnerable to further insect attacks.

Tent caterpillar moth

Plants:

Tent caterpillars enjoy dining on birch (*Betula*), flowering cherry (*Prunus*), junipers (*Juniperus*), linden (*Tilia*) and many other types of trees. Watch for the telltale tents in tree branches.

Controls:

Physical: Dormant season

- Check for eggs, resembling a ring around a branch, the width of a pencil or thicker. Prune the branches out and burn them, then spray the tree with dormant oil, according to directions.

Chemical: Growing season

If the tent wraps around a small branch, prune it out and burn it. It should be noted that spraying alone, without pruning, is often ineffective as the spray will not always penetrate the tent itself. After pruning, to discourage further infestation, spray the tree with an insecticide containing:

- Diazinon, or carbaryl, or bacillus thuringiensis, according to the label directions.

Weevils:

Identification:

Weevils are most active during the night so you may not see them at all during the daytime. The damage they cause, however, will be obvious! There are five or six weevil species, ranging in size from 3 cm to 11 cm (1 in to 4 in). Weevils are slow-moving beetles, making them easy to catch.

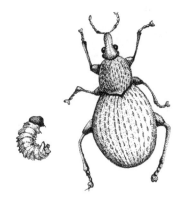

Weevil adult
and larva

Damage:

Vine weevils can cause clusters of grapes to drop off of vines. Root weevil larvae feed on roots and, if the infestation is bad enough, they can seriously weaken plants or cause them to die. Adult weevils feed on plant leaves, chewing large sections out of the leaves edges, giving them a scalloped or notched appearance. A favourite for weevils is the *Rhododendron*. In this case, ragged looking leaves will provide the evidence of a weevil infestation.

Weevil damage

Plants:

Weevils are attracted to many types of berries and ornamental plants, as well as azalea (*Rhododendron*), hemlock (*Tsuga*), *Rhododendron* and yew (*Taxus*).

Controls:

Physical:

- Placing small boards around the base of plants and collecting the weevils hiding under them during the day can be a very effective method of control.

- As previously mentioned in this chapter, weevils can be manually picked up. After dusk, take a flashlight, go outside and spread an old white sheet under the affected shrub. Gently shake the shrub to make the weevils fall off of the plant and onto the sheet. As they do not move quickly, you will be able to scoop them up without difficulty and dispose of them.

- You could also wrap a barrier, such as tape with a sticky substance on it, around the trunk of larger shrubs. See the reference to banding trees under "Wintermoth/Bruce Spanworm".

Chemical:

- Weevil bait is available commercially and will help control most species.

- Another partial method of control is to use an insecticide containing malathion that

should, ideally, be applied when you see fresh notches taken out of plant leaves. Use it only when the outside temperature registers above 20°C (68°F).

Natural Enemies:

- There is a nematode that is a natural enemy of weevil larvae. It is available at most garden centres.

- The only predators we have ever heard of that eat weevils, are chickens!

Whitefly:

Identification:

Whiteflies are small white, winged insects and are most often found on the underside of a leaf or fluttering around plants. If an infested plant is disturbed, swarms of whiteflies will rise.

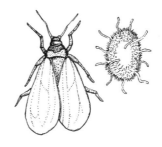

Whitefly adult and larva

Damage:

Whiteflies suck the juice from plant leaves. Like the aphid, they will leave a sticky "honeydew" substance behind, coating the leaves. If leaves become pale or discoloured, it could be an indication that whitefly is present.

Plants:

Whitefly is particularly damaging in greenhouses as the conditions present are ideal for the pest. Consequently, they thrive there. *Coleus, Fuchsia, Hibiscus* and *Impatiens* are all favourites of the whitefly.

Controls:

Chemical:

- When first evidence of whitefly is found, use an insecticide containing permethrin, according to label instructions. If the problem is severe, spray every three days until control is achieved. Be prepared to spray up to ten times. Keep watch for new whitefly infestations and use yellow sticky traps to monitor them.

- If you are bringing in a plant from the outdoors, remove most of the foliage, pruning it well, and dip the plant and its roots in an insecticidal soap solution before placing it indoors.

Wintermoth/Bruce Spanworm:

Wintermoth

Identification:

Full-grown larvae measure up to 2 cm (¾ in) in length, are bright green and have three narrow white stripes on each side of their body. The male moth is a pale tan-grey colour with a wing span of about 3 cm (1¼ in). The females are unable to fly. Young larvae dangle from "threads", hanging from tree branches. The larvae are carried by the wind, from one tree to another, effectively spreading the infestation, so it is best that entire neighbourhoods exercise precautions to control these destructive pests.

Damage:

Damage becomes evident in early April to late May while the worms feed on the buds, flowers and leaves of plants. Defoliation, the total destruction of all leaves, may occur when an infestation is severe.

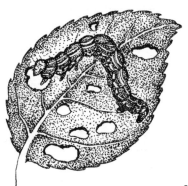

Wintermoth damage

Plants:

Larvae attack birch (*Betula*), blueberry (*Vaccinium*), cherries (*Prunus*), both fruiting and ornamental, maple (*Acer*), as well as many other shrubs and trees.

Controls:

Physical:

- A physical barrier can be constructed to deter the female moth from climbing trees in autumn, effectively preventing her from laying her eggs on them. Two sticky bands, approximately 15 cm (6 in) wide, or one wider band, should be applied to the trunks of your trees in late October. Apply a substance that will stop female moths from climbing. Some gardeners use heavy motor oil, but there are many commercially made products available at local nurseries. Keep a close watch on the bands, as sometimes they become crowded with dead females. If this happens, others will just climb over their unfortunate cohorts. It is therefore important to replace the bands whenever necessary. Ensure that the bands completely encircle the tree and that deep furrows in the tree's trunk are filled and treated. This is critical. Bands can be removed in February, and should be burned.

Chemical:

As an additional aid, if the infestation is particularly severe, use a chemical spray in spring, at the time when apple blossoms are budding (before reaching the "pink" stage), and spray again immediately after apple blossom time is finished. Use an insecticide containing:

- Methoxychlor or permethin, according to label directions.
- Or use insecticidal soap.

Plant Diseases… causes and cures!

Insects are not the only pests that can cause harm to plants. Diseases also wreak havoc in the garden. Such problems are triggered by the environment, incorrect nutrition, or by a living microorganism too tiny to be seen without a microscope. Disease can affect a plant at any stage in its life cycle.

Living organisms that cause harm take different forms and belong to distinct families. Those that you are most likely to come into contact with are fungus, bacteria, viruses and nematodes. These microorganisms not only cause damage in their own right, but also encourage the growth of other diseases by weakening a plant to the point where it becomes vulnerable to pestilence of all descriptions.

As with insect control, Integrated Pest Management (IPM) principles can be employed when dealing with plant diseases. For instance, one can use specific cultivars of plants that are less susceptible to disease. A case in point is illustrated by the dogwood (*Cornus*) family, which is particularly vulnerable to anthracnose, a fungus. There are, however, specific *Cornus* varieties that are less likely to succumb to this fungal parasite (note: In the *Plant Encyclopaedia*, we have only included plants that are proven to be less susceptible to disease).

Regular garden cleanup will also greatly reduce the incidence of disease in the garden. Simply raking up and destroying diseased leaves and pruning out cankered twigs and limbs will help to prevent disease from spreading. This is especially important in autumn, in order to discourage fungus from multiplying or overwintering in your garden. Also, keeping your garden tools clean will lessen the likelihood of a disease spreading from plant to plant. Sterilizing garden tools, especially pruners, by dipping them in a weak solution of bleach and water, is recommended.

Fungus

Fungus is a plant that is unable to manufacture its own food, so it feeds off of other plants in a parasitic manner. Some kinds of fungi are beneficial because they aid in decomposition. Other fungi feed off of plants that are still living, and these, naturally enough, are the ones we do not want in our backyards.

Fungus first appears as a fluffy or fuzzy area on a plant, very much like the "green stuff" that grows on food left in the refrigerator too long!

Fungus reproduces by releasing spores that can travel great distances through the air, on water, on insects, or on garden tools. Problems begin when fungus penetrates the surface of a plant and becomes a parasite.

To control fungal disease, improve ventilation and reduce dampness, wherever possible. Also, remove dead leaves, branches and flowers from your plants. Keeping the garden clean and tidy is important because infected leaves that litter the ground harbour spores that are splashed up onto plants when it rains. During wet summers, some gardeners go so far as to remove the lower leaves of tomato plants to prevent the spread of fungus.

There are commercially sold fungicides that have proven effective, but be sure to read the labels and follow all directions when using them, as they can be toxic.

Bacteria

Bacteria, in general, can be either good or bad. Without bacteria, we would not be able to make cheese or yogurt as well as many pharmaceutical drugs. However, bacteria can also cause disease in humans, animals and plants. Like fungi, bacteria cannot produce its own food and must seek an appropriate host to feed upon.

Bacteria thrive in a warm and damp environment. By itself it cannot penetrate the surface of a plant, so it enters through natural openings or wounds instead. Contamination can be spread by, water containing bacteria that has been splashed up onto a plant, through plants touching each other due to crowding, or from insects transferring bacteria from plant to plant. Bacteria can also thrive on plant debris, making regular cleanup essential.

Symptoms of bacterial disease vary greatly from plant to plant and from one part of a plant to another. On leaves, bacteria have a distinctive appearance, much like that of a water mark. Bacteria cause blights, wilts, scabs, cankers, rots and other symptoms. To protect your garden, propagate transplants only from bacteria-free plants and keep the garden clean. The only way to get rid of bacteria is through soil sterilization, but this is not a practical option.

Viruses

Viruses represent the third category of organisms that infect plants, humans, and animals. Plant viruses operate the same way as do human viruses, such as the common cold. Viruses can live and reproduce only within other living cells. Unlike fungus or bacteria that remain within an infected area, a virus, once it has taken hold, will spread throughout the plant. Therefore the whole plant will exhibit the symptom rather than the problem being isolated to a mere spot on a leaf.

Viruses are easily spread by insects, seeds, pollen, or simply by rubbing up against an infected plant as you walk through the garden, brushing other plants as you go along. Pruning shears are another source of viral transmission, so dip your shears in a weak solution of bleach and water to sterilize them before moving on to other plants.

Viruses can overwinter in perennial or biennial weeds and in some seeds. Most viruses can survive on a variety of hosts, unlike bacteria and fungus, which are more host-specific.

There is no cure or chemical that will fight a virus. The only thing to do is to remove the infected plant from the garden before it infects other plants. Also, when propagating, only use plants that you are sure are healthy.

Nematodes

Nematodes generally do not present too much of a problem for the average home gardener - they are of greater concern to commercial growers.

Nematodes attack the root system of a plant. The effects are not visible above ground until the roots are so damaged that the entire plant dies. The root systems of infected plants will display excessive growth, or knobs.

As nematodes are not as mobile as some other organisms, they must be transported through the agency of unwitting humans or animals. They are able to survive because they can remain in the egg stage, in the soil, until a suitable carrier host is available. If nematodes are discovered at a commercial grower's operation, the crop is usually quarantined.

When a plant has become infected with nematodes, there is not much that can be done. Prevention is the best protection. Use sterile potting soil and ensure that the plants brought into your garden are free of nematodes.

Other Causes

Disease can also be caused by malnutrition or through a nutrient imbalance. Such conditions can usually be easily remedied if correctly diagnosed. For example, a lack of nitrogen could be the cause of leaves turning yellow. With the correct additions to the soil, the plant would soon be healthy and green. In order to better understand nutritional disease, you need to know the type of soil you have in your garden, particularly its acidity level (pH), and the requirements of the plant. It is easier to grow a plant suited to the existing garden environment than to try and change the environment to suit a less tolerant plant.

Sometimes, environmental factors can cause problems in the garden. If there is an extreme and sudden change in the weather, plants may not be able to tolerate it. They may become stunted and never recover. This is one of the reasons why you should always *slowly* introduce transplants from the greenhouse into the garden. They need to become acclimatized in order to do well.

Damage can also be caused by toxic pollutants in the air and from the misuse of herbicides and insecticides.

A lack of moisture will place excessive stress on a plant and reduce its vigour. Also, poor drainage causes water to settle in the root area, which could drown the plant.

Diagnosing Disease

A symptom can result from many different causes. Here are some common factors to watch for to enable you to discover what is ailing your plant:

1. Environment:

A strong, healthy plant will be better able to fight off disease, so do all you can to keep your plants robust.

2. Sun Exposure:

Ensure each plant has the sun exposure it requires to keep it growing vigorously. For example, too much sun on a Japanese aralia (*Fatsia*) will cause its leaves to turn yellow.

3. *Wind*:

The wind is a major factor with regard to plant health. It can dry out the soil under trees as easily as the potting soil in a hanging basket of annuals. Understand how much wind each plant can tolerate in order to ensure that sufficient moisture is not lacking. For example, a windmill palm (*Trachycarpus*) will develop ratty-looking limp leaves if it is exposed to too much wind.

4. Moisture:

Know the amount of moisture required for each plant, and place plants with similar moisture requirements together. Do not, for example, plant a bog plant and a desert plant in the same area because, in order to keep one happy, you will likely kill the other!

5. Nutrients:

Learn what nutrients your plants require to stay healthy. Do not overlook the importance of micronutrients. While the quantities of micronutrients in soil are extremely small, they are nevertheless vital to the health of your plants. A soil test will reveal which nutrients, if any, are lacking.

6. Chemical Contaminants:

Ensure that the soil is not contaminated. Do not allow soaps or other chemicals to be washed into the garden soil or into the lawn as they can burn or kill plants. Also, keep an eye out for a neighbourhood dog that favours a shrub and persists in "marking" it... not the best way to water a plant! Heavy salting on roads in wintertime can also burn shrubs. The salty water is often splashed onto them by passing vehicles.

7. Microclimate:

Realize that changes made to the design of your yard could also alter the microclimate surrounding specific plants. For example, adding a large tree will create a new area of shade. Also, choose carefully which plants to place against walls or fences or near windows. Such locations can become extremely hot due to reflected heat.

Look out for These Plant Symptoms

SPOTS:

Spots on leaves and stems are often the first warning signs you will notice. Such blemishes can arise from many different causes, including fungi, bacteria, or simply the environment. Analysing the size, shape and colour of the spots can aid you in correctly diagnosing the disease.

BLIGHT:

If the growing tips of a plant die, a blight is probably to blame. Blight is a fungal disease for which no reliable cure is available. Destroy diseased branches, stems and leaves.

SCORCH:

Browning, bleaching or shrivelling of leaves is caused by scorching, which is due to the effect of sudden hot, dry spells or from the soil being too high in salts.

WILT:

Plants wilt when they are not absorbing enough water into their tissues. A plant's water transporting system can become clogged through disease, or the roots may be damaged by larvae. Causes of wilt can vary. Then again, it may be that you simply need to water more frequently.

Woe to Weeds... identification, treatment and prevention!

Weeds are unwelcome intruders in our gardens. Really, the only way to define a weed is as a plant that is growing in a spot where we, as gardeners, do not want it to grow! Pansies poking up through a crack in the driveway may be considered a weed whereas they would be welcome if they were growing in the flower bed. Despite their delicious berries, blackberry bushes can be considered weeds because the brambles rapidly take over a garden.

Like all plants, weeds are classified as being annual or perennial. Annual weeds are weeds that seed themselves each year, therefore if you are diligent in removing the flower heads before they turn to seed, their numbers will be reduced. Perennial weeds, on the other hand, are weeds that grow from part of a root that overwinters and sends out new shoots each spring. When pulling these weeds, you must be particularly careful to get all of the roots. There are also biennial weeds that take two years to go to seed, but are nevertheless treated as if they were annuals.

Unfortunately, weeds grow happily in any part of the garden, wherever they are able to find enough soil in which to thrive. The method used to control weeds will largely depend upon where they are growing in your yard.

Pull weeds that grow in the vegetable patch. There are many different types of edible foliage that could be damaged if you spray with chemicals. Chemicals that kill weeds may also kill your vegetables. And remember, you will be eating these vegetables and you certainly do not want to spray the ones you plan to consume.

Normally, weeds in ornamental beds should be pulled, but can sometimes be sprayed depending on the weed and what plant it is growing next to. Read the label of the chemical product you have chosen and check for its effect on sensitive or specific plants before using it.

Weeds in the lawn present another problem. Pulling is sometimes effective, but sprays are often used. Use a spray that will kill your specific type of weed. If the lawn is kept in a healthy state, it should overtake most weeds and choke them out. If the weed being treated is one that grows on runners or stems that lay on the ground and root as they grow, it is advantageous to aggressively rake the area with a steel-toothed rake. This will pull up the main portion of the weed, allowing for partial removal when mowing over the

area. The smaller portion of weed left over will be easier to remove. One important thing to remember is not to compost the grass clippings of a lawn full of weeds. Some weed seeds are very hardy and, when the compost is spread, the seeds will also be spread throughout your garden.

If you choose to spray the lawn, do not compost the clippings until you have cut the grass several times and can be reasonably certain that no chemicals remain.

Weed Control - Points to Ponder

1. Prevention:

As with any problem, in the garden or otherwise, prevention is the best policy. Weeds can be prevented in a number of ways. First of all, be sure that new soil does not contain weeds. By allowing the soil to sit a few days before spreading it, you will quickly discover if you will be spreading unwanted weeds throughout your yard. It is best to inspect the soil before having it delivered to see if there are many weeds growing in it.

Secondly, check all plants that are brought into the garden. If weeds are growing in the nursery pot, they will also grow in your yard. Pull out the weeds before planting nursery stock. Lastly, be careful of what you put into your compost pile. A compost pile that does not generate enough heat may not kill weed seeds and, as a result, they will likely sprout wherever the compost is spread.

2. Maintenance:

Making an effort to keep up with weeds in their early stages of growth, in spring, will prevent most problems later. Mulching also helps since seed will not germinate if it is not exposed to sunlight. Mulch the beds with well-aged mushroom manure, peat moss or clean compost.

3. Chemical Control:

If chemical control is your choice, be sure to read the product label on the container and use sprays designed for use on specific weeds. Understand the differences between the following types of weed killers:

- Systemic herbicides are designed to kill the entire plant, roots and all. The chemical is transmitted throughout the plant.

- Contact herbicides kill only the part of the plant that they touch. They kill annual weeds by ensuring that they do not go to seed and multiply.

- There are also chemicals called soil sterilants. If one of these is used on an area of soil, *nothing* will grow there. Take this into consideration!

- Selective sprays are chemicals that are designed to kill specific plants. Generally speaking, they should not harm the plants surrounding your weeds, but read the label in order to be certain. There are many types of selective sprays that will kill weeds, but not the grass in your lawn. Check at your local nursery.

- Non-selective herbicides kill all living plants that they land on. Ensure that there is no wind or breeze when using them, as chemical drift could cause extensive damage to existing plants in the garden.

Common Weeds:

Although the weeds listed below will grow in any part of the garden, they are commonly found in lawns, where harsher sprays are most often used. The flowering times mentioned within the descriptions that follow may not correspond exactly with flowering times in your area, as these can vary, depending on local weather factors as well as microclimatic conditions.

Before spraying weeds, be sure to read and carefully follow the instructions on the container or box of the product you are using. Take care not to spray too heavily. Do not use sprays where tender plants could be damaged and never use sprays on or near edible plants unless it is clearly stated on the label that it is safe to do so.

Read the *Pesticide Safety Code*, at the end of this chapter, before using any chemical spray.

Black Medic:

Description:

This weed has a well-defined stalk and produces yellow flowers followed by black seed pods.

Black medic

Control:

Spray it with a herbicide containing mecoprop (MCPP).

Clover:

Description:

Many varieties of clover exist. Its flowers are either pink or white and the plant itself grows on runners. Clover is usually found in lawns and is very attractive to bees.

Clover

Control:

Clover prefers a non-acidic soil as well as a dry soil, so be sure to maintain moisture during periods of drought. If it is found in the lawn, mow it down regularly and spray it with a herbicide containing mecoprop (MCPP).

Common Chickweed:

Description:

Common chickweed is an annual or winter annual with horizontal stems that root at the nodes. The stems are bright green and leafy with a line of hair down one side. This weed produces small white flowers about .5 cm (¼ in) across, and green leaves that vary greatly in shape. The root system forms a mat underground. The plant matures from seed to weed quickly and then seeds once more during its growing season. Common chickweed blooms from early July through late September.

Control:

Applying a herbicide, containing MCPP, to the weed when it is growing will have the best effect.

Creeping Buttercup:

Description:

A perennial weed of significant length, characterized by horizontal stems that root at the nodes. Its shiny black seeds are produced in green or brown clusters and its flowers consist of five shiny yellow petals. Creeping buttercup usually blooms from May to September.

Creeping buttercup

Control:

Creeping buttercup prefers a heavy, wet soil. Therefore proper maintenance will help to prevent and control further invasion. Hand-rake and physically pick the weed out of the lawn or mow away as much of it as possible. If this is not sufficient, use a herbicide containing MCPA or mecoprop as its active ingredient.

Dandelion:

Description:

Dandelions stand 11 cm to 61 cm (4 in to 2 ft) tall. This perennial weed has a deep, thick tap root and a hollow stalk containing milky juice. The yellow flower transforms into a fluffy mass of slender parachute-type seeds. It usually blooms from July to late September.

Dandelion

Control:

When pulling the weed out of the ground by hand, be sure to get the entire root. A little bit left in the soil will form a new weed very quickly. If using a chemical spray, buy one containing 2,4-D or MCPA and spray only the weed itself. It may be necessary to spray the dandelion again after a few weeks.

False Dandelion:

Description:

Unlike the dandelion, which has a deep root, the false dandelion has a very short tap root with a fibrous root system. This weed produces a bright yellow flower and has feathery brown hair on its seeds.

Control:

Treat it the same as you would a dandelion. Pull it out by hand or spray it with a herbicide containing 2,4-D or MCPA.

Horsetail (or Marestail):

Horsetail

Description:

Horsetail is a perennial weed with annual stalks. This means that the stems die off in winter, but the roots continue to live, though dormant, underground. The roots grow horizontally to the ground surface and new shoots grow from them. Stems are upright, hollow and jointed. When pulling up the weed by hand, the stem easily breaks at the joints, making it difficult to remove the entire plant unless you excavate down to 31 cm (12 in) deep. Even a tiny bit of root left in the ground will produce another weed. Horsetail does not flower or produce seeds, as it multiplies only through root growth. It will grow from 11 cm to 61 cm (4 in to 24 in) tall. The weed lasts until frost and returns by early May, although in warmer climates it thrives all year. Horsetail prefers poor drainage and dry areas, for example, along railway tracks, but will happily invade any part of your garden if it is allowed a foothold.

Control:

Horsetail is a very stubborn and hard-to-kill weed. Use a spray containing MCPA. Sometimes, pouring boiling water on horsetail growing in cracks (eg. between bricks and paving stones) will temporarily control it. Perseverance is the key word when dealing with this weed! .

Morning Glory:

Description:

This perennial weed is especially difficult to control due to its deep and extensive root system. It can take the form of a climbing vine or grow prostrate on the ground. Morning glory will strangle most plants with which it comes into contact by twining tightly around their branches. Each branch of this weed can grow up to 3 m (10 ft) long. The leaves are arrow or heart-shaped and green. Its flowers are large and white in colour, growing from long stalks. It blooms from mid-June to September.

Morning glory

Control:

Morning glory is a very difficult perennial to eradicate. If the infestation is severe, it may take up to two years of persistent effort to gain control of it. The first step is to dig out the roots with a trowel. The roots are very fine and it is important to remove all of them. Simply pulling the weed will not be effective because the soft stems will break off, leaving the roots behind to continue growing. Once all the vines have been removed, watch for new shoots. Use the chemical 2,4-D, or mecoprop, on these. You could use glyphosate as an alternative, but be very careful because it will kill or damage all plants that it comes into contact with. If, as is usually the case, morning glory is growing amongst other tender plants, it is best to mix a solution of the chemical and "paint" it onto the weed. This way you will not risk damage to other plants.

Pesticide Safety Code

Ministry of Agriculture and Fisheries - Province of British Columbia

1. Buy and use only a pesticide with a DOMESTIC label. Domestic or home and garden products are in small containers and are easy to use. Do not use a product marked AGRICULTURAL, COMMERCIAL, INDUSTRIAL, or RESTRICTED. These products are often more toxic and are only available in large containers.

2. Use only the pesticide recommended for the problem. The recommended uses are on the label.

3. Before opening the container, READ THE LABEL. Read it all, even the small print.

4. Follow the label directions and measure the dosage exactly. Do not use a little extra for good measure as too much may cause injury to plants, kill beneficial insects, or leave harmful residues on edible crops. Rates lower than recommended may result in unsatisfactory pest control.

5. Use a special measuring container for pesticides, not kitchen utensils.

6. Do not leave pesticide containers open or unguarded while spraying.

7. To avoid drift, do not apply pesticides on a windy day.

8. Spraying fruit and vegetable crops with insecticides when they are in bloom can reduce pollination and yield by killing bees that pollinate the flowers.

9. Never smoke, eat, or drink while applying pesticides.

10. Cover feed and water containers when using pesticides around livestock or pets. Do not contaminate fish ponds or waterways.

11. Take care that poison baits do not accidentally poison children or pets.

12. Avoid inhaling sprays or dusts. Always wear protective clothing and masks when the label calls for them.

13. Wash hands and face after applying pesticides.

14. If dusts or sprays are spilled on skin or clothing, remove clothing immediately and wash contaminated skin with warm, soapy water. Clothing must be thoroughly cleaned before it is worn again.

15. After applying pesticides, clean the application equipment thoroughly. Clean and store your clothing and protective equipment. Wash yourself.

16. Observe the required waiting period before harvesting.

17. Store pesticides safely.

18. Dispose of unwanted pesticide containers safely.

CHAPTER 7

Calendar of Garden Chores and Plant Availability

THIS CHAPTER IS divided into monthly sections, each containing a summary of garden chores to be performed and practical advice to keep you abreast of various important tasks related to planting, pruning and generally maintaining the flowers, trees, shrubs and turf in your garden. Also included for each month is a list of plant availability at local nurseries, highlighting popular plant species and the time when you may expect to find the best selection.

Finally, at the end of each section, is a space where you can write down your own observations, such as the garden chores you performed, what plants were in bloom, pest infestations you had to deal with, what pest control methods proved most effective, etc. By recording your observations this year, you will find that they provide a wonderful reference for subsequent years!

Temperatures and geography are not consistent from one zone to another. This being the case, please be aware that the timings mentioned here, in relation to planting, pruning and plant availability, may vary somewhat, depending on where you live. The time frames used here relate primarily to zones seven and eight. If you live within a different zone, be sure to make note of any variations. In this way you will know exactly what timings apply to your area. Use the space provided at the end of each monthly section for your personal garden notes.

January

In this, the coldest month of the year, not much is in bloom, but it is a good time for catching up with maintenance chores. You are not likely to be out in the garden digging and hoeing, but there are other tasks to be done. Give your gardening tools a good cleaning and sharpening, ready for use in spring. You can also clean out and disinfect pots and plant containers or, if you are handy with a hammer and saw, you may wish to build some new planters.

January is also a good month for planning changes to your garden. Curl up in front of a fire and glean ideas from some gardening and landscape design books. Check out your local library or book store for books and magazines that look interesting.

On cold, blustery days, seed and plant catalogues can provide great comfort and offer hope for warmer spring days… and you can make your orders right away! Bring out your garden photos and videos and enjoy them all over again. Most of all, take heart, for you will once again be busy in your garden in a few weeks time.

Plant Availability at Local Nurseries:

- Fresh stocks of assorted flower and vegetable seeds are beginning to arrive.
- Primroses are coming into bloom: light mauve, followed by yellow and blue varieties, with more colours available each week.
- No increase in outdoor plant stock, as yet.

Your Personal Garden Notes for January:

February

Flowers:

Flower and vegetable seeds should be purchased now, but do not get too carried away. Read all the information that accompanies each package to discover how soon to plant the seeds. Some seeds can be planted straight into the garden come springtime, while others need a head start and will, consequently, have to be sown indoors. Be aware of individual seed requirements before ordering, or you may find yourself bogged down with a lot of unforeseen work and bother.

You will soon be enjoying spring bulbs in bloom, but watch for those tenacious slugs. Tender shoots are a tempting meal for them.

Trees and Shrubs:

This is the time to spray deciduous trees and shrubs, especially fruit trees and roses, with dormant oil. Only spray on a calm, windless day with temperatures above freezing. Spraying must be done before buds begin to break open on the plants or they will suffocate. Also, be careful that you do not spray the evergreens in your garden as they could die as a result.

In general, mid-February is the time to prune fruit trees and summer-flowering shrubs and trees. However, do not prune the spring-blooming plants or you will remove their flower buds. A rule-of-thumb is to prune roses when *Forsythia* is in bloom, so have your clippers handy when the yellow flowers appear in early spring.

Turf:

Nothing to do, as yet!

Plant Availability at Local Nurseries:

- All seeds from different seed companies should be available now.
- Packaged rare bulbs and tubers will be arriving, many of which are specialty bulbs and, consequently, may not be listed in the *Plant Encyclopaedia*.
- Also, a large variety of other packaged plants should be available. These can be planted at the end of the month or into March, depending on the weather.
- Perennials in small pots are being stocked. The larger pots will arrive in March. Plant the small potted plants now to allow them a good start. The larger ones can be planted throughout the spring, summer and autumn.

- By the end of the month, nursery workers will be pruning and potting bare root roses as they arrive. You will find these for sale in March.
- Primroses are still available in many colours: blues, mauve, pink, yellow, white and red.
- The more unusual shrubs will be arriving in March and April. If you have a special shrub or tree you wish to purchase, it is a good idea to let your nursery representative know about it now. She/he should be able to order it for you if it is available. However, be aware that this is a busy time for nursery staff and you are well advised to give them plenty of advance notice of your requirements.

Your Personal Garden Notes for February:

March

Flowers:

Finish any leftover winter cleanup of flower beds. Remove the overwintered tops of perennials, being careful not to damage any new sprouts, and divide the plants that have outgrown their area.

Check at your local nursery for the perennials you wish to add to your garden. If annuals are available, you can purchase them as well, but it is too early to plant them in the garden, as yet. Bring them home and put them in your greenhouse or coldframe, remembering to water them regularly.

Spring bulbs should be blooming beautifully by now. Remove the spent flower heads so that the plants will not go to seed. When the bulbs are finished blooming, leave the foliage on until it browns, and fertilize the plants that have finished flowering to encourage good growth for next year.

Trees and Shrubs:

Prune off winter damage on branches, taking care to make the cut just above a leaf bud. Be sure the wood is healthy all the way through the fresh cut you have made. If the wood shows discolouration, prune it back until it is creamy white in colour. Do not be afraid to prune damaged branches extensively. If they are not pruned back far enough, the diseased part of the branch will eventually die and make the plant more vulnerable to disease and insects.

You can fertilize most shrubs now. However, do not overdo it or you could burn the plants. Also, do not fertilize plants if the weather is cold and wet.

Hopefully, by now the weather is getting warmer and you can begin planting trees and shrubs. If you are uncertain as to whether it is the best time to plant a particular species, speak with your nursery representative. Some varieties transplant better if planted at certain times of the year.

Turf:

You can spread a dolomite lime on your lawn at this time of year, if the soil is acidic, but it is still too cool to fertilize and too wet to mow in most areas.

Other:

Keep watch for pests and weeds.

Plant Availability at Local Nurseries:

- The best selection of perennials is available in March and April. Most are sold in small pots. If the ground is not frozen they can be planted.
- Trees and shrubs are also increasingly available at this time. Most are sold in one, two, or five-gallon containers. Larger trees are priced according to the calliper or the diameter of their trunks.
- Many annuals are available in multi-packs, ie. more than one plant per container. This is a very economical way in which to purchase bedding plants. Once the weather is warmer and there is no longer a fear of frost these can be planted outdoors.

- Hedging material should now be available in significant quantities. It is a good time to purchase your hedging plants if you need many of the same species or variety. Look for cedars (*Thuja*) as well as many other types.
- The best selection of roses (*Rosa*) is available now, so go down to the nursery and take a look. Choose a plant with at least two strong stems, or with three stems, each being at least the thickness of a pencil.

Your Personal Garden Notes for March:

April

Flowers:

By now, the soil has warmed up sufficiently for planting and all necessary soil amendments can be added. When doing so, be careful not to disturb and damage any existing roots. If you are putting in a new bed, it is a good idea to add an 11 cm (4 in) layer of compost, mushroom manure or well-rotted steer manure and dig it into the soil. You may wish to do the same for the vegetable patch before it is planted.

Some of the summer and autumn flowering bulbs, like *Dahlia*, can be planted now, but not the tender bulbs and tubers, such as *Begonia*.

Plant out the perennials that were not planted in the preceding autumn.

If you have sufficient space in a greenhouse, this is a good time to plant up your hanging baskets and pots. Outdoor temperatures are too cool in the evening for them to be hung outside, but if you plant them now, they will be more advanced in growth and flower production when you do take them outside. When making up your pots, be sure to pinch off the flower buds as you plant. This will encourage strong root growth and ultimately result in large and prolific blossoms. Properly maintain the containers once they are planted. If they are kept in a greenhouse, be sure to open the door or windows on warmer days in order to increase ventilation and reduce heat buildup. This will ensure that the temperature change from daytime to nighttime is less drastic.

Spring bulbs should be completing their blooming phase about now. Once they have, give them some fertilizer high in phosphate (ie. the middle number in the ratio), to strengthen them for next year's blooms.

Watch for pests in the garden and continue to weed your beds regularly.

Trees and Shrubs:

This is a great time to be planting trees and shrubs. Availability is excellent and the weather will likely be cooperative. Prune any shrubs that have finished blooming.

Turf:

By now, the lawn should be starting to grow again. To prepare the turf for strong summer growth, give it a good raking with a steel rake. This will loosen up and remove most of the moss that took hold over the winter. If you plan to power rake (to remove thatch buildup from your lawn), this is the month to do it in. Most lawns also benefit from an aeration in springtime. You can have this done professionally or you can rent a machine, or simply do it by hand by poking holes all over the lawn with a pitchfork.

You should begin mowing the lawn now (if it is dry enough), remembering to never remove more than one third of the grass blade at a time. Make sure your mower blade is sharp.

Finally, edging the lawn at this season will give it a "facelift".

Plant Availability at Local Nurseries:

- If you have not planted your perennials yet, there is still time to do it. At local nurseries, some will already be in bloom and you will be able to see what the different flowers look like. This can be a bonus if you are unfamiliar with the species.
- The best selection of unusual trees, shrubs and perennials is available now. Plants that are novel or uncommon are often bought up quickly, so go to the nursery and browse every other week or you may miss out. If you request a specific plant, be sure to submit your order at least two weeks in advance.

Your Personal Garden Notes for April:

May

Flowers:

Watch for slugs and snails. Their appetites are voracious and they can consume your tender transplants overnight. Aphids are also out in force now.

At the end of the month it should be safe, in most zones, to plant out all bedding plants. However, if they have been stored in a greenhouse, harden them off for a few days before planting them in the garden. This means that a plant must be introduced gradually to the outdoors. To harden off a plant, place it in a very sheltered area outside, for a couple of days, before planting it in the ground. This will avoid "shocking" the plant. If a plant is shocked, it will never grow to the same size as a plant that has been properly hardened off.

Hanging baskets can be planted and placed outside by the middle or the end of the month.

Fertilize plants in planters and hanging baskets, and water them as required.

It is now safe to plant tender, summer-flowering bulbs, such as *Dahlia*, and *Begonia*.

Trees and Shrubs:

Finish pruning spring-flowering shrubs.

Turf:

This month will see the first fertilizing of the lawn. Use a fertilizer containing a higher nitrogen level (ie. the first number of the three in the ratio). Repeat as required during the growing season and, as always, be sure to read the label on the bag for the correct rate of application.

This is also a good time to sow grass seed or seed over bare areas in your lawn.

Plant Availability at Local Nurseries:

- At the beginning of May you will find quite a wide selection of annuals. The most tender annuals arrive at nurseries at the end of May and should be planted out at the beginning of June.
- The selection of trees and shrubs will still be adequate, but some of the larger sizes will have been sold, as well as many of the rarer plants.
- Local nurseries will also be bringing in their water plant stock and supplies at this time.

Your Personal Garden Notes for May:

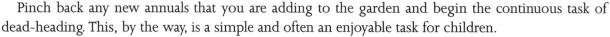

June

Flowers:

Sow the seeds of biennials in June so that they will bloom for you next year.

Pinch back any new annuals that you are adding to the garden and begin the continuous task of dead-heading. This, by the way, is a simple and often an enjoyable task for children.

Maintain your regular schedule of watering and fertilizing bedding plants, especially as the weather gets warmer.

Summer-flowering bulbs can still be planted out.

Trees and Shrubs:

Prune shrubs that have just finished blooming. Keep an eye on your newly planted trees and shrubs to be sure they receive adequate water.

Turf:

By now, you ought to be on a regular schedule of watering and mowing. Be careful not to over water your lawn. Remember that 3 cm to 5 cm (1 in to 2 in) of water each week is all the moisture that a mature lawn requires. If, however, the soil is very sandy, more water may be needed.

Plant Availability at Local Nurseries:

- Annual bedding plants are arriving daily to provide the *instant* colour you need in your garden. These mature plants are a little more expensive, but well worth the price for the beauty they bring to the garden.
- Perennials are still available, but the more unusual varieties will likely have been snapped up by now.
- Trees and shrubs are still available at nurseries, but you may have to phone around if you are looking for specific specimens.

Your Personal Garden Notes for June:

July and August

Flowers:

Continue with regular watering, fertilizing and dead-heading activities.

If the summer is dry, watch for spider mites. In late August, you can begin taking perennial cuttings for propagation. You can also continue to sow biennial seeds for blooms next year.

Trees and Shrubs:

Ensure that newly planted trees and shrubs receive sufficient moisture. Many coastal areas, as well as inland regions, experience drought in the summer. Slow, deep watering is important to encourage deep root growth and to help the plants survive hot and dry spells.

Turf:

When mowing the lawn during periods of drought, leave it a little longer to encourage deeper root growth.

Other:

If the weather is dry, the compost pile may need to be moistened in order for it to do its job properly.

It is best not to water the garden from above because moisture sitting on leaves can make plant foliage more susceptible to disease, especially in the heat. If you can, use a drip or slow soaker system and water the root areas only. Also, much less water is wasted this way as more is absorbed by the plants and less is evaporated into the air.

Plant Availability at Local Nurseries:

- Most of the bedding plants in flats will be gone by now, but the smaller sized pots are still available.
- If you have not been able to plant up your own containers and hanging baskets, there are usually many available to choose from at nurseries.
- Shrubs that are B&B (Balled and Burlapped) do not transplant well during hot weather and, generally, are not available at nurseries at this time. In any case, it is not advisable to plant these in the summertime as they run a risk of drying out.

Your Personal Garden Notes for July and August:

September

Flowers:

The blooming of annuals can be prolonged if you continue to dead-head plants regularly. Bedding plants in containers will still require a lot of water, especially now that the containers will be full of roots. Continue to fertilize, but do it gently. Now is also the time to take cuttings of your favourite annuals to propagate them for a ready supply next year.

Perennials can once again be planted. Fresh ones are beginning to arrive at nurseries and, if planted now, will continue to grow until the weather turns cold. You may even find them on sale at your local nursery.

You may think it is a bit early to be purchasing spring-flowering bulbs and certainly too early to plant them (after all, your summer annuals are still in fine form). Nevertheless, the best choice of colours is available now. Different varieties of bulbs bloom at different times. To achieve the best possible display, find out *what* blooms *when* and plant the combinations accordingly. When considering bulbs for the garden, you may also wish to purchase a few for forcing in pots. They can be brought into the house in winter. During a dark, cold January, nothing bears more hope of a coming spring than a cheerful pot of tulips or *Crocus*.

Trees and Shrubs:

At the end of the month you should band the deciduous trees that are susceptible to Winter Moth infestations. The bands can be removed anytime from the end of December until February, depending on seasonal temperatures.

Be sure that shrubs do not become parched. Flowering shrubs, like *Camellia*, will not put on a good show of blooms in spring if they are allowed to dry out in autumn. They require moisture to store up for the winter ahead.

New trees and shrubs can be planted during September. Check the local nursery for sales. Nursery owners would rather sell a plant than have to keep it over winter. Be sure they are well watered in, once planted, but do not give them fertilizer, other than some bone meal sprinkled in the planting hole. You do not want to encourage new growth when freezing temperatures are just around the corner.

Turf:

At the end of the month, fertilize the lawn with a fertilizer low in nitrogen (ie. the first number listed in the ratio). It is best to use a slow release or "Winterizing" formula.

Lawns have less stress tolerance during winter, so ensure that the final cutting does not leave the grass too short.

Water the lawn if there is little rainfall.

If there are some areas of the lawn that suffered over the summer, now is a good time to sow grass seed. You can seed over a specific area, or start an entirely new lawn.

Plant Availability at Local Nurseries:

Autumn is a beautiful time of year and your garden should not be without colour.

- Pansies (*Viola*), Chrysanthemum, and dusty miller (*Senecio*) are all beginning to arrive at local nurseries.
- Spring bulbs are being stocked and the selection is excellent. Look for tulips (*Tulipa*), daffodils (*Narcissus*), Crocus, Iris, and Hyacinth (*Hyacinthus*), as well as many rare and unusual bulbs and tubers.

Your Personal Garden Notes for September:

October

Flowers:

This is the month in which to plant bulbs for blooms next spring. Most spring-flowering bulbs should be planted by the end of the month. The earlier blooming varieties can be planted earlier in the month and the later blooming ones can be planted right up to and including the beginning of November.

It is now time to dig up tender bulbs, such as *Dahlia* and *Begonia*. If you wish, let the first frost blacken the tops, but be sure the tender bulbs are not left out during a heavy freeze.

Bring in plants for overwintering, such as *Fuchsia*. Store them in a greenhouse, or another suitable area.

You can dig up, divide and transplant most perennials in October.

October is also the month for garden cleanup. The annual bed and the vegetable garden should be ready for some winterizing. To do this, remove the dead annuals and put them into the compost pile. You can also remove the top parts of perennials that are looking really tired, but you should not prune them right down to the ground. Cut them back moderately, because if too much is removed and the winter is harsh, the plant may freeze into the root system and die. Mulch your tender perennials as nighttime temperatures become close to freezing.

Trees and Shrubs:

You may wish to prune back a little bit of some of your shrubs, but do not cut them back more than one third of the desired size. As with perennials, this will allow leeway for winter dieback.

Some trees and shrubs can still be planted, but watch the weather carefully. If the temperature drops, wait until early spring.

Other:

The garden may still need periodic weeding. After all, you do not want to leave a home for disease and insects to overwinter.

Turn your attention, now, to house plants. The days are getting shorter and they may need to be moved closer to the windows in order to receive sufficient sunlight.

Plant Availability at Local Nurseries:

- Unusual shrubs continue to be added to the stock of plants that exhibit features of winter interest, such as the colourful berries of wintergreen (*Gaultheria*) and beautyberry (*Callicarpa*). For other shrubs with strong autumn and winter interest, refer to the *Quick Check Chart of Trees and Shrubs* at the end of Chapter 2.
- Most nurseries will be bringing in their final selection of perennials for autumn planting. Plant them now for a head start come spring.

Your Personal Garden Notes for October:

November and December

Flowers:

If you have not yet cleaned up the flowerbed (and it is not too cold to go outside and do so) do it now so that slugs and snails will not have a place to hide when they emerge in spring.

Spring bulbs can continue to be planted until mid-November.

Trees and Shrubs:

Trees and shrubs can be planted only if the weather continues to be mild and the ground is not frozen.

After a heavy snow fall, gently brush the snow off of delicate tree branches in order that they are not broken or misshapen by the weight of the snow on them.

Other:

It is time to get out your garden journal and recall the delights and the disasters of the past growing season. Ask yourself what you particularly liked and why. Take note of the colour, the size and the names of the plants that pleased you. Was there a plant or a landscape design element that you observed in a park, in a garden or at a garden show that you would like to incorporate into your own garden next year? Write it all down or you may not remember it when it comes time to plant again next year.

Why not borrow some library books or read the gardening magazines that you could not find the time to do more than browse through during the summer. Relax and take heart that spring is just around the corner!

Another thing you can do is to order your seed catalogues. They are a great source of information and ideas.

It is very festive to bring some fir (*Abies*), pine (*Pinus*), juniper (*Juniperus*) or cedar (*Thuja*) boughs into your home close to Christmas. Just be sure to look them over thoroughly to ensure you do not bring in any unexpected "guests" as well! Look for festive materials, such as holly, in your garden. There are also a multitude of indoor and outdoor nursery plants to use. There are many craft classes as well as books that can teach you how to make cedar wreaths and other decorative Christmas items.

Plant Availability at Local Nurseries:

- Poinsettias begin arriving at nurseries at the end of November. In December, the poinsettia selection is extensive as well as the availability of tropical azalea and other Christmas plants.

Your Personal Garden Notes for November/December:

CHAPTER 8

Your Personal Garden Journal

THE FOLLOWING PAGES have been added so that you can record observations about your own garden. Review your monthly personal garden notes (*Chapter 7*) to recall your gardening successes and what mistakes you would prefer not to repeat.

Plant Encyclopaedia

THE PLANT ENCYCLOPAEDIA features plants suited to the climatic and geographic conditions prevailing in zones seven and eight, and in the Pacific West Coast region, specifically. However, many of the species we have listed will also grow very well in zones five and six.

The plants we have chosen to include, exhibit outstanding features to complement your garden. They are suitable for residential gardens and can be defined as low maintenance, meaning that they need little or no pruning, spraying or "fussing". All the plants listed are disease and pest resistant and therefore do not require continuous applications of chemical herbicides and insecticides that could prove damaging to the environment.

The plants appear in alphabetical order under their botanical or scientific name (ie. genus), which is capitalized for easier reference. Scientific names are assigned according to the universally recognized *International Code of Botanical Nomenclature* (1988). Our sources for nomenclature include, *Hortus Third* (New York: Macmillan Publishing Company, 1976) and, *The Hillier Manual of Trees & Shrubs* (Great Britain: Redwood Press Ltd., 1993). We have also referenced various wholesale catalogues for the names of the more recent plant introductions.

Following the "genus" name is the plant's family name, indicated in small capitals. Directly below the genus is the species and variety, and following that is its common name, in brackets. The darkened circle indicates the coldest zone in which the plant can ideally thrive (note: zones are not given for annuals or for the summer flowering tubers or bulbs, as few of them are hardy and, generally, will not survive more than one warm season outdoors). The example below shows the format used for all plants listed in the pages that follow:

If you are familiar with only the common name of a plant, do not despair! The common names of many plants appear alphabetically throughout the Encyclopaedia with a cross-reference to the proper genus name. In cases where the common name is the same as the botanical name, it is not listed for cross-reference.

Next, is a brief description of the plant's rate of growth, including its growing habit (shape), the type of plant it is (ie. deciduous, broadleaf evergreen, semi-deciduous or evergreen), and lastly, whether the plant is an annual, a bulb, a perennial, a shrub or a tree.

The term *feature*, describes any outstanding or notable attribute of the plant (eg. outstanding autumn colour, berries or flowers).

Size, includes the height that the plant can be expected to reach *at five to ten years of age*, as well as its spread (ie. the width of the plant or how widely to space it apart from other plants).

Location, indicates how much sun or shade a plant requires and what type of soil conditions it thrives in. Again, we have chosen plants that will generally tolerate regular, well-drained soil as opposed to extreme conditions of wetness or dryness (eg. conditions for water plants or alpine plants).

Finally, under *comments*, we have described interesting characteristics of the plant that were not already discussed under the heading, *feature*. For example, under *comments*, we may recommend a particular use of a plant within a garden landscape or suggest complementary plant groupings.

If you are unsure as to the meaning of certain terms or technical expressions used here, please refer to the *Glossary of Gardening Terms*.

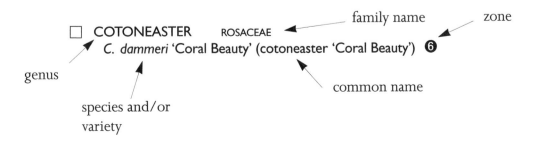

☐ **ABELIA** CAPRIFOLIACEAE

A. 'Edward Goucher' ('Edward Goucher' pink abelia) ❻

A medium growing, mounding, broadleaf, semi-deciduous shrub.

Feature: Fragrant, light pink flowers all summer with showy, bronze bracts in the autumn.

Size: 1.2 m (4 ft) tall / 1.5 m (5 ft) spread.

Location: Sun or light shade, in regular well-drained soil.

Comments: Adds a "fine" texture to a garden and is one of the few broadleaf evergreens that flower all summer long. During cold winters, abelias may lose their leaves. Try planting them in masses or use them to create a border along a retaining wall.

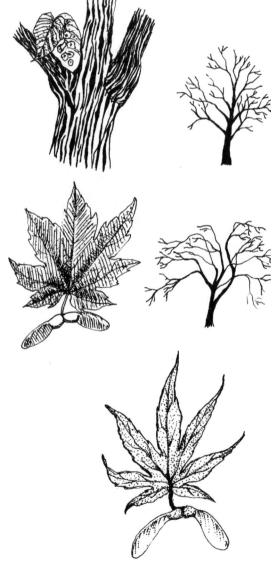

☐ **ACER** ACERACEAE

A. *capillipes* (snakebark maple or Davidii Serpentine) ❻

A slow growing, upright, broadleaf, deciduous tree.

Feature: As the tree ages, the bark develops a striking appearance, with white vertical markings. This maple also provides outstanding autumn colour.

Size: Over 5 m (16 ft) tall / over 2.5 m (8 ft) spread.

Location: Full sun, in average well-drained soil.

Comments: The leaves of the snakebark maple unfurl in the spring, a reddish colour at first, turning green as they mature, and changing to scarlet before they drop in the autumn. With showy bark and exceptional autumn colour, this tree provides a perfect focal point for any garden and, an added bonus, it adapts well to container planting.

A. *circinatum* (vine maple) ❺

A medium growing, upright, broadleaf, deciduous tree.

Feature: Excellent autumn colours of orange, red and yellow with an airy, open manner of growth to provide visual interest.

Size: Over 4.5 m (15 ft) tall / 2.5 m (8 ft) spread.

Location: Sun or partial shade, in moist soil, rich in organic matter.

Comments: Ideal in a woodland setting with a background of conifers to highlight its beautiful autumn colours. Evergreen azaleas, ferns and *Rhododendrons* retain a more natural look when planted within the vicinity of this multi-purpose tree. It does well in containers and is native to coastal regions, from British Columbia to northern California.

A. *palmatum* 'Atropurpureum' (red Japanese maple or red ribbonleaf maple) ❺

A medium growing, vase-shaped, broadleaf, deciduous tree.

Feature: Reddish-purple leaves that hold their colour throughout the summer.

Size: 4.5 m (15 ft) tall / 2 m (6½ ft) spread.

Location: Sun or part sun, in moist, rich well-drained soil.

Comments: *Acer palmatum* 'Atropurpureum' and, another variety, *Acer palmatum* 'Bloodgood', are great additions to any garden due to their unusual foliage. They also display lovely fall colour and grow well in containers.

126

A. *palmatum* 'Bloodgood' ('Bloodgood' Japanese maple) ❺

A medium growing, upright, broadleaf, deciduous tree.

Feature: Large, deep purple-red foliage throughout spring and summer, turning scarlet in autumn.

Size: 4.5 m (15 ft) tall / 1.8 m (6 ft) spread.

Location: Sun or part shade, in moist, rich well-drained soil.

Comments: You will have the beginnings of an oriental garden if you plant this tree close to a pine tree, and add a concrete garden ornament surrounded by pebbles alongside it. This eye-catching plant provides an excellent contrast to a garden full of greenery.

A. *palmatum* 'Burgundy Lace' ('Burgundy Lace' Japanese maple) ❺

A slow growing, upright, broadleaf, deciduous tree.

Feature: Deeply cut leaves with showy, purple-red summer colour.

Size: 3 m (10 ft) tall / 1.8 m (6 ft) spread.

Location: Sun or partial shade, in well-drained soil.

Comments: The lacy margin of the leaves, along with an interesting branching habit, lends a light and airy effect to a garden. This tree also adapts well to container planting.

A. *palmatum* 'Dissectum Crimson Queen' ('Crimson Queen' laceleaf maple) ❺

A low growing, spreading, broadleaf, deciduous shrub.

Feature: Dark crimson leaves throughout spring and summer, turning scarlet in the fall.

Size: 60 cm (2 ft) tall (taller, if trained up on a stake) / 1.5 m (5 ft) spread.

Location: Sun or partial sun (too much shade will cause the leaves to become greenish-red), in rich well-drained soil.

Comments: A very striking plant when cascading over a wall. Try planting *Crocus* or dwarf *Iris* beneath it for early spring colour. Laceleaf maples retain their red colour all summer, and grow well in containers. A variety that is often substituted for *Acer palmatum* 'Dissectum Crimson Queen', is *Acer palmatum* 'Dissectum Atropurpureum' (red cutleaf Japanese maple).

A. *palmatum* 'Dissectum Viridis' (green laceleaf Japanese maple or green cutleaf maple) ❺

A low growing, spreading, broadleaf, deciduous shrub.

Feature: Light green, finely cut leaves turn brilliant yellow before dropping in autumn.

Size: 60 cm (2 ft) tall (taller, if trained) / 1.5 m (5 ft) spread.

Location: Sun or partial sun, in regular well-drained soil.

Comments: Excellent fall colour and, with its drooping branches, it looks superb cascading over a wall. It also grows well in a container, and makes an excellent bonsai subject.

A. *palmatum* 'Sango Kaku' (coral bark maple or 'Senkaki' maple) ❺

A medium growing, vase-shaped, broadleaf, deciduous tree.

Feature: Spectacular bright-coral bark with yellow autumn foliage.

Size: 4.5 m (15 ft) tall / 1.8 m (6 ft) spread.

Location: Sun or part sun, in well-drained soil.

Comments: Striking coral-red branches make this a treasure in the garden. This tree also grows well in a container. During the spring and summer the leaves are green with slightly reddish margins. In autumn, the yellow foliage provides a pleasing contrast to the red branches. Highly recommended!

A. *palmatum* 'Shindeshojo' ('Shindeshojo' Japanese maple) ❺

A slow growing, spreading, broadleaf, deciduous tree.

Feature: This tree displays bright pinkish-crimson new leaf growth in spring followed by reddish-green and orange foliage in autumn.

Size: 2.5 m (8 ft) tall / 1.5 m (5 ft) spread.

Location: Sun or partial sun, in well-drained soil.

Comments: Its vibrant, pinkish branches and foliage in March and April make this an eye-catching plant in the spring. As a relatively small tree, it is ideal for a small garden. It grows well in containers and can be successfully grown on a balcony.

A. *rubrum* 'Red Sunset' ('Red Sunset' maple) ❺

A fast growing, upright, broadleaf, deciduous tree.

Feature: Its green leaves turn a brilliant scarlet colour in autumn in frosty areas.

Size: over 6 m (20 ft) tall / over 4 m (13 ft) spread.

Location: Best in full sun, with ample moisture.

Comments: Used widely as a shade tree along streets and in gardens. Its bright scarlet autumn colour lasts a long time and is accentuated when planted alongside a *Liriodendron tulipifera* (tulip tree), the leaves of which turn a brilliant yellow in autumn.

☐ ACHILLEA   COMPOSITAE

A. *tomentosa* 'Aurea' (woolly yarrow) ❸

A medium growing, spreading perennial.

Feature: Yellow clusters of blooms in early summer into August.

Size: 20 cm (8 in) tall / 30 cm (12 in) spread.

Location: Sun, in regular well-drained soil.

Comments: Yarrows are known for their ability to tolerate hot, dry locations. They are also very popular as fresh cut or dried flowers for arrangements. *Achillea* 'Summer Pastels' displays a range of pastel colours, in a mixture of plants, and grows to 60 cm (2 ft) high. Try planting yarrow with ornamental grasses. Regularly remove the spent flowers to promote continual blooms.

☐ ADIANTUM   POLYPODIACEAE

A. *pedantum* (maidenhair fern) ❹

A fast growing, upright, broadleaf, deciduous perennial.

Feature: Fine textured foliage, tropical in appearance.

Size: Just over 60 cm (2 ft) tall / up to 60 cm (2 ft) spread.

Location: Cool, moist, shady to partly shady location, in well-drained soil, rich in humus.

Comments: This fern can be grown in a container and is especially pleasing when placed against large rocks or allowed to gracefully arch over a pond. Its light green, fan-shaped fronds contrast well with its blackish, striped stem.

☐ AJUGA   LABIATAE

A. *reptans* 'Bronze Beauty' (bugleweed 'Bronze Beauty') ❸

A medium growing, low spreading perennial.

Feature: This plant has dark bronze leaves and violet-blue flowers that bloom for four to six weeks in the spring.

Size: 15 cm (6 in) tall / 30 cm (12 in) spread.

Location: Grows well in sun or shade, in well-drained soil.

Comments: This plant makes an excellent ground cover and can be planted between rocks, or placed to cascade over them. Another excellent variety is *Ajuga reptans* 'Silver Beauty', with its variegated cream and green leaves and violet-blue flowers.

☐ AKEBIA   LARDIZABALACEAE

A. *quinata* (fiveleaf akebia or chocolate vine) ❻b

A vigorously growing, semi-deciduous, twining vine.

Feature: Dark-green leaves with fragrant, rose-purple flowers in April, and long, purple fruit in the summer.

Size: Over 4.5 m (15 ft) long.

Location: Sun or part shade, in rich well-drained soil.

Comments: A fast grower, it will easily cover a fence or trellis; it is especially good for lattice barriers erected for privacy. It is native to China, Japan, and Korea.

☐ ALASKA FERN - SEE POLYSTICHUM.

☐ ALBIZIA   LEGUMINOSAE

A. *julibrissin* (mimosa tree or silk tree) ❼b

A medium growing, flat-topped, spreading, broadleaf, deciduous tree.

Feature: Feathery light green foliage with many leaflets and fluffy pink blooms in July.

Size: 2.7 m (9 ft) tall / over 3 m (10 ft) spread.

Location: Prefers a protected, sunny spot in rich well-drained soil.

Comments: Though not large, this airy, tropical-looking tree can provide a substantial amount of shade. The leaflets are light-sensitive and fold up at night. It requires ample water and protection during very cold winters. It is native to Asia.

☐ ALYSSUM   CRUCIFERAE

A. *saxatile* 'Gold Dust' (alyssum 'Gold Dust' or basket of gold) ❹

A medium growing, cascading perennial.

Feature: Fragrant golden flowers bloom for six weeks or more, beginning in April.

Size: 30 cm (12 in) tall / 30 cm (12 in) spread.

Location: Best in full sun, in well-drained soil.

Comments: Try planting this bright golden, flowering perennial with an evergreen hybrid azalea, 'Hino Crimson', and a dwarf, mauve-flowered *Rhododendron*. The grey foliage of the 'Gold Dust' alyssum also is very attractive when combined with other green-leaved plants.

☐ ANDROMEDA   ERICACEAE
A. *polifolia* (bog rosemary)

A compact, low growing, broadleaf evergreen shrub.

Feature: Light-pink, globe-shaped flowers in late April and May.

Size: 25 cm (10 in) tall / 30 cm (12 in) spread.

Location: Sun or partial shade, in moist acidic soil.

Comments: It has leathery, 2.5 cm (1 in) long, narrow, grey-green leaves with undersides that are grey or almost white. This dwarf shrub combines well with azaleas and other acid-loving plants.

☐ ANDROMEDA,'MOUNTAIN FIRE' - SEE PIERIS

☐ ANEMONE   RANUNCULACEAE
A. *coronaria* (poppy-flowered or windflower anemone) ❸

A fast growing, upright, tuberous-rooted bulb.

Feature: Its large, 5 cm (2 in) wide, blue, red or white flowers bloom in spring or summer.

Size: 25 cm (10 in) tall / 8 cm (3 in) spread.

Location: Sun or partial sun, in rich, moist, sandy soil.

Comments: Before planting, it is best to first soak the bulb overnight, then plant it 8 cm (3 in) deep. If you do not know which end of the bulb is up, simply plant it on its side and the roots will automatically grow downwards with the stems growing upwards. Poppy-flowered anemones are purchased and planted either in the spring, so that they bloom in the summer, or in the autumn, so that they bloom in the spring. Sometimes, it is possible to plant them in the late summer for blooms during winter (only if the winter is mild). Two popular types are, 'De Caen', which has a single flower, and 'St. Brigid', which has a double flower.

A. x *hybrida* (Japanese anemone) ❺

A medium growing, upright, fibrous-rooted perennial.

Feature: Semi-double, pink flowers bloom in late summer into October.

Size: 60 cm (2 ft) tall / 60 cm (2 ft) spread.

Location: Sun to partial sun, in well-drained soil.

Comments: The Japanese anemone is an excellent perennial for providing fall colour. It is also highly prized as a cut flower. Some noteworthy varieties include: 'Alice', which has a semi-double, light pink bloom; 'September Charm', with its single, silvery-pink blooms; and 'Whirlwind', a semi-double, white-flowering variety. Mulch it for the first winter and it will naturalize into an outstanding, low-maintenance perennial.

☐ AQUILEGIA   RANUNCULACEAE
A. x *hybrida* (columbine) ❸

A medium growing, low spreading perennial.

Feature: Lacy blue-green leaves with flowers of mixed colours of blue, crimson, yellow, pink, red and white. Blooms from May to June.

Size: Depending upon the variety, they range from 15 cm to 91 cm (6 in to 3 ft) tall / 30 cm to 60 cm (12 in to 2 ft) spread.

Location: Sun to filtered shade, in moist, sandy soil.

Comments: Remove the spent flowers to prolong the blooming period. Some commonly known *Aquilegia hybrida* include: 'Biedermeier', 45 cm (18 in) tall; 'Crimson Star', 60 cm (2 ft) tall; and 'McKana's Giant', 91 cm (3 ft) tall.

☐ ARABIS   CRUCIFERAE

   A. caucasica 'Snow Cap' (arabis 'Snow Cap') ❺

   A medium, low trailing or cascading perennial.

   Feature: Fragrant white flowers, bloom in early spring for a month or more.

   Size: 20 cm (8 in) tall / 30 cm (12 in) spread.

   Location: Full sun or part shade, in well-drained, or even in poor soil.

   Comments: Use it in rock gardens to cascade over walls and around bulbs. The white flowers are luminescent and provide early spring colour.

☐ ARBORVITAE - SEE THUJA

☐ ARBUTUS   ERICACEAE

   A. unedo 'Compacta' (strawberry arbutus) ❼

   A medium growing, broadleaf evergreen shrub.

   Feature: Edible strawberry-like fruit appears in the fall along with white, globe-shaped flowers.

   Size: over 1.8 m (6 ft) tall / 1.5 m (5 ft) spread.

   Location: Sun or part shade, in well-drained soil.

   Comments: It grows well in containers. It is considered to be an unusual evergreen tree, and it makes an interesting specimen plant. It is lime-tolerant and fairly drought-tolerant, as well.

☐ ARCTOSTAPHYLOS   ERICACEAE

   A. uva-ursi 'Vancouver Jade' (kinnikinnick or bearberry) ❹

   A rapidly spreading, broadleaf evergreen ground cover.

   Feature: Dark, glossy green leaves with fragrant, pinkish-white flowers in spring and red berries in autumn.

   Size: 10 cm (4 in) tall / 91 cm (3 ft) spread.

   Location: Sun or partial shade, in dry sandy soil (preferably acidic soil).

   Comments: Bright leaves make this a valuable ground cover. It is also well suited to cascading over walls. The University of British Columbia first introduced this species.

☐ ARMERIA   PLUMBAGINACEAE

   A. maritima 'Dusseldorf Pride' (sea thrift 'Dusseldorf Pride') ❹

   A low growing, tufted, evergreen perennial.

   Feature: Its rose-red flowers bloom for weeks at the end of spring, into the summer.

   Size: 20 cm (8 in) tall / 25 cm (10 in) spread.

   Location: Full sun, and best in well-drained soil.

   Comments: Rounded flowers in clusters stand upright above evergreen, grass-like foliage. This compact perennial is an ideal plant to use beside narrow borders and walkways. Remove spent flowers to prolong blooming time.

☐ ARTEMISIA   COMPOSITAE

A. *stelleriana* 'Silver Brocade' (wormwood) ❸

A low growing, rapidly spreading perennial.

Feature: Its lacy, silver-grey foliage makes it an excellent accent plant.

Size: 20 cm (8 in) tall / 60 cm (2 ft) spread.

Location: Full sun or light shade, in well-drained soil.

Comments: Although it dies back during winter, this hardy perennial is an excellent rockery plant. It is also used in planting hanging baskets, to soften or blend in with red carnations, blue lobelia and many other flowers. During August and September, *Artemisia* will sometimes produce small yellow blooms.

☐ ASTER   COMPOSITAE

A. *novae-angliae* 'September Ruby' (Michaelmas daisy or 'September Ruby' aster) ❸

A fast growing, upright perennial.

Feature: It provides lovely, long-lasting cut flowers with ruby-red blooms, 5 cm (2½ in) across. It flowers in August and September.

Size: 91 cm (3 ft) tall / 45 cm (18 in) spread.

Location: Full sun, in moist well-drained soil.

Comments: 'September Ruby' is desirable for its late summer colour that lasts for almost eight weeks.

☐ ASTILBE   SAXIFRAGACEAE

A. x *arendsii* 'Deutschland' (false spiraea or meadow sweet) ❹

A medium growing, upright perennial.

Feature: Fragrant, plume-like flowers and tropical-looking foliage.

Size: 45 cm (18 in) tall / 60 cm (2 ft) spread.

Location: Sun or part shade, and best in rich, moist soil.

Comments: 'Deutschland' has creamy white flowers in June that can be used in arrangements or dried. *Astilbe* is especially pleasing when planted near the edge of a pond or when combined with *Aquilegia* (columbine), *Bergenia*, and *Hosta* (plantain lily). *Astilbe* is available in shades of white, pink and red.

☐ ATHYRIUM   POLYPODIACEAE

A. *filix-femina* (lady fern) ❹

A medium growing, upright, broadleaf, deciduous perennial.

Feature: Large, soft fronds of triangular shape.

Size: Over 91 cm (3 ft) tall / 60 cm (2 ft) spread.

Location: A cool, moist, partially shaded area, in humus-rich soil.

Comments: The delicate fronds of *Athyrium* are especially effective when combined with *Hosta* and *Bergenia* or other bold-leaved plants. It is also a good background plant.

A. *niponicum* 'Pictum' (Japanese painted fern) ❺

A slow growing, upright, broadleaf, deciduous perennial.

Feature: Silver-grey fronds growing from a dark coloured leaf-stalk.

Size: 30 cm (12 in) tall / 30 cm (12 in) spread.

Location: A moist shady spot, in rich well-drained soil.

Comments: The unusual colour of the fronds adds interest to a shady garden. Use it in a focal area, near water (eg. pond or creek) or combined with *Rhododendrons* in a woodland setting.

☐ **AUBRIETA**   CRUCIFERAE
    A. deltoidea 'Cascade Blue' (aubrieta) ❺

    A medium growing, cascading perennial.
    Feature: Blue-mauve flowers, blooming from April to June.
    Size: 20 cm (8 in) tall / 30 cm (12 in) spread.
    Location: Best in full sun, and well-drained soil.
    Comments: *Aubrieta* is an excellent plant for borders and for cascading over walls. Shear the plant after it finishes blooming to encourage flower production for a few weeks later.

☐ **AUCUBA**   CORNACEAE
    A. japonica 'Gold Dust' (Japanese 'Gold Dust' Aucuba) ❼

    A medium growing, rounded, broadleaf evergreen shrub.
    Feature: Large, evergreen, gold speckled leaves. If there is a male *Aucuba* nearby, the female plant will develop large red berries, creating a festive display of colour in autumn and throughout the winter.
    Size: Over 1.5 m (5 ft) tall / 1.5 m (5 ft) spread.
    Location: Shade to semi-shade, in acidic soil.
    Comments: Many gardeners prefer the female *Aucuba* because of its more colourful leaves. However, the berries can prove to be a bit messy if they fall near a pathway. Due to its showy leaves, it is often used as a background plant, among ferns, *Fatsias*, *Rhododendrons*, and other shade-loving plants. Another cultivar that exhibits the same qualities as shown by the *Aucuba japonica* 'Gold Dust', is *Aucuba japonica* 'Picturata'. *Aucuba j.* 'Picturata' has leaves with green margins and large golden centres. Both these plants grow well in containers and are fairly smog resistant. Keep them pruned to control their height. They are native to both the Himalayas and Japan.

☐ **AUSTRIAN PINE** - SEE PINUS

☐ **AUTUMN FERN** - SEE DRYOPTERIS

☐ **AZALEA** - SEE RHODODENDRON

☐ **BABY'S BREATH** - SEE GYPSOPHILA

☐ **BAMBOO** - SEE PHYLOSTACHYS

☐ **BARBERRY** - SEE BERBERIS

☐ **BASKET OF GOLD** - SEE ALYSSUM

☐ **BEARBERRY** - SEE ARCTOSTAPHYLOS

☐ **BEAUTYBERRY** - SEE CALLICARPA

☐ **BEGONIA**   BEGONIACEAE
    B. x *semperflorens-cultorum* (fibrous begonia)
    A medium growing, rounded, upright annual.
    Feature: Small white, pink or red flowers, and green or dark bronze succulent leaves.

Size: 25 cm (10 in) tall / 25 cm (10 in) spread.

Location: Sun or partial shade, in moist, rich well-drained soil.

Comments: This bedding plant is just as attractive in baskets as it is in beds. It is slug-resistant, and, if fed correctly with 20-20-20 or a root transplanting substance, it will cover the ground rapidly. It requires very little care, once established, and is lovely when planted in large masses.

B. x *tuberhybrida* (tuberous begonia)

A medium growing, upright and trailing, annual bulb.

Feature: A tuberous bedding plant with large double and single blooms in pure white, yellow, pink, red, coral, orange, and some bicolour varieties.

Size: Over 30 cm (12 in) tall / over 30 cm (12 in) spread.

Location: Part sun to shade, in rich well-drained soil.

Comments: If an upright or trailing type is to be planted in a container or hanging basket, two to three bulbs will be sufficient to fill the pot, depending on its size. A hint to remember, when planting them in a planter, is to ensure that the leaf tips point towards you so that the flower itself is facing you. Water it in the morning hours, beneath the leaves to prevent mildew.

☐ BERBERIS   BERBERIDACEAE

B. *darwinii* (Darwin barberry) ❼

A slow growing, fountain-like, broadleaf evergreen shrub.

Feature: Orange-yellow flowers in bell-shaped clusters during spring, followed by blue-black berries in late summer.

Size: 1.2 m (4 ft) tall / 1.2 m (4 ft) spread.

Location: Full sun or part shade, in well-drained soil.

Comments: The shiny, dark, 2.5 cm (1 in) long, green leaves, with a greyish-white underside, are three-pointed. Birds are attracted to the berries. It is native to Argentina and Chile.

B. *julianae* (wintergreen barberry) ❺

A medium growing, upright, broadleaf evergreen shrub.

Feature: Lightly scented yellow flowers in spring, along with 2.5 cm (1 in) long thorns, and blue-black berries in late summer.

Size: 1.5 m (5 ft) tall / 1.2 m (4 ft) spread.

Location: Sun or part shade, in well-drained soil.

Comments: This is one of the most thorny varieties and it makes a great barrier hedge. The leathery, 6 cm (2½ in) long, spine-toothed, dark green leaves turn a reddish colour in autumn. It is native to China.

B. *verruculosa* (warty barberry) ❻

A slow growing, compact, but spreading, broadleaf evergreen ground cover.

Feature: Yellow blooms in early spring, followed by blue-black berries in late summer.

Size: 60 cm (2 ft) tall / 91 cm (3 ft) spread.

Location: Full sun or part shade, in well-drained soil.

Comments: The dark green 2.5 cm (1 in) long leaves are shiny on the top and white underneath, with scattered reddish autumn colour. This compact shrub makes a good foundation plant for placement in front of more leggy shrubs.

☐ BERGENIA   SAXIFRAGACEAE
B. *cordifolia* (heartleaf bergenia) ❸

A medium growing, broadleaf evergreen perennial.

Feature: Mauve-pink, pendulous, clustered blooms in April/May and large 15 cm (6 in) long by 10 cm (4 in) wide, glossy green leaves that turn reddish bronze in colder weather.

Size: 30 cm (12 in) tall / 45 cm (18 in) spread.

Location: Sun or part shade, in rich, moist soil.

Comments: The large succulent leaves lend a tropical effect when this plant is used along borders, near water features and among ferns. It originated in Mongolia and Siberia.

☐ BETULA   BETULACEAE
B. *jacquemontii* (Himalayan white birch) ❺

A medium growing, tall, narrow, broadleaf, deciduous tree.

Feature: This tree has attractive white bark year-round, and dark green leaves with strong autumn colour.

Size: Over 6 m (20 ft) tall / 3 m (10 ft) spread.

Location: Full sun, in moist well-drained soil.

Comments: The luminous white bark is interesting in all seasons, making this tree an outstanding focal point in any garden. *Rhododendrons*, *Pieris* and pines (*Pinus*), complement this stunning birch. At night, try shining a light up its trunk and into its branches for added drama.

B. *pendula* 'Youngii' (Young's weeping birch) ❷b

A slow growing, drooping, broadleaf, deciduous tree.

Feature: This is a small tree with attractive autumn colour, and graceful, arching branches that grow downwards.

Size: Most varieties are top grafted, 1.2 m (4 ft) or 2.2 m (7 ft) above the ground / 1.8 m (6 ft) spread.

Location: A sunny spot, in moist well-drained soil.

Comments: As with all birches, small catkins or cone-like fruit hang on the branches throughout winter. Lacy, graceful branches make this an excellent accent plant.

☐ BIRCH - SEE BETULA

☐ BLACK LOCUST - SEE ROBINIA

☐ BLECHNUM   POLYPODIACEAE
B. *spicant* (deer fern or hard fern) ❹

A medium growing, upright, broadleaf evergreen perennial.

Feature: Two types of fronds grace this plant.

Size: 30 cm to 91 cm (1 ft to 3 ft) tall / 45 cm to 61 cm (18 in to 2 ft) spread.

Location: Prefers a cool, shady, moist environment, and an acidic soil.

Comments: It has sterile evergreen fronds with fewer fertile deciduous fronds springing from the centre of the crown. This is a common fern found west of the Pacific coastal mountains and is an ideal plant for inclusion in a natural garden setting.

☐ BLIRIEANA FLOWERING PLUM - SEE PRUNUS

☐ BLUE FESCUE - SEE FESTUCA

☐ BLUE OAT GRASS - SEE HELICTOTRICHON

☐ BOG ROSEMARY - SEE ANDROMEDA

☐ BOXWOOD - SEE BUXUS

☐ BRACHYCOME   COMPOSITAE
    B. iberidifolia (Swan River daisy)
      A medium growing, spreading annual.
      Feature: Masses of light mauve, daisy-like flowers, 1.2 cm (½ in) across, cover the finely cut leaves of this plant.
      Size: 25 cm (10 in) tall / space them 25 cm (10 in) apart, especially in a hanging basket.
      Location: Sun or part sun, in rich well-drained soil.
      Comments: The Swan River daisy is very attractive when mixed with other bedding plants in a basket, or by itself in a larger container or border. Its fine texture compliments bolder bedding plants, such as trailing or upright geraniums and canna lilies.

☐ BROOM - SEE CYTISUS OR GENISTA

☐ BUDDLEIA   LOGANIACEAE
    B. davidii (butterfly bush or summer lilac) ❺
      A fast growing, vase-shaped, broadleaf, deciduous shrub.
      Feature: Small fragrant flowers bloom from July to September.
      Size: 1.5 m (5 ft) tall / 1.5 m (5 ft) spread.
      Location: Full sun or part sun, in well-drained poor soil.
      Comments: A perfect plant for seaside conditions. Its small flowers appear at the tips of the branches, in arching, spike-like clusters, over 15 cm (6 in) long, in shades of blue, lilac, pink, purple, and white. The plant has 15 cm (6 in) long, tapering leaves that are dark green and leathery above and white and felt-like underneath. To keep the plant bushy, it should be pruned down to a few inches from the ground in early spring. It grows well in coastal areas and attracts butterflies.

☐ BULBS - SEE ANEMONE, BEGONIA, CROCUS, GALANTHUS, HYACINTHUS, IRIS, NARCISSUS AND TULIPA

☐ BUNCHBERRY - SEE CORNUS

☐ BUTTERFLY BUSH - SEE BUDDLEIA

☐ BUXUS   BUXACEAE
    B. sempervirens (common boxwood or English boxwood) ❻
      A slow growing, rounded, broadleaf evergreen shrub.
      Feature: A great plant for hedges, or for use as a topiary accent.
      Size: 30 cm to 1.8 m (1 ft to 6 ft) tall / 15 cm to 1.2 m (6 in to 4 ft)

spread, depending on the species.

Location: Full sun or shade, in well-drained soil.

Comments: This easy to maintain shrub lends itself well to being sheared into various shapes, including animal shapes. It grows well in containers. Dwarf varieties, such as *Buxus sempervirens* 'Suffruticosa' and *Buxus sempervirens* 'Rotundifolia', are widely used as hedge plants in narrow areas, and for surrounding formal rose gardens.

☐ CALLICARPA   VERBENACEAE
C. bodinieri (beautyberry) ❺

A medium growing, rounded, broadleaf, deciduous shrub.

Feature: It has 8 cm (3 in) long leaves that turn rosy purple in autumn and clusters of bright purple, pea-size berries that last into winter.

Size: Over 1.5 m (5 ft) tall / 1.2 m (4 ft) spread.

Location: Sun or part sun, and well-drained soil.

Comments: This is one of the most notable winter-fruiting shrubs due to its "neon" purple berries. It shows best with evergreen shrubs planted around it, such as *Euonymus japonica* 'Silver Queen', or cedars, *Rhododendrons*, or any lower growing evergreen.

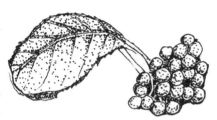

☐ CALLUNA   ERICACEAE
C. vulgaris 'H. E. Beale' (Scotch heather) ❺

A medium growing, rounded, broadleaf evergreen shrub.

Feature: It has 15 cm (6 in) long spikes of very tiny bell-shaped flowers.

Size: 45 cm (18 in) tall / 45 cm (18 in) spread.

Location: Best in full sun, but will also tolerate partial shade, in moist, well-drained peat-rich soil.

Comments: 'H. E. Beale' is one of the best "true" Scotch heathers for cutting and drying because of its long flower spikes. Scotch heathers come in shades of pink, lilac or mauve, also in white and a darker reddish-purple colour. Most varieties bloom for two or three months. The early varieties begin in July and the late varieties flower until October. Trim early heathers to just below the dead flowers, immediately after they bloom. The later blooming varieties should not be trimmed until March. Plant heaths (*Erica carnea*) in front of them for flowers year-round.

☐ CAMELLIA   THEACEAE
C. japonica (camellia) ❽

A medium growing, upright, broadleaf evergreen shrub.

Feature: It has 8 cm (3 in) wide, peony-like blooms during March or April, in shades of pink, red and white.

Size: Over 1.5 m (5 ft) tall / 1.5 m (5 ft) spread.

Location: Best in part shade, sheltered from the hot sun by being planted under tall trees or on the north or east side of a building, in well-drained peat-rich soil.

Comments: Some varieties best suited for a coastal climate include, 'Kumasaka' (the hardiest camellia, with rosy-pink, compact 7.5 cm (3 in) wide flowers), 'Mrs. Charles Cobb' (large, deep red flowers and tall growing), and 'Mrs. Tingley' (delicate, double, salmon-pink flowers). These dark, glossy green-leaved shrubs can be kept compact by pruning just above the previous year's growth, where the bark is thicker and rougher.

Camellias grow very well in containers on a protected deck or patio, in partial shade. Check at your local nursery for varieties best suited to your area.

☐ **CAMPSIS**   BIGNONIACEAE
C. radicans (trumpet vine or creeper) ❺
A medium growing, broadleaf, deciduous, twining vine.
Feature: It features dark orange, trumpet-like blooms that are 5 cm (2 in) long, from mid to late summer.
Size: Over 3 m (10 ft) spread.
Location: Best in full sun, in well-drained soil.
Comments: This vine produces showy masses of brilliant flowers in the summer. The fullness of the leaves makes it an ideal summer screen.

☐ **CANDYTUFT** - SEE IBERIS

☐ **CARNATION** - SEE DIANTHUS

☐ **CEANOTHUS**   RHAMNACEAE
C. thyrsiflorus 'Victoria' (California lilac) ❽
A fast growing, upright, broadleaf evergreen shrub.
Feature: Light blue tiny clusters of flowers appear in late spring.
Size: Over 1.5 m (5 ft) tall / 1.5 m (5 ft) spread
Location: Full sun, in well-drained soil.
Comments: This drought-tolerant shrub has dark green, glossy leaves and showy flowers. It grows well in seaside conditions. Clip it lightly right after it blooms.

☐ **CEDAR** - SEE CEDRUS OR THUJA

☐ **CEDRUS**   PINACEAE
C. atlantica 'Glauca' (blue atlas cedar) ❼
A medium growing, upright, open, coniferous evergreen tree.
Feature: It has grey-blue needles, 2.5 cm (1 in) long, in tufted clusters.
Size: Over 6 m (20 ft) tall / 4.5 m (15 ft) spread.
Location: Full sun, in well-drained soil.
Comments: Once established, these "true" cedars are drought-tolerant. A cedar is attractive in a large garden containing other tall evergreens.

C. atlantica 'Glauca Pendula' (weeping blue atlas cedar) ❻
A medium growing, weeping, coniferous evergreen shrub.
Feature: It has silvery, grey-blue needles and has a cascading form.
Size: It can be staked to any height, for example, 3 m (10 ft) tall, and may be supported to any length, even over 4.5 m (15 ft) long.
Location: Full sun, in well-drained soil.
Comments: This unusual evergreen is at its best cascading over large rocks and down overhangs. Two of these plants could be trained on either side of a large archway, crossing over one another in the centre, to create a stunning focal point in a garden.

☐ **CERCIDIPHYLLUM**   CERCIDIPHYLLACEAE

    C. japonicum (katsura tree) ❺

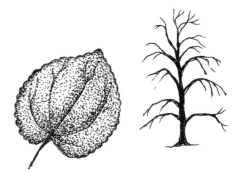

A slow growing, upright, broadleaf, deciduous tree.

Feature: This is a small to medium-size tree, resistant to pests, with attractive red or yellow fall colour.

Size: Over 6 m (15 ft) tall / 2.5 m (8 ft) spread.

Location: Sun to part sun, in moist well-drained soil.

Comments: The katsura tree is used as a screen and has dainty, 6 cm (2 in) long, nearly round leaves that are blue to grey-green in colour. A weeping variety of katsura, *Cercidiphyllum japonicum* 'Pendula', has an interesting shape that complements a garden containing medium to low growing, broadleaf evergreen shrubs, such as David's viburnum and *Rhododendron* 'Unique'.

☐ **CHAENOMELES**   ROSACEAE

    C. japonica (flowering quince) ❺

A medium growing, upright, broadleaf, deciduous shrub.

Feature: This shrub blooms in early spring. Its flowers can be pink, red, peach or white, followed by yellow quince fruit.

Size: Over 1.5 m (5 ft) tall / 1.5 m (5 ft) spread. It may require some pruning to maintain this size.

Location: Full sun, in average garden soil.

Comments: The flowering quince may be pruned any time of the year to achieve a preferred size or to impart an "oriental" appearance. Many gardeners cut off the budded branches in early spring and bring them indoors to enjoy. Place the cuttings in water near a bright, warm window.

☐ **CHAMAECYPARIS**   CUPRESSACEAE

    C. nootkatensis 'Pendula' (weeping Alaska cedar or weeping Nootka cypress) ❺

A fast growing, pyramidal, coniferous evergreen tree.

Feature: Its graceful, hanging branches give this tree an interesting form.

Size: Over 5 m (16.5 ft) tall / 1.5 m (5 ft) spread.

Location: Full sun, in well-drained soil.

Comments: This choice example of a weeping variety makes an excellent narrow-growing tree for small gardens. It is also attractive when planted in groups, and does well in containers.

    C. obtusa 'Nana' (dwarf hinoki cypress or dwarf false cypress) ❼

A very slow growing, rounded, coniferous evergreen shrub.

Feature: Dense, emerald green foliage in fan-shaped tiers.

Size: 91 cm (3 ft) tall / 91 cm (3 ft) spread.

Location: Best in full sun, but will tolerate light shade, in well-drained soil.

Comments: The dwarf hinoki is an excellent container plant, and an appropriate addition to a Japanese garden or a rock garden. It is easy to care for and is especially well suited to narrow, constricted spaces, eg. beside walkways. A choice plant!

    C. pisifera 'Filifera Aurea Nana' (golden thread cypress or golden thread-branch cypress) ❹

A medium growing, semi-spreading, coniferous evergreen shrub.

Feature: It features showy, golden, drooping thread-like branches.

Size: 91 cm (3 ft) tall / 1.5 m (5 ft) spread.

Location: To retain its golden colour, it is best placed in full sun, in well-drained soil.

Comments: The golden colour provides an effective contrast when the plant is placed between shrubs such as *Rhododendrons*, dwarf balsam fir, blue star juniper, red laceleaf maple or most other sun-loving shrubs.

☐ CHERRY, ORNAMENTAL FLOWERING - SEE PRUNUS

☐ CHINESE WITCH HAZEL - SEE HAMAMELIS

☐ CHOISYA   RUTACEAE
   C. *ternata* (Mexican mock orange) ❽
   A medium growing, rounded, broadleaf evergreen shrub.
   Feature: This shrub produces fragrant white flowers during spring and sporadically throughout the year. It has shiny, green, trifoliolate leaves, 5 cm (2 in) long, that are aromatic when crushed.
   Size: 1.5 m (5 ft) tall / 1.5 m (5 ft) spread
   Location: Sun or part shade, in well-drained soil.
   Comments: Prune it lightly, when required, to shape it or just to cut some fragrant, flowering stems to enjoy indoors. This relatively dense shrub is ideal as a screen during summer or winter.

☐ CHRYSANTHEMUM   COMPOSITAE
   C. *frutescens* (marguerite daisy)
   A fast growing, upright annual.
   Feature: Its 5 cm (2 in) wide, bright yellow, daisy-like flowers bloom all summer and into the autumn.
   Size: 91 cm (3 ft) tall / 91 cm (3 ft) spread.
   Location: Sun or part sun, in well-drained soil.
   Comments: Plant this rapidly growing bedding plant to create a summer hedge or use it as a background plant.
   C. x *superbum* or *Leucanthemum maximum* (Shasta Daisy) ❹
   A slow to medium growing, upright perennial.
   Feature: White, daisy-like flowers bloom from early summer into September (for many weeks, depending on the variety).
   Size: Most varieties grow 30 cm to 45 cm (12 in to 18 in) tall / 45 cm (18 in) spread.
   Location: Best in sun, in regular well-drained soil.
   Comments: Chrysanthemums are widely used as cut flowers. Perennial chrysanthemums (or garden mums) are normally used in borders and should be divided every two years to keep them in top flowering condition. Some common varieties available (all with white blooms) include: 'Alaska', with single flowers; 'Esther Read', with double blooms; 'Marconi', with large, double and semi-double blooms; 'Silver Princess', compact with single blooms; and 'Snow Lady', which grows to only 25 cm (10 in) tall and has slightly larger blooms that appear earlier than other varieties of shasta daisy.

☐ CLEMATIS   RANUNCULACEAE

C. *armandii* (evergreen clematis) ❼

A fast growing, broadleaf evergreen vine.

Feature: Sweetly scented white blossoms burst forth in April. The flowers are 5 cm (2 in) wide with five narrow petals. Its leaves are usually 2.5 cm (1 in) wide and 15 cm (6 in) long.

Size: It grows more than 1.8 m (6 ft) long in one season / it eventually spreads over 6 m (20 ft).

Location: Full sun or part shade. It prefers a slightly protected area in well-drained soil.

Comments: The evergreen clematis is one of few climbing evergreen vines, other than ivy (see *Hedera*). Prune it after it blooms to tidy it. It flowers on old wood only.

C. 'Jackmanii' ❹

A fast growing, broadleaf, deciduous vine.

Feature: It produces large, 10 cm (4 in) wide, violet-purple flowers in June through August.

Size: Spreads over 6 m (20 ft) long.

Location: Any position, sun or shade, as long as the roots are shaded (covered by other plants, for example), in well-drained soil.

Comments: As this summer blooming clematis only flowers on new wood, it is recommended to prune it hard in February or March when the buds begin to swell.

C. *montana rubens* ❺

A fast growing, broadleaf, deciduous vine.

Feature: It produces lightly fragrant, small 5 cm (2 in) wide, pinkish flowers in April or May.

Size: Spreads over 4.5 m (15 ft) long.

Location: Sun or shade (the roots must be shaded), in well-drained soil.

Comments: Try planting this showy spring-blooming clematis beside a tall tree and allow the vine to twine through the tree's branches for a charming effect. This clematis should be pruned after it flowers, if it needs tidying. A suggestion for keeping the roots shaded is to place a piece of tile over them.

C. 'Nelly Moser' ❺

A fast growing broadleaf, deciduous vine.

Feature: It produces large, mauve-pink flowers, each with a darker pink bar in the centre, from May to June and again in August through September. Its flowers measure over 12.5 cm (5 in) across.

Size: Spreads over 3 m (10 ft) long.

Location: Best facing north, west, or east (with the roots in the shade), in well-drained soil.

Comments: Prune it lightly in February or March. It grows well in a container and has attractive seed heads.

☐ COLEUS   LABIATAE

C. x *hybridus* or *blumei* (coleus or painted leaves)

A medium growing, rounded, upright annual.

Feature: Attractive, multi-coloured leaves, 5 cm (2 in) long.

Size: 30 cm (12 in) tall / 25 cm (10 in) spread.

Location: Part shade to shade, in moist, rich well-drained soil.

Comments: Outstanding, coloured leaves, ranging from a shade of velvety dark maroon to tricolours of lime-yellow, hot pink, scarlet and red. Coleus makes a wonderful contrast to begonias or impatiens, it brightens up shady spots in the garden, and can even add spice to a hanging basket. Pinch off the flower spikes to enhance the "bushiness" of the plant.

☐ COLUMBINE - SEE AQUILEGIA

☐ CORALBARK MAPLE - SEE ACER

☐ CORAL BELLS - SEE HEUCHERA

☐ CORDYLINE　　AGAVACEAE

C. indivisa (blue dracaena palm) ❾

A fast growing, stiff, upright, broadleaf evergreen, hardy annual.

Feature: Palm-like in appearance with 2.5 cm (1 in) wide by 91 cm (3 ft) long leaves.

Size: Grows 60 cm (2 ft) per year and can easily reach 2.5 m (8 ft) in height / 1 m (3 ft) spread.

Location: Sun or part shade, in well-drained soil.

Comments: The dracaena grows very well in containers. Due to its height and texture, it enhances the look of bedding plants growing around it. It also tolerates seashore and drought conditions. To give it the highest chance of survival, it should be brought under cover (eg. into the garage) during winter. If the dracaena is grown in the garden, it can be given winter protection by wrapping burlap around the root and lower stem area. A variety with a similar appearance is the *Cordyline australis* (dracaena or grass palm), which has a slightly wider leaf blade.

☐ CORNUS　　CORNACEAE

C. canadensis (bunchberry or puddingberry) ❷

A slow growing, spreading, broadleaf, deciduous perennial.

Feature: Features white flowers in May or June, and red fruit in August and September.

Size: 15 cm (6 in) tall / it spreads slowly by underground stems, so space them about 30 cm (12 in) apart.

Location: Sun or part shade, in acidic soil with chunks of rotten bark added to augment the moist humus content in the soil.

Comments: Once established, this rare ground cover (which is related to the dogwood) makes a great companion plant for evergreen hybrid azaleas, ferns, and *Rhododendrons*.

C. kousa (Korean dogwood) ❺b

A medium growing, oval-shaped, broadleaf, deciduous tree.

Feature: This dogwood produces white flower bracts in June and July, and red fruit in October.

Size: Over 3 m (10 ft) tall / 2.5 m (8 ft) spread.

Location: Sun or part shade, in well-drained soil.

Comments: This clean and attractive tree is ideal for a small garden and displays lovely yellow and red fall colours.

☐ **CORTADERIA**   GRAMINEAE

C. selloana (pampas grass) ❺

A fast growing, upright, broadleaf evergreen, ornamental, clump-forming grass.

Feature: It produces white, feathery plumes in late summer through autumn.

Size: 1.8 m (6 ft) tall / 1.8 m (6 ft) spread.

Location: Sun or part sun, in average soil.

Comments: This plant tolerates soggy or drought conditions and is often used on sloped areas. Some winters it will die back, but the roots usually survive, allowing the plant to quickly grow more of its long, serrated leaves in the spring. If, at the end of winter, the foliage appears to be dried out, give the plant a good clipping in early spring.

☐ **CORYLUS**   CORYLACEAE

C. avellana 'Contorta' (Harry Lauder's walking stick) ❹

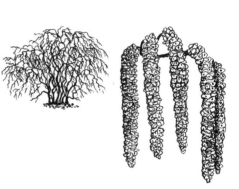

A medium growing, rounded, broadleaf, deciduous shrub.

Feature: This interesting shrub features unusual, twisted corkscrew-like branches and shows to advantage in the winter because of its drooping catkins.

Size: Over 2 m (6½ ft) tall / 1.8 m (6 ft) spread.

Location: Best in full sun, in well-drained soil.

Comments: The spiralling, bare branches are this shrub's best attribute during the winter months. It also makes an unusual screen during the rest of the year (when the plant is in leaf).

☐ **COSMOS**   COMPOSITAE

C. bipinnatus (cosmos)

A fast growing, upright annual or half-hardy annual.

Feature: Its daisy-like flowers, 8 cm (3 in) across, are pink, purple, white, or mauve-red. Cosmos blooms from mid-summer into fall.

Size: 1 m to 1.2 m (3 ft to 4 ft) tall / 30 cm to 45 cm (12 in to 18 in) spread.

Location: Full sun, in average or poor well-drained soil.

Comments: The fine-textured, bright green foliage of cosmos makes a great filler behind lower shrubs or annuals. It also makes an excellent cut flower when newly opened. To keep it bushy, dead-head the spent blooms regularly. As it is fast growing, avoid planting cosmos too close to sidewalks. It is drought-tolerant, once established, and it self-seeds, which attracts birds.

☐ **COTINUS**   ANACARDIACEAE

C. coggygria 'Royal Purple' (royal purple smoke tree) ❺

A medium growing, upright, broadleaf, deciduous tree.

Feature: It has round, dark purple leaves and smoke-like puffs of flowers.

Size: Over 2 m (6½ ft) tall / 2 m (6½ ft.) spread.

Location: Best in full sun, in poor well-drained soil (sandy or rocky).

Comments: The purple leaf colour is showy and makes a great addition to a garden. It is especially attractive when placed among evergreen shrubs. During the fall, the leaves turn orange-yellow to orange-red. Gently pinch off new branches to keep the plant to a manageable size, or let it grow into a small tree and just trim off the dried up flower puffs, to keep it looking tidy.

☐ **COTONEASTER**   ROSACEAE

C. dammeri 'Coral Beauty' (cotoneaster 'Coral Beauty') ❻

A medium growing, spreading, broadleaf evergreen shrub.

Feature: This plant produces many small white flowers in late April or in May, followed by coral-red, 1 cm (¼ in) round berries at the end of summer.

Size: 45 cm (18 in) tall / 60 cm (2 ft) spread.

Location: Sun or part sun, in well-drained soil.

Comments: The berries are plentiful and the shrub itself may be trained on a trellis.

C. horizontalis (fish-bone cotoneaster) ❻

A medium growing, spreading, broadleaf, deciduous shrub.

Feature: Pinkish buds open to white flowers near the end of April or in early May. A profusion of red berries appears in late summer. The plant's leaves and berries provide lovely fall colour.

Size: 91 cm (3 ft) tall / 1.8 m (6 ft) spread.

Location: Sun or part sun, in well-drained soil.

Comments: Espalier this plant on a light-coloured wall or fence to produce a striking contrast with the dark silhouette and herringbone shape of the shrub. The small glossy leaves remain on the shrub for most of the year until they turn orange and red in autumn. This plant should be given plenty of room to grow so that the tips of the branches will not require pruning.

C. salicifolius floccosus (willowleaf cotoneaster) ❻

A fast growing, semi-upright, broadleaf evergreen shrub.

Feature: It produces white flowers during April or May followed by bright red, 1 cm (¼ in) round fruit in 5 cm (2 in) long clusters.

Size: Over 2.5 m (8 ft) tall / 1.8 m (6 ft) spread.

Location: Sun or part sun, in well-drained soil.

Comments: This tall growing shrub also makes an excellent small tree with its graceful arching branches. It has narrow willow-like leaves, 8 cm (3 in) long that are dark green and wrinkled on the surface and greyish underneath.

☐ **CRANESBILL** - SEE GERANIUM

☐ **CREEPING PHLOX** - SEE PHLOX

☐ **CROCUS**   IRIDACEAE

all zones

A slow growing, spreading corm or bulb.

Feature: Oval flowers appear in early spring, in shades of white, yellow, blue and white stripes, solid blue, light mauve, mauve and white stripes, and dark mauve. The foliage is grass-like and usually displays a silvery midrib or leaf centre.

Size: 10 cm (4 in) tall / 8 cm (3 in) apart.

Location: Sun or partial shade, in well-drained soil.

Comments: These popular bulbs are extremely easy to care for. Once planted, they naturalize quickly. After blooming, the leaves and flowers shrivel up and disappear into the soil leaving the garden neat and tidy. Combine these bulbs with primula or with dwarf iris (see *Iris*). The crocus can also be forced for indoor use. For information on forcing bulbs, see *Chapter 5*.

☐ **CUPHEA**   LYTHRACEAE

C. ignea (cigar flower or firecracker plant)

A fast growing, upright, broadleaf annual.

Feature: This annual produces masses of 2.5 cm (1 in) long, orange tubular flowers with unusual black and grey open tips, resembling the ashes of a cigar.

Size: 25 cm (10 in) tall / 25 cm (10 in) spread.

Location: Sun or partial sun, in well-drained soil, rich in organic matter.

Comments: This is a unique bedding plant and its availability may be limited. A visit, once a week at the end of April and into May, to local retail nurseries would be advisable if you do not want to miss out. Try growing it in a raised container or even in a hanging basket.

☐ **CYPRESS** - SEE CHAMAECYPARIS

☐ **CYTISUS**   LEGUMINOSAE

C. x praecox (Warminster or moonlight broom) ❻

A medium growing, upright, broadleaf, deciduous shrub.

Feature: It produces creamy yellow flowers in spring.

Size: 1.5 m (5 ft) tall / 1.5 m (5 ft) spread

Location: Best in full sun, in well-drained sandy or rocky soil.

Comments: Prune it immediately after it blooms to keep it compact. It is sometimes used for mass planting on slopes or as a filler in larger plant borders.

☐ **DAFFODIL** - SEE NARCISSUS

☐ **DAHLIA**   ASTERACEAE

D. hybrids (dahlia)

A fast growing, upright, broadleaf annual.

Feature: There are many cultivars in assorted sizes and with a variety of flower types and colours. Dahlias bloom from May until frost.

Size: Dwarf cultivars are 30 cm (12 in) round while the regular cultivars are 45 cm to 1.2 m (18 in to 4 ft) tall / regular cultivars have a 45 cm (18 in) spread.

Location: Full sun, in rich well-drained soil.

Comments: Dahlias are available in packages at retail nurseries by early March. In May, dwarf dahlias can be purchased in pots. By late April, dahlias should be planted in the garden (especially if they are the packaged variety). When they finally start to bloom, it is recommended to remove spent flowers to encourage the plant to produce more. With the arrival of autumn, dig up the tuberous roots and cut off the top growth to about 10 cm (4 in) in length. Let the tubers dry and store them in a frost-free area for the winter.

☐ **DAISY** - SEE CHRYSANTHEMUM

☐ **DAPHNE**   THYMELAEACEAE
D. cneorum (rock daphne or garland flower) ❷
A slow growing, spreading, broadleaf evergreen shrub.
Feature: It produces very sweetly scented pink flowers in April.
Size: 30 cm (1 ft) tall / 91 cm (3 ft) spread.
Location: Prefers a sunny spot, in well-drained soil.
Comments: The pink clusters of flowers provide a very showy contrast when combined with white candytuft and a dwarf mauve *Rhododendron*, or even a yellow alyssum. It does not like to be moved and prefers to be planted in the ground rather than in a container.

☐ **DEER FERN** - SEE BLECHNUM

☐ **DIANTHUS**   CARYOPHYLLACEAE
D. gratianopolitanus 'Tiny Rubies' (tiny rubies carnation or cheddar pink) ❹
A slow growing, compact, mounding, evergreen perennial.
Feature: Fragrant pink flowers bloom during April and May.
Size: 5 cm (2 in) tall / 20 cm (8 in) spread.
Location: Best in full sun, in well-drained soil.
Comments: To complement its sweet smelling flowers, this perennial has tufts of attractive narrow, grey leaves. It is a great dwarf plant for a rock garden. An interesting variety is *Dianthus gratianopolitanus* 'Spotty', due to the unusual dark pink and white markings on its flowers.

☐ **DOGWOOD** - SEE CORNUS

☐ **DORONICUM**   COMPOSITAE
D. cordatum (leopard's bane) ❹
A medium growing, upright perennial.
Feature: Bright yellow daisy-like flowers that bloom in early spring.
Size: 45 cm (18 in) tall / 60 cm (2 ft) spread.
Location: Best in partial shade, in well-drained soil.
Comments: The flowers are 5 cm (2 in) across, borne singly above heart-shaped leaves. It is best to divide the clumps every two or three years. Plant in large masses under high-branching trees. It makes a good cut flower. During the spring, and sometimes in the fall, it is available at retail nurseries.

☐ **DRACAENA** - SEE CORDYLINE

☐ **DRAGON'S BLOOD SEDUM** - SEE SEDUM

☐ **DRYOPTERIS**   POLYPODIACEAE
D. erythrosora (autumn or Japanese sword fern) ❼
A medium growing, spreading, broadleaf, evergreen perennial.
Feature: This fern has dark, glossy, drooping fronds.
Size: 61 cm (2 ft) tall / 61 cm (2 ft) spread.
Location: Part shade or shade, in well-drained soil.
Comments: This is a fairly drought-tolerant fern. The new fronds are a rusty brown colour when they unfurl, a contrast to the existing dark, glossy fronds. It is a particularly good "filler" plant.

☐ DWARF FOUNTAIN GRASS - SEE PENNISETUM

☐ ELEPHANT EAR PLANT - SEE GUNNERA

☐ EMERALD CEDAR - SEE THUJA

☐ ENGLISH IVY - SEE HEDERA

☐ ENGLISH YEW - SEE TAXUS

☐ ENKIANTHUS   ERICACEAE

E. campanulatus (redvein enkianthus) ❺

A medium growing, upright, broadleaf, deciduous shrub.

Feature: This shrub provides excellent fall colour and produces bell-shaped clusters of creamy yellow flowers with red veins in spring.

Size: 1.8 m (6 ft) tall / 91 cm (3 ft) spread.

Location: Sun or part sun, in well-drained acidic soil.

Comments: A rare and beautiful shrub with a vertical growing habit and side branches that grow almost horizontally. Red-veined flowers hang below the whorled leaves at the end of each branch. The leaves are 2.5 cm (2 in) long and are a blue-green colour. Plant this unusual shrub among other acid-loving plants, like heathers. Use some taller evergreens as a background to the brilliant red to orange fall colours produced by the enkianthus.

☐ ERICA   ERICACEAE

E. carnea 'King George' (spring or winter heather) ❻

A slow growing, spreading, broadleaf evergreen shrub.

Feature: Long lasting, bell-shaped, pink-mauve flowers bloom through the winter.

Size: 30 cm (12 in) tall / 91 cm (3 ft) spread.

Location: Sun or part sun, in well-drained acidic soil.

Comments: The flowers of the 'King George' Heather last for at least eight weeks (around Christmas time). After the blooms are spent, soft new growth emerges from the needle-like leaves. Light shearing is recommended immediately after flowering. Two other varieties are *Erica c.* 'Vivellii' and *Erica* x *darleyensis* 'Silberschmelze'. 'Vivellii' is slightly smaller growing than 'King George' and has deep carmine coloured flowers and dark bronzy foliage. 'Silberschmelze' grows slightly larger than 'King George', and has sweetly scented, white blooms in winter, lasting into spring. Heathers make an excellent ground cover, whether planted in planters or in borders, and look especially attractive when massed in larger groups. All varieties attract bees.

☐ ERODIUM   GERANIACEAE

E. chamaedryoides (Heron's bill or alpine geranium) ❼

A slow growing, spreading perennial.

Feature: This plant produces cup-shaped, 1.3 cm (½ in) wide flowers from May through October.

Size: 8 cm (3 in) tall / 30 cm (12 in) spread.

Location: Sun or partial shade, in well-drained soil.

Comments: Heron's bill is a mat-forming, dense perennial with scalloped

.8 cm (⅓ in) wide leaves. The flowers are either white or a shade of light pink with darker veins. It is highly recommended for a small-scale rock garden or alpine environment. Two noteworthy varieties include *reichardii* (lower growing than Heron's bill) and x *variabile* 'Bishop's Form'.

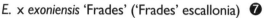

☐ **ESCALLONIA**   SAXIFRAGACEAE
    E. x *exoniensis* 'Frades' ('Frades' escallonia) ❼

A medium growing, rounded, slightly drooping, broadleaf evergreen shrub.

Feature: Long lasting colour throughout the summer and into the fall.

Size: 1.5 m (5 ft) tall / 1.5 m (5 ft) spread

Location: Sun to part shade, in well-drained soil.

Comments: Escallonia is one of the few broadleaf evergreens that produce masses of summer colour (*Abelia* runs a close second). This shrub has glossy evergreen leaves with clusters of small, soft pink flowers from spring to autumn. Wind, drought and seashore conditions are tolerated by this plant. Two other notable varieties include, 'Pink Princess' and 'C. F. Ball', both of which have slightly larger and darker leaves and blooms. Gentle pruning may be done as the flowers fade, or one third of the growth may be removed in the spring to keep the plant more compact.

☐ **EULALIA GRASS** - SEE MISCANTHUS

☐ **EUONYMUS**   CELASTRACEAE
    E. fortunei 'Emerald Gaiety' ('Emerald Gaiety' euonymus) ❺

A medium growing, spreading, broadleaf evergreen shrub.

Feature: It features variegated foliage throughout the year.

Size: 60 cm (2 ft) tall / 91 cm (3 ft) spread.

Location: Sun or shade, in well-drained soil.

Comments: It is a valuable plant as it complements azaleas, other broadleaf evergreens, and conifers such as the 'Blue Star' juniper (*Juniperus squamata* 'Blue Star'). Another notable variety is *Euonymus fortunei* 'Emerald n' Gold'. It has the same growing pattern as that of 'Emerald Gaiety', except that its green leaves are edged with golden-yellow instead of silver-white.

    E. japonicus 'Aureovariegatus' (evergreen euonymus) ❽

A medium growing, rounded, upright, broadleaf evergreen shrub.

Feature: Variegated foliage year-round.

Size: Over 1.2 m (4 ft) tall / 1.2 m (4 ft) spread.

Location: A sunny location will produce the best colour (in part shade the foliage will be lighter green with less colour contrast), in well-drained soil.

Comments: The name 'Aureovariegatus' implies a golden variegated colour. For this variety, the margins are dark green while the centre is golden, while a similar variety, *Euonymus japonica* 'Aureo-marginata', has dark leaves with golden-yellow margins. A slightly hardier variety is the *Euonymus japonica* 'Silver Queen', which has green leaves with creamy white leaf margins. All these varieties are drought-tolerant once established. Their shape can be maintained through light shearing in the spring.

☐ **EUROPEAN BEECH** - SEE FAGUS

☐ **EUROPEAN HORNBEAM** - SEE CARPINUS

☐ **FAGUS**   FAGACEAE

F. sylvatica 'Purpurea' (copper beech) ❹

A medium growing, pyramidal, broadleaf, deciduous tree.

Feature: This tree has reddish or purple leaves.

Size: 8 m to 23 m (26 ft to 75 ft) tall / over 3.6 m (12 ft) spread

Location: Best in full sun, in rich well-drained soil.

Comments: The Copper Beech makes a good lawn specimen and its dark purple leaves provide a great contrast to *Gleditsia triacanthos* 'Sunburst' or *Robinia pseudoacacia* 'Frisia', both of which have golden-yellow foliage. Another feature is that the leaves turn brown in the fall and hang in place well into winter, instead of dropping off.

F. sylvatica 'Purpurea Pendula' (weeping copper beech) ❻

A slow growing, weeping, dwarf, broadleaf, deciduous shrub.

Feature: This is a graceful, weeping, purple-leaved shrub.

Size: 1.2 m to 5 m (4 ft to 16 ft) / 1.5 m (5 ft) spread.

Location: Best in full sun, in rich well-drained soil.

Comments: The weeping copper beech is a great substitute for the red cut-leaf Japanese maple (*Acer palmatum dissectum* 'Atropurpureum'). This beech grows especially well in containers and is a splendid specimen for cascading over rocks or walls.

☐ **FATSIA**   ARALIACEAE

F. japonica (Japanese aralia or fatsia) ❽

A medium growing, upright, rounded, broadleaf evergreen shrub.

Feature: It features large, tropical-looking leaves.

Size: Over 2 m (6½ ft) tall / 1.8 m (6 ft) spread

Location: Best in a shady or semi-shady protected area, in fairly rich, well-drained acidic soil.

Comments: *Fatsia japonica* grows well in a container in a sheltered spot, or under the canopy of large evergreens. Unlike *Rhododendrons* and azaleas, the Japanese aralia is not fancied by root weevils and therefore sustains no damage. The leaves are deeply lobed, over 25 cm (10 in) wide, and lend tropical ambience to a garden (they are attractive subjects to place near pools, as well). If fatsias receive too much sun, they become yellowish; but if they are planted in a shady area and still look yellowish, try adding iron to the soil.

☐ **FERNS** - SEE ADIANTUM, ATHYRIUM, BLECHNUM, DRYOPTERIS AND POLYSTICHUM.

☐ **FESTUCA**   GRAMINEAE

F. ovina 'Glauca' (blue fescue or sheep fescue) ❸

A medium growing, rounded, broadleaf evergreen, ornamental grass.

Feature: Attractive silver-blue, needle-fine blades characterize this grass.

Size: 30 cm (12 in) tall / 30 cm (12 in) spread.

Location: Sun or part sun, in well-drained average soil.

Comments: The mounding blue-grey blades combine well with other dwarf ornamentals, such as the dwarf hinoki cypress (*Chamaecyparis obtusa* 'Nana'), and the dwarf balsam fir (*Abies balsamea* 'Nana'). It is also attractive when paired with candytuft, and other perennials. To keep it looking tidy, clip off the seed heads in August.

☐ FIRETHORN - SEE PYRACANTHA

☐ FLOWERING ORNAMENTAL CHERRIES - SEE PRUNUS

☐ FLOWERING QUINCE - SEE CHAENOMELES

☐ FORSYTHIA   OLEACEAE

F. x *intermedia* 'Lynwood Gold' ('Lynwood Gold' forsythia) ❻

A medium growing, upright, vase-shaped, broadleaf, deciduous shrub.
Feature: Plentiful yellow flowers bloom in late winter to early spring.
Size: Over 1.8 m (6 ft) tall / 1.5 m (5 ft) spread.
Location: Prefers a sunny spot, and regular soil.
Comments: The *Forsythia* begins to bloom anytime from late February to early April. Branches may be cut and brought indoors during the winter to be forced into bloom. Prune it after it blooms by cutting the oldest stems to the ground. Remove one third of each branch that flowered.

☐ FRAGARIA   ROSACEAE

F. x 'Pink Panda' ('Pink Panda' strawberry) ❸

A medium growing, creeping perennial.
Feature: Large, clear pink blossoms, 2.5 cm (1 in) across, that bloom from May into autumn. Edible sweet fruit.
Size: 15 cm (6 in) tall / 30 cm (12 in) spread.
Location: Sun to part sun, in well-drained average soil.
Comments: The 'Pink Panda' strawberry is a hardy, semi-evergreen container or ground cover plant. This strawberry is a new hybrid between *Fragaria* and *Potentilla*. 'Pink Panda' is often planted to create a low border and is also used in hanging baskets. The foliage is interesting in the fall when it takes on a red tint.

☐ FUCHSIA   ONAGRACEAE

F. x *hybrida* (fuchsia)

A medium growing, trailing or semi-trailing, broadleaf annual.
Feature: Prolific single or double blooms from June until first frost.
Size: 25 cm (10 in) tall / 45 cm (18 in) spread
Location: Part shade in an area sheltered from too much wind, in rich well-drained soil.
Comments: There are hundreds of varieties to choose from, and a wide range of colourful blooms. The sepal is the outer part of the flower and is normally in shades of white, pink, or red. The corolla is the inner part of the bloom, with stamens in the centre. This part of the flower can be almost any colour, such as white, purple, red, violet, peach or coral. Normally fuchsias are planted in hanging baskets along with other annuals, but it is common to find baskets containing fuchsias alone. It is important to remove the spent blooms to keep the messy cherry-like fruit from forming.

F. *magellanica* 'Riccartonii' (hardy Riccartoni fuchsia) ❽

A fast growing, upright or arching, broadleaf perennial.
Feature: This hardy plant produces reddish-purple flowers from early summer until first frost.
Size: 91 cm (3 ft) tall / 91 cm (3 ft) spread.
Location: Sun, partial shade or shade, in rich, moist soil.

Comments: A very popular and dependable fuchsia that blooms for the entire summer. It makes a great "filler" plant behind azaleas. Another unusual hardy fuchsia, called *Fuchsia hybrida* 'Island Sunset', has colourful grey-green leaves with creamy margins and has sunset-pink new growth and red stems. The 'Island Sunset' fuchsia has better leaf colour when planted in a sunny or partly sunny spot.

☐ GALANTHUS   AMARYLLIDACEAE

G. nivalis (snowdrop)

all zones

A medium growing, spreading, upright bulb.

Feature: This bulb produces double or single, white, 2.5 cm (1 in) long, flowers in late winter.

Size: 15 cm (6 in) tall / 7 cm (3 in) spread.

Location: Sun or part shade, in well-drained, but moist soil rich in humus.

Comments: This wonderful bulb naturalizes well and is most often planted under deciduous shrubs or trees. It grows well in containers. Plant it in the autumn, 8 cm (3 in) deep and, if possible, try not to disturb the plants by dividing them. If it must be moved or divided, do so after it blooms.

☐ GAULTHERIA   ERICACEAE

G. procumbens (teaberry or wintergreen) ❹

A slow growing, spreading, broadleaf evergreen ground cover.

Feature: This plant features small, white flowers in early summer and red, edible berries in early autumn.

Size: 15 cm (6 in) tall / 30 cm (12 in) spread.

Location: Part shade, in rich, moist acidic soil.

Comments: When squeezed, the berries produce a marvellous wintergreen scent. Not only are the bright red berries very striking, but the small glossy, 2.5 cm (1 in) long leaves turn an attractive reddish colour in the fall.

G. shallon (salal) ❻

A medium growing, spreading, broadleaf evergreen shrub.

Feature: White, urn-shaped flowers bloom in early summer, followed by dark, blue-black, edible berries in late summer

Size: 61 cm (2 ft) tall when planted in a sunny spot and over 1.5 m (5 ft) tall when grown in the shade / 1 m (3 ft) spread, depending on light conditions.

Location: Sun or shade, in acidic soil rich in organic matter.

Comments: This versatile broadleaf evergreen remains compact when planted in a sunny area and grows taller in the shade. It has large glossy, leathery leaves that are often used as greenery in flower arrangements. It combines well with other acid-loving plants and can be used as a filler plant underneath trees.

☐ GENISTA   LEGUMINOSAE

G. lydia (Lydia broom) ❸

A medium growing, spreading, broadleaf, deciduous shrub.

Feature: Its golden yellow flowers bloom in early spring.

Size: 61 cm (2 ft) tall / 1.2 m (4 ft) spread.

Location: Best in full sun, in well-drained sandy or rocky soil.

Comments: This is a hardy, low-growing broom that produces masses of flowers. Use as a ground cover on steep, rocky slopes or as a foreground plant when grouped with other plants. All brooms are drought-tolerant.

G. pilosa 'Vancouver Gold' ('Vancouver Gold' broom) ❺

A medium growing, spreading, broadleaf, deciduous shrub.

Feature: Bright, golden-yellow blooms appear at the end of April and last into May.

Size: 15 cm (6 in) tall / 1 m (3 ft) spread.

Location: Best in full sun, in rocky or sandy soil.

Comments: This broom is an introduction by the University of British Columbia Botanical Garden. The low, dense, mounding habit of this plant is ideal for cascading over walls and combining with other low perennials, such as candytuft and *Aubrieta*.

☐ GERANIUM   GERANIACEAE

G. cinereum 'Dwarf Ballerina' (cranesbill or hardy geranium) ❺

A slow growing, spreading, perennial.

Feature: Its flowers are pink with dark veins, and bloom throughout the summer.

Size: 20 cm (10 in) tall / 45 cm (18 in) spread.

Location: Sun or partial shade, in average well-drained soil.

Comments: This hardy geranium is an easy-care perennial with compact growth. The leaves are slightly lobed and the flowers resemble saucers. Another popular type of hardy geranium used for borders is x 'Johnson's Blue', with its large, medium blue flowers. It grows to 45 cm (18 in) tall.

☐ GIANT RHUBARB - SEE GUNNERA

☐ GINKGO   GINKGOACEAE

G. biloba (maidenhair tree or ginkgo tree) ❺

A slow growing, pyramidal, broadleaf deciduous coniferous tree.

Feature: This tree has fan-shaped leaves that turn golden-yellow in the autumn.

Size: 6 m to 23 m (20 ft to 75 ft) tall / 3.5 m to 7 m (12 ft to 24 ft) spread.

Location: Full sun, in well-drained soil.

Comments: This graceful tree has leaves resembling the leaflets of the maidenhair fern. It appears ungainly when young, but it grows to be more pyramidal with age. The maidenhair tree is a conifer, although it resembles a deciduous tree. Only the male of the species should be used since female trees produce messy, odorous fruit. Once thought to be extinct in the wild, it was rediscovered in Southeast China.

☐ GLEDITSIA   LEGUMINOSAE

G. triacanthos 'Sunburst' (sunburst honeylocust) ❹ or zone 4b

A medium growing, pyramidal, broadleaf, deciduous tree.

Feature: Bright, golden-yellow new growth appears from long leaflets.

Size: 5 m to 15 m (16 ft to 50 ft) tall / 3 m to 6 m (10 ft to 20 ft) spread.

Location: Best in full sun, in well-drained soil.

Comments: The honeylocust is an ideal lawn tree, given that the yellow leaves that have dropped in autumn, dry up and filter into the grass. No raking of leaves is required. If the area is large enough to accommodate three trees, an ideal combination would be the honeylocust (yellow autumn colour), the red sunset maple (scarlet autumn colour) and the red Japanese maple (rich crimson colour lasting many months).

☐ GOLDSTEM BAMBOO - SEE PHYLOSTACHYS

☐ GOLDTHREAD CYPRESS - SEE CHAMAECYPARIS

☐ GRAPE HOLLY - SEE MAHONIA

☐ GRASSES - SEE CORTADERIA, FESTUCA, HELICTOTRICHON, IMPERATA, MISCANTHUS, PENNISETUM, PHYLLOSTACHYS (BAMBOO) AND STIPA.

☐ GUNNERA   GUNNERACEAE
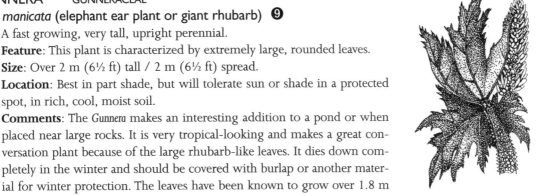

G. manicata (elephant ear plant or giant rhubarb) ❾

A fast growing, very tall, upright perennial.

Feature: This plant is characterized by extremely large, rounded leaves.

Size: Over 2 m (6½ ft) tall / 2 m (6½ ft) spread.

Location: Best in part shade, but will tolerate sun or shade in a protected spot, in rich, cool, moist soil.

Comments: The *Gunnera* makes an interesting addition to a pond or when placed near large rocks. It is very tropical-looking and makes a great conversation plant because of the large rhubarb-like leaves. It dies down completely in the winter and should be covered with burlap or another material for winter protection. The leaves have been known to grow over 1.8 m (6 ft) wide under ideal conditions.

☐ GYPSOPHILA   CARYOPHYLLACEAE

G. paniculata 'Bristol Fairy' (baby's breath) ❹

A medium growing, tall, upright perennial.

Feature: This perennial has double, white, rosette-like flowers measuring 1 cm (⅓ in) across. The flowers are commonly used in dried or fresh flower arrangements.

Size: 91 cm (3 ft) tall / 91 cm (3 ft) spread.

Location: Prefers full sun, in good well-drained soil.

Comments: The perennial dies down in the winter, but blooms for three months or more throughout the summer. The best types to purchase are those grown from cuttings rather than from seed. They are usually available at nurseries in March or April.

☐ HAMAMELIS   HAMAMELIDACEAE

H. mollis (Chinese witch hazel) ❻

A medium growing, upright, broadleaf, deciduous shrub.

Feature: Bright yellow fragrant flowers bloom in late winter before the leaves appear.

Size: Over 2 m (6½ ft) tall / 1.8 m (6 ft) spread.

Location: Sun or light shade, in moist soil rich in humus.

Comments: Witch Hazel can grow into a small tree and therefore should be given sufficient room to do so. It has 15 cm (6 in) long, oval leaves that turn yellow in the fall. The branches, which may be forced for late winter blooms indoors, are often used in flower arrangements.

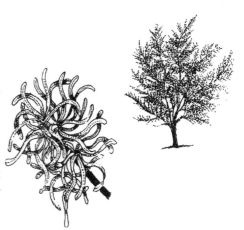

☐ HARDY GERANIUM - SEE GERANIUM

☐ HARRY LAUDER'S WALKING STICK - SEE CORYLUS

☐ HART'S TONGUE FERN - SEE PHYLLITIS

☐ HEARTLEAF BERGENIA - SEE BERGENIA

☐ HEATHER - SEE ERICA

☐ HEAVENLY BAMBOO - SEE NANDINA

☐ HEDERA   ARALIACEAE
H. helix (English ivy) ❺
A medium growing, climbing, broadleaf evergreen vine.
Feature: A hardy evergreen vine or groundcover.
Size: Over 3 m (10 ft) long / space 60 cm (2 ft) apart.
Location: Sun or shade, in fairly moist soil.
Comments: There is a saying that the first year the ivy sleeps, the second year it creeps, and the third year it leaps. Keep the ivy well watered when young and soon it will climb large structures or control any erosion problems you have. Due to its roots, which can cling to almost any surface, it will cover walls or fences as well as ground features. Its glossy dark green leaves are 8 cm (3 in) wide, usually with three or five lobes. Some smaller leaved varieties are: *Hedera helix* 'Baltica' (Baltic ivy), with white veins contrasting with dark leaves; and *Hedera helix* 'Glacier', with grey-green leaves tinged with pink and white along the leaf margin. Ivy is drought-tolerant once established.

☐ HELIANTHEMUM   CISTACEAE
H. nummularium (rock rose or sun rose) ❻
A medium growing, spreading, broadleaf evergreen shrub.
Feature: Showy flowers, 2.5 cm (1 in) wide, bloom for six weeks, beginning in late May and into July.
Size: 30 cm (12 in) tall / 91 cm (3 ft) spread.
Location: Best in full sun, and it must be planted in well-drained soil.
Comments: This plant truly is an asset to a sunny garden. The soft grey-green, narrow, 2.5 cm (1 in) long leaves are interesting year-round. Try planting it in combination with other shrubs or perennials in a border. Its flowers are eye-catching, and mixing varieties with different colours can be quite effective. The rock rose usually produces single flowers in white, pink, red, orange and a new variety called 'Raspberry Ripple' (a bicolour of red and white). Double-blooming varieties are also available. Rock roses can usually be found at retail nurseries in March through May. Shear them lightly after they finish blooming to encourage more flowers later in the season.

☐ **HELICTOTRICHON**   GRAMINEAE
   H. sempervirens (blue oat grass) ❹

A medium growing, upright, broadleaf evergreen, ornamental grass.
Feature: Coarse silver-blue, arching blades characterize this grass.
Size: 60 cm to 90 cm (2 ft to 3 ft) tall / 60 cm (2 ft) spread.
Location: Best in full sun, in well-drained average soil.
Comments: Tan coloured spikes appear in late spring through mid-summer, but it is the intense blue foliage for which this ornamental grass is noted.

☐ **HELLEBORUS**   RANUNCULACEAE
   H. orientalis (Lenten rose) ❺

A medium growing, upright, broadleaf evergreen perennial.
Feature: This plant has leathery, sharply toothed leaflets and produces greenish, purple or rose coloured flowers on long stems, appearing in February and lasting into May.
Size: 45 cm (18 in) / 45 cm (18 in) spread.
Location: Shade or partial shade, in moist, well-drained soil rich in organic matter.
Comments: *Helleborus* is often used as a cut flower. Like snowdrop bulbs, it is best to avoid moving them or dividing them too often as it takes a long time for them to recover.

☐ **HEMLOCK** - SEE TSUGA

☐ **HERON'S BILL** - SEE ERODIUM

☐ **HEUCHERA**   SAXIFRAGACEAE
   H. sanguinea (coral bells) ❹

A medium growing, spreading, broadleaf, deciduous perennial.
Feature: Bright coral, bell-shaped flowers bloom in late May into July.
Size: 45 cm (18 in) tall / 30 cm (12 in) spread.
Location: Sun or part sun, in moist, rich well-drained soil.
Comments: The delicate sprays of flowers on twiggy stems are often used as cut flowers. Below these stems are masses of rounded leaves with scalloped edges. An excellent variety, *Heuchera micrantha* 'Palace Purple', has purplish-red foliage to contrast with green-leaved perennials or shrubs, and white flowers that appear in early summer. The 'Palace Purple' variety has an especially interesting effect when placed beside blue fescue grass or combined with heathers.

☐ **HIBISCUS**   MALVACEAE
   H. syriacus (Rose-of-Sharon or shrub althea) ❻

A medium growing, upright, broadleaf, deciduous shrub.
Feature: Large, trumpet-shaped flowers, 6.5 cm (2½ in) long, bloom from July into October.
Size: Over 2 m (6½ ft) tall / 1.5 m (5 ft) spread.
Location: Sun or part sun, in well-drained soil.
Comments: Four notable varieties of *Hibiscus syriacus* are: 'Blue Bird', with a single blue flower and a slightly darker throat; 'Collie Mullens', with a double rosy-purple flower and a crimson centre; 'Red Heart', with a single

white flower and a red eye; and 'Woodbridge', with a single rosy-purple flower and a red throat. Once established, Rose-of-Sharon is fairly drought-tolerant. It can be pruned to produce a tree-like top with a single trunk.

☐ HOLLY GRAPE - SEE MAHONIA

☐ HONEYLOCUST - SEE GLEDITSIA

☐ HONEYSUCKLE - SEE LONICERA

☐ HOSTA   LILIACEAE

H. undulata (funkia or plantain lily) ❹

A medium growing, spreading, broadleaf, deciduous perennial.

Feature: Lush clumps of bold, heart-shaped foliage. Its stalks are topped with lily-like, mauve or white flowers.

Size: Ranges from 20 cm to 60 cm (8 in to 24 in) tall, depending on the variety / 20 cm to 60 cm (8 in to 24 in) spread.

Location: Shade or part sun, in rich well-drained soil.

Comments: The bold, textured leaves of this plant brighten up dark corners. It is a choice plant for areas viewed from close up. *Hosta undulata* 'Variegated', is a first class hosta. It has wavy, two-tone green leaves with a creamy-white centre, and it grows only 25 cm (10 in) high. Other popular varieties include: 'Blue Cadet', featuring lavender flowers in July with taller growing blue-grey leaves; 'Honeybells', featuring fragrant mauve flowers in late summer with light green foliage of medium-low height; *montana* 'Aureo-marginata', featuring white blooms in late July, and taller green leaves with yellow margins; and *sieboldiana* 'Frances Williams', featuring lavender flowers in July, and taller, rounded, wrinkled, blue-green foliage with yellow borders. Valued not only for its ability to grow in the shade and in containers, hostas also add texture and interest to a garden due to the pleasing combination of variegated leaf colours and attractive flowers. Many golden coloured varieties tolerate full sun.

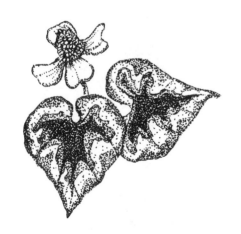

☐ HOUTTUYNIA   SAURURACEAE

H. cordata 'Variegata' (chameleon plant) ❺

A medium growing, spreading, broadleaf, deciduous perennial.

Feature: This plant has multi-coloured, small, heart-shaped leaves measuring 6.5 cm (2½ in) long.

Size: 30 cm (12 in) tall / spreads underground, over 30 cm (12 in), and can become invasive in wet soil.

Location: Sun or shade, in well-drained soil.

Comments: The foliage of the chameleon plant displays patches of cream, green, bronze, red and yellow on the upper side of the leaf. When the leaves are crushed or bruised they produce a strong citrus scent that makes your mouth water. Since this plant has the tendency to spread underground, consider planting it only in an area where it can be contained and thereby controlled.

☐ HYACINTH - SEE HYACINTHUS

☐ HYACINTHUS   LILIACEAE

H. orientalis (common hyacinth)

all zones

A slow growing, upright bulb.

Feature: In early spring, this bulb produces extremely fragrant, dense spikes of waxy blooms in shades of white, pale pink or blue, dark pink or blue, reddish-peach, yellow and purple.

Size: 25 cm to 30 cm (10 in to 12 in) tall / 15 cm (6 in) apart

Location: Sun or partial shade, in well-drained soil.

Comments: Hyacinth bulbs can be purchased between September and December but must be planted before the ground freezes. The best colour selection will be available in September or October and the safest time to plant them is in mid-October. Hyacinth bulbs for forcing can be purchased at this time, and, if planted, watered and cared for as recommended, they will flower indoors in about twelve weeks (possibly in time for Christmas). Some people have an allergic reaction to Hyacinth bulbs, so wash your hands after handling them. See details of caring for and planting bulbs in *Chapter 5*.

☐ HYDRANGEA   saxifragaceae

H. anomala petiolaris (climbing hydrangea) ❺

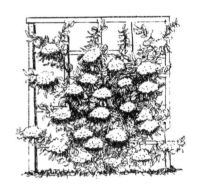

A slow growing, broadleaf, deciduous, clinging vine.

Feature: This vine produces white, flat clusters of flowers throughout the summer.

Size: 3 m (10 ft) spread.

Location: Partial shade, in moist, rich well-drained soil.

Comments: In addition to the attractive flower clusters, are heart-shaped leaves. In the autumn the leaves turn yellow and drop cleanly off the branches. The branches of the vine cling to fences or wall by aerial rootlets, much like ivy.

H. macrophylla (bigleaf hydrangea or hortensia) ❻

A fast growing, rounded, broadleaf, deciduous shrub.

Feature: Clusters of tiny flowers form balls of colour that cover the shrub. Flowers are blue, pink, red or white, blooming throughout the summer.

Size: Over 1.5 m (5 ft) tall / 1.5 m (5 ft) spread.

Location: Best in part sun (but will tolerate full sun), in moist, rich well-drained soil.

Comments: This shrub is famous for its dried flowers, which are normally harvested at the end of the summer. When grown on the Pacific West Coast, the flowers of the Garden Hydrangea, also known as *Hydrangea hortensia*, are blue or purple due to the acidic soil of the region. To retain the blue colour, add aluminum sulphate to the soil, well before blooming time. If you prefer the pinker shades, you will need to have alkaline soil conditions, or you could try sweetening the soil by adding gypsum lime or superphosphate. To obtain larger blooms, thin out some stems in spring and, for a more compact plant, remove one third of the growth in early spring.

H. macrophylla 'Winning Edge' ('Winning Edge' hydrangea) ❻

A medium growing, rounded, broadleaf, deciduous shrub.

Feature: This is a dwarf hydrangea with dark pink flower heads that bloom throughout the summer.

Size: 46 cm (18 in) tall / 60 cm (2 ft) spread.

Location: Part sun in moist, rich well-drained soil.

Comments: 'Winning Edge' hydrangea originated in Australia and was introduced to commemorate the 1994 Commonwealth Games in Victoria, British Columbia, Canada. The blooms virtually cover this miniature hydrangea from late spring into early fall. Another notable dwarf pink hydrangea is *Hydrangea macrophylla* 'Pia' or pink elf miniature French hydrangea.

H. paniculata 'Grandiflora' (Peegee or P.G. hydrangea) ❸

A fast growing, pyramidal, broadleaf, deciduous shrub.

Feature: This shrub features cone-shaped flower clusters, over 25 cm (10 in) long, that change slowly from white to a medium pink colour. It blooms from late August until frost.

Size: Over 2 m (6½ ft) tall / 1.8 m (6 ft) spread.

Location: Sun to part sun, in moist well-drained soil.

Comments: If left to grow without pruning, this hydrangea could grow to a height of 4.6 m (15 ft). This shrub is often trained into a small tree. The long-lasting blooms make it an ideal plant as a focal point, or specimen, in a garden.

☐ HYPERICUM   HYPERICACEAE

H. calycinum (Aaron's beard or St. John's wort) ❼

A fast growing, spreading, broadleaf evergreen ground cover.

Feature: Bright golden flowers, 6.5 cm (2½ in) wide, composed of five petals, and many golden stamens. It blooms throughout the summer.

Size: 30 cm (12 in) tall / 45 cm (18 in) spread.

Location: Sun or part sun, in poor, well-drained soil.

Comments: St. John's wort competes successfully against tree roots and is a good plant for erosion control because of its vigorous underground stems. The best way to ensure a lush appearance is to shear off the top one third of the plant in early spring, every couple of years.

☐ IBERIS   CRUCIFERAE

I. sempervirens 'Little Gem' ('Little Gem' candytuft) ❹

A slow growing, mounding, broadleaf evergreen perennial.

Feature: Pure white flower clusters appear in the spring.

Size: 20 cm (8 in) tall / 30 cm (12 in) spread.

Location: Sun or part shade, in rich, moist well-drained soil.

Comments: This compact plant has dark green leaves and is an attractive perennial in any season. To encourage flower production, give candytuft a light "haircut" after the blooms are spent. Candytuft is a delightful addition to a low border and provides a lovely contrast for the bright purple flowers of *Aubrieta* and the hot pink flowers of the evergreen hybrid azalea 'Hino-Crimson'. It is also a wonderful plant for a twilight garden.

☐ ICEPLANT - SEE LAMPRANTHUS

☐ ILEX   AQUIFOLIACEAE

I. crenata 'Convexa' (convex leaf Japanese holly) ❻

A slow growing, rounded, broadleaf evergreen shrub.

Feature: This shrub is easy to clip into a low hedge.

Size: 1.2 m (4 ft) tall / 1.2 m (4 ft) spread.

Location: Sun or shade, in rich, well-drained acidic soil.

Comments: This holly is compact and finely textured due to its glossy, medium green, small, 1.3 cm (½ in) long, convex leaves. It also produces many tiny black berries. *Ilex crenata* 'Golden Gem' is another favourite holly; a variety that has golden-yellow, flat leaves, making it a bright addition to a winter garden.

☐ IMPATIENS   BALSAMINACEAE

I. wallerana (impatiens or busy Lizzy)

A medium growing, upright, spreading, broadleaf annual.

Feature: This favourite annual provides a profusion of blooms all summer, until the first frost.

Size: 25 cm (10 in) tall / 20 cm (8 in) spread.

Location: Partial sun, in rich well-drained soil.

Comments: Nurseries stock impatiens at the end of April, but it is wise to wait until at least mid-May before planting them directly into the garden. Just one cold night will suffice to stunt the impatiens' growth for weeks. Many gardeners choose their favourite colours early, then repot them into a larger container and harden them off until it is safe to plant them outdoors. If the location chosen is too shady, the impatiens will not grow as quickly as they could. If the plants are well fertilized and are kept on the dry side, they will grow nicely in containers, in moss baskets or in the ground.

☐ IMPERATA   GRAMINEAE

I. cylindrica 'Rubra' (Japanese blood grass) ❺

A slow growing, upright, broadleaf, deciduous, ornamental grass.

Feature: The upper half of the blade is red to bright scarlet, providing excellent autumn colour to a garden.

Size: 60 cm (2 ft) tall / 30 cm (12 in) spread.

Location: Sun or part sun, in average soil.

Comments: The striking colours of Japanese blood grass are best appreciated when the sun shines through the blades (especially at sunset). It is very attractive when mass planted near yellow-flowering perennials (*Alyssum*, for example) or bedding plants. Ensure that there are no plants situated behind the grass, to cut off the light shining through the blades.

☐ IRIS   IRIDACEAE

I. danfordiae (dwarf iris)

A slow growing, spreading bulb.

all zones

Feature: Lightly scented, long, tubular flowers appear in late winter. The blooms are bright yellow with a dark, speckled throat.

Size: 15 cm to 20 cm (6 in to 8 in) tall / 7 cm (2¾in) spread.

Location: Sun or partial sun, in well-drained soil.

Comments: These short bulbs are outstanding in any garden and should be used more often for their showy display of colour. They are also easy to care for as they naturalize quickly. These bulbs are well worth their price and are available at nurseries in September and October. The flowers of another variety, *Iris reticulata*, are a beautiful clear blue called 'Harmony', and have spotted throats. Dwarf iris leaves are extremely narrow and appear after the plant blooms. They are lovely in pots and in rock gardens, especially when seen poking through a thin layer of snow. There are many taller varieties of iris available that bloom in late spring and in the summer.

☐ IRISH YEW - SEE TAXUS

☐ IVY - SEE HEDERA

☐ JAPANESE ANEMONE - SEE ANEMONE

☐ JAPANESE ARALIA - SEE FATSIA

☐ JAPANESE BLOOD GRASS - SEE IMPERATA

☐ JAPANESE HOLLY - SEE ILEX

☐ JAPANESE MAPLE - SEE ACER

☐ JAPANESE PAINTED FERN - SEE ATHYRIUM

☐ JAPANESE SPURGE - SEE PACHYSANDRA

☐ JAPANESE UMBRELLA PINE - SEE SCIADOPYTIS

☐ JASMINUM   OLEACEAE
  J. nudiflorum (winter jasmine) ❻
    A medium growing, broadleaf, deciduous, vine-like shrub.
    Feature: This shrub produces yellow, 2.5 cm (1 in) long flowers during late winter.
    Size: 91 cm (3 ft) tall / 2 m (6½ ft) spread.
    Location: Sun to part sun, in well-drained soil.
    Comments: Winter jasmine is one of few winter-flowering plants. It has long slender branches, much like broom, except that the leaves have three leaflets and are larger than those of broom. Although normally trained as a vine, it is also a good shrub for cascading over rocks or to enhance water features.

☐ JUNIPERUS   CUPRESSACEAE
  J. chinensis 'Pfitzeriana Old Gold' ('Old Gold' juniper) ❹
    A medium growing, spreading, coniferous evergreen shrub.
    Feature: Low growing, wide, golden foliage characterizes this shrub.
    Size: 60 cm (2 ft) tall / 1.5 m (5 ft) spread.
    Location: Best in full sun, in average well-drained soil.
    Comments: This juniper is widely used for erosion control on slopes or for planting in containers. It retains its golden colour well into winter and has a compact growth habit.
  J. chinensis 'Torulosa' (Hollywood juniper) ❺
    A medium growing, upright, coniferous evergreen shrub.
    Feature: It is easy to train into various shapes and has bright emerald-green foliage. In the winter, and early spring the blue-grey berries attract robins.
    Size: Over 2.5 m (8 ft) tall / 1.5 m (5 ft) spread.
    Location: Sun to partial sun, in average well-drained soil.
    Comments: This juniper grows well in containers and tolerates seashore

conditions. It has a twisted appearance and can be used to create a dense screen or it can be pruned into a large bonsai. Try planting winter heather all around it for an outstanding effect.

J. squamata 'Blue Star' ('Blue Star' juniper) ❺

A slow growing, spreading, coniferous evergreen shrub.

Feature: A compact dwarf evergreen with steel-blue, short needle-like foliage.

Size: 45 cm (18 in) tall / 1 m (3 ft) spread.

Location: Sun to part sun, in average well-drained soil.

Comments: This dwarf juniper is a favourite among gardeners. It is particularly eye-catching when interplanted with 'Little Gem' candytuft and winter heather. If possible, plant it near an area where it will have artificial light focused on it; when water droplets or frost covers the juniper, the whole plant seems to shimmer with silver when bathed in light.

J. virginiana 'Skyrocket' ('Skyrocket' juniper) ❺

A medium growing, upright, coniferous evergreen shrub.

Feature: This juniper has dense, soft, blue-green, scale-like foliage.

Size: Over 2.5 m (8 ft) tall / 1 m (3 ft) spread.

Location: Best in full sun, in well-drained soil.

Comments: This evergreen provides a lovely colour contrast to other coniferous evergreens. It is also one of few tall, narrow plants that can be used in a confined area.

☐ KALMIA   ERICACEAE

K. latifolia (mountain laurel or calico bush) ❺

A slow growing, rounded, broadleaf evergreen shrub.

Feature: Mountain laurel produces showy red, pink or white flowers in late spring.

Size: Over 1.5 m (5 ft) tall / 1.5 m (5 ft) spread.

Location: Partial shade, in well-drained acidic soil rich in organic matter.

Comments: A member of the ericacea family, the mountain laurel has the same requirements as rhododendrons. The blooms burst from a bud that opens up to form a miniature, cup-shaped flower.

☐ KINNIKINNICK - SEE ARCTOSTAPHYLOS

☐ KOREAN DOGWOOD - SEE CORNUS

☐ KOREAN LILAC 'MISS KIM' - SEE SYRINGA

☐ LABURNUM   LEGUMINOSAE

L. x watereri 'Vossii' (goldenchain tree) ❺

A medium growing, upright, broadleaf, deciduous tree.

Feature: This tree features 30 cm (12 in) long clusters of golden flowers in late spring.

Size: Over 8 m (26 ft) tall / 6 m (20 ft) spread.

Location: Sun to part sun, in well-drained soil.

Comments: Brown seed pods develop after the flowers are spent. The seed pods are poisonous and should be removed as they also drain the strength of the tree. The blooms are very attractive and the tree has the added feature of eye-catching green bark.

☐ LADY FERN - SEE ATHYRIUM

☐ LAMPRANTHUS   AIZOACEAE
    L. multiradiatus (ice plant or mesembryanthemum)
    A slow growing, spreading annual.
    Feature: Florescent pink, 5 cm (2 in) wide, daisy-like flowers bloom all summer, until the first frost.
    Size: 20 cm (8 in) tall / 20 cm (8 in) spread.
    Location: Best in full sun, in a well-drained sandy soil.
    Comments: The ice plant is a very easy bedding plant to care for. It is often used in containers and grows well in a rockery. Ice plants are fairly drought-tolerant and have narrow succulent leaves, 4 cm (1½ in) long.

☐ LAVANDULA   LABIATAE
    L. angustifolia (English lavender) ❺
    A medium growing, upright perennial.
    Feature: Attractive grey foliage with spikes of scented lavender flowers in early summer into fall.
    Size: 30 cm to 60 cm (1 ft to 2 ft) tall / 45 cm (18 in) spread.
    Location: Best in full sun, in well-drained soil.
    Comments: Lavender has a long history as a scented herb and is most often observed in cottage gardens or perennial borders. Popular varieties of *Lavandula angustifolia* include: 'Hidcote Blue', with rich, deep purple flower spikes (compact growth); 'Munstead', with bright lavender-blue blooms; and 'Rosea', with pink flowers. The flower spikes are used as cut flowers, and for perfume and scented sachets. To keep the plant compact, it is best to prune it in early spring. In cold winters, lavender benefits from being mulched.

☐ LAVATERA - SEE MALVA

☐ LENTEN ROSE - SEE HELLEBORUS

☐ LEOPARD'S BANE - SEE DORONICUM

☐ LEUCOTHOE   ERICACEAE
    L. fontanesiana 'Rainbow' (drooping 'Rainbow' leucothoe) ❺
    A medium growing, rounded, broadleaf evergreen shrub.
    Feature: White bell-shaped flowers appear in the spring. The eye-catching leaves of this shrub are multicoloured (yellow, cream, and pink).
    Size: 91 cm (3 ft) tall / 91 cm (3 ft) spread.
    Location: Best in partial shade (but will tolerate full sun), in peat-rich well-drained soil.
    Comments: The narrow, leathery leaves, 10 cm (4 in) long, of this variety provide a showy accent when used in combination with pines and rhododendrons. *Leucothoe* does well in containers and displays excellent fall colour.

☐ LILAC 'MISS KIM' - SEE SYRINGA

☐ LILY-OF-THE-VALLEY SHRUB - SEE PIERIS

☐ LINDEN - SEE TILIA

☐ **LIQUIDAMBAR**   HAMAMELIDACEAE

L. styraciflua (sweet gum) ❼

A medium growing, pyramidal, broadleaf, deciduous tree.

Feature: Excellent autumn colour and interesting wrinkled bark characterize this tree.

Size: Over 9 m (30 ft) tall / over 3.7 m (12 ft) spread.

Location: Best in full sun, in average soil.

Comments: The maple-shaped leaves turn from medium green to a conglomeration of yellow, orange and scarlet in the fall. Sweet gum makes an unusual specimen tree when underplanted with a shade-loving ground cover (eg. Japanese spurge or periwinkle) and some widely spaced evergreen shrubs (eg. *Pieris japonica* 'Mountain Fire' or *Kalmia*).

☐ **LITHODORA** OR **LITHOSPERMUM**   BORAGINACEAE

L. diffusa 'Grace Ward' (lithodora 'Grace Ward') ❼

A fast growing, spreading, broadleaf evergreen perennial.

Feature: Bright royal-blue flowers bloom throughout the summer and into the autumn.

Size: 15 cm (6 in) tall / 45 cm (18 in) spread.

Location: Full sun or partial shade, in well-drained acidic soil.

Comments: The gentian blue flowers are spectacular when viewed with other perennials, such as candytuft and alyssum basket of gold. During cold winters, mulch it to prevent it from drying out and to protect it from frost damage.

☐ **LOBELIA**   LOBELIACEAE

L. erinus 'Crystal Palace' ('Crystal Palace' lobelia)

A medium growing, spreading annual.

Feature: Bright royal-blue flowers bloom all summer long.

Size: 20 cm (8 in) tall / 20 cm (8 in) spread.

Location: Sun or partial sun, in compost-rich soil.

Comments: This bedding plant is most often used in hanging baskets or in containers. The bright blue flowers are outstanding and striking when combined with bedding plants. For a partly shaded garden, try planting some bright orange tuberous begonias with 'Crystal Palace' lobelia. Three upright varieties of lobelia include: 'Cambridge Blue', with light blue flowers; 'Rosamond', with carmine red blooms, each with a white eye; and 'White Lady', with white flowers. Two trailing types are: 'Blue Cascade', a medium blue; and 'Sapphire', a bright blue with a white eye. Do not allow *Lobelia* to dry out in their containers as they will have difficulty recovering from the setback.

☐ **LOBULARIA**   CRUCIFERAE

L. maritima (sweet alyssum)

A rapidly growing, spreading or trailing annual.

Feature: A profusion of fragrant, tiny clusters of four-petalled blooms covers this plant from spring until first frost.

Size: 10 cm (4 in) tall / 25 cm (10 in) spread.

Location: Sun or partial sun, in regular soil.

Comments: Sweet alyssum can be used in hanging baskets or containers, but is more often planted for edging in borders, with slightly taller bedding plants placed behind it. Good compact, white varieties are 'Carpet of Snow' and 'Tiny Tim'. Two popular coloured varieties are 'Rosie O'Day', a rosy colour, and 'Oriental Night', with darker pinky-mauve flowers. All alyssum plants attract bees.

☐ LONICERA   CAPRIFOLIACEAE

L. 'Gold Flame' (gold flame honeysuckle) ❹

A fast growing, broadleaf, deciduous, twining vine.

Feature: Gold and red blooms last from early summer until frost.

Size: Over 3.7 m (12 ft) spread.

Location: Sun to part shade, in well-drained soil.

Comments: The flowers of all honeysuckles are tubular and many varieties are fragrant. The flowers attract hummingbirds and bees.

L. japonica 'Halliana' (Hall's honeysuckle) ❻

A fast growing, broadleaf, semi-deciduous vine.

Feature: Fragrant white and yellow flowers bloom during the summer and into the autumn.

Size: Over 4.6 m (15 ft) spread.

Location: Sun to part shade, in well-drained soil.

Comments: The rapid growth of honeysuckle enables it to cover a small trellis in one season, while providing a lovely display of flowers. Another popular variety is *Lonicera japonica* 'Purpurea' (purple Japanese honeysuckle), which has darker coloured leaves with a purple hue on the underside, and reddish-purple blooms with white centres.

☐ MAGNOLIA   MAGNOLIACEAE

M. grandiflora (evergreen magnolia or southern magnolia) ❽

A medium growing, upright, broadleaf evergreen tree.

Feature: Fragrant flowers cover the tree all summer, turning from white to a creamy colour when finished blooming.

Size: Over 15m (50 ft) tall / 9 m (30 ft) spread.

Location: Sun or partial sun, near a warm wall, in rich moist soil.

Comments: This *Magnolia* not only has large flowers, 25 cm (10 in) across, when open, but it also has leaves that measure over 15 cm (6 in) long, with a waxy, green upper surface and a fuzzy, rusty coloured underside. Two varieties suited to smaller sized yards are, *Magnolia grandiflora* 'Little Gem', and *Magnolia grandiflora* 'Majestic Beauty'. The M. g. 'Little Gem' grows 4.6 m (15 ft) tall and 2.4 m (8 ft) wide. Its flowers are smaller, 7 cm (5 in) across, and its branches normally touch the ground. The M. g. 'Majestic Beauty' is 9 m (30 ft) tall, 4.6 m (15 ft) wide, with blooms that measure almost 30 cm (12 in) across. Its leaves are also darker in colour and larger. These two varieties look very exotic when placed near hot tubs and swimming pools. Since these are grafted varieties, they will almost certainly bloom during the first year after they are purchased.

M. sieboldii (Oyama magnolia or Siebold's magnolia) ❼b

A medium growing, rounded, broadleaf, deciduous tree.

Feature: This tree produces fragrant, white, cup-shaped flowers, 10 cm (4 in) across, with crimson centres, all summer long.

Size: 4.5 m (15 ft) tall / 4.5 m (15 ft) spread.

Location: Full to part sun, in rich, moist well-drained soil.

Comments: Carefully consider where to locate a magnolia, keeping in mind its eventual size. They are difficult to transplant once they grow larger. To achieve the best effect from a Siebold's magnolia, situate the plant near the top of a slope. This tree is also highly recommended for smaller garden spaces.

M. x *soulangiana* (saucer magnolia) **5**a

A medium growing, vase-shaped, broadleaf, deciduous tree.

Feature: The large, 15 cm (6 in) wide, white flowers have a rose-purple base, and last for almost four weeks.

Size: 7.6 m (25 ft) tall / 7.6 m (25 ft) spread.

Location: Full to partial sun, in moist, rich well-drained soil.

Comments: This magnolia is most commonly found in British Columbia and is often incorrectly termed the "tulip tree" because of the tulip-shaped flowers it produces (note: the true "tulip tree" is actually a *Liriodendron*, which has a tulip-shaped leaf). The saucer magnolia makes a wonderful lawn specimen, although care must be taken to avoid soil compaction around the base of it (ie. avoid too much foot traffic near this tree). Also, do not allow grass to grow near the area surrounding the trunk.

M. *stellata* (star magnolia) **5**b

A slow growing, rounded, large, broadleaf, deciduous shrub, or small tree.

Feature: Showy, fragrant, pure white, flowers, 8 cm (3 in) wide, with thin petals bloom in early spring.

Size: 2.4 m (8 ft) tall / 2.4 m (8 ft) spread.

Location: Sun to part sun, in rich, moist well-drained soil.

Comments: A profusion of luminescent blooms appears before the leaves emerge. The flowers on bare branches provide a remarkable contrast to a dark background of coniferous evergreens or broadleaf evergreens such as *Photinia x fraseri*, with its bright red new leaves. It also grows very well in containers.

☐ MAHONIA   BERBERIDACEAE

M. *aquifolium* (Oregon grape or holly barberry) **5**

A slow growing, spreading, broadleaf evergreen shrub.

Feature: This shrub produces fragrant yellow flowers in the spring, followed by edible blue-black berries in late summer that attract birds.

Size: 1.5 m (5 ft) tall / 1.5 m (5 ft) spread.

Location: Sun or partial shade, in well-drained acidic soil.

Comments: The Oregon grape grows well in containers. In the autumn, some leaves turn bright red. It is an excellent landscape plant because of its minimal maintenance requirements and the fact that it is fairly drought-tolerant. The holly-shaped, dark, glossy leaves turn a bronzy-purple in the winter. A smaller-growing variety is *Mahonia aquifolium* 'Compacta'.

M. *nervosa* (longleaf or Cascades mahonia) **7**

A slow growing, spreading, broadleaf evergreen shrub.

Feature: Fragrant yellow flowers bloom in spring, followed by blue-black, edible berries in the summer.

Size: 60 cm (2 ft) tall / 91 cm (3 ft) spread.

Location: Best in partial shade, in well-drained acidic soil.

Comments: This is another mahonia native to the Pacific West Coast. It is also low maintenance. As it spreads by underground roots, it makes an excellent ground cover.

☐ MAIDENHAIR FERN - SEE ADIANTUM

☐ MAIDENHAIR TREE - SEE GINKGO

☐ MALVA   MALVACEAE

M. trimestris (lavatera or mallow)

A fast growing, upright, broadleaf hardy annual.

Feature: Showy, florescent, almost silky, 7.5 cm (3 in) wide, clear pink flowers bloom from June into August.

Size: 45 cm (18 in) tall / 30 cm (12 in) spread.

Location: Full sun, in average soil.

Comments: Lavatera is usually planted in groups of three or five, behind lower-growing annuals such as petunias. Although it is eye-catching, its trumpet-shaped flowers do not last into the fall. Unlike most other bedding plants, they go to seed quickly.

☐ MAPLE - SEE ACER

☐ MARIGOLD - SEE TAGETES

☐ MEXICAN MOCK ORANGE - SEE CHOISYA

☐ MICHAELMAS DAISY - SEE ASTER

☐ MISCANTHUS   GRAMINEAE

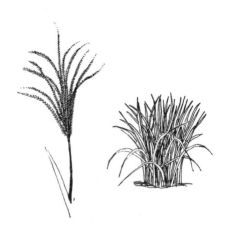

M. sinensis (eulalia grass) ❺

A medium growing, upright, broadleaf evergreen, ornamental grass.

Feature: This grass has erect, slightly arching, bold leaves, with loose seed heads appearing in autumn and lasting through the winter.

Size: 1.8 m (6 ft) tall / 1.5 m (5 ft) spread.

Location: Sun or shade, in any garden soil.

Comments: Trim it in the spring, before the new growth appears, the same as you would for any ornamental grass. Some notable garden varieties of *Miscanthus sinensis* include: 'Gracillimus', or maiden grass, with feathery, white blooms and silver-green blades; 'Silberfeder', or silver feather grass, with silver-white flowers in early autumn; and 'Zebrinus', or zebra grass, with horizontal bands of yellow to mark the leaves.

☐ MOCK ORANGE - SEE PHILADELPHUS

☐ MORUS   MORACEAE

M. alba 'Pendula' (weeping mulberry) ❹

A rapidly growing, weeping, broadleaf, deciduous tree.

Feature: The graceful branches of this tree drape the ground and are covered by bright green, deeply cut foliage.

Size: 2.4 m (8 ft) tall (though they are usually grafted lower down on the trunk) / 2.4 m (8 ft) spread.

Location: Full sun, in well-drained regular soil.

Comments: This is one of few weeping-style trees and is ideal for small gardens.

☐ MOSS PHLOX - SEE PHLOX

☐ MOUNTAIN HEMLOCK - SEE TSUGA

☐ MOUNTAIN LAUREL - SEE KALMIA

☐ MUGHO PINE - SEE PINUS

☐ MULBERRY - SEE MORUS

☐ NANDINA   BERBERIDACEAE
N. domestica (heavenly bamboo or sacred bamboo) ❼

A slow growing, upright, broadleaf evergreen shrub.

Feature: A narrow-growing shrub with good fall colour.

Size: 1.5 m (5 ft) tall / 91 cm (3 ft) spread.

Location: Sun or shade (the foliage is more colourful in a sunny location), in regular soil.

Comments: Despite its name, it is not a bamboo, but is actually related to barberry. It has a similar growth habit to bamboo and the foliage has a delicate texture with 4 cm (1½ in) long, pointed oval leaflets, like bamboo. In the fall and winter, the leaves become a fiery crimson, especially if the plant is in a sunny spot. If the weather becomes very cold, heavenly bamboo will lose its leaves, but do not worry as it will recover quickly. Planted in larger groups, the *Nandina* produces small, inconspicuous white flowers followed by small red berries. Other varieties, which have smaller leaves and a more compact dwarf growing habit, are *Nandina domestica* 'Gulf Stream' and *Nandina domestica* 'Moon Bay'.

☐ NARCISSUS   AMARYLLIDACEAE
N. hybrids (daffodils)

all zones

A slow growing, upright bulb.

Feature: These bulbs feature extremely showy, often fragrant, yellow, orange and white flowers in early spring (for dwarf varieties) or in mid-spring.

Size: 15 cm to 40 cm (6 in to 16 in) tall, depending on the variety / 15 cm (6 in) spread.

Location: Sun or part sun, in well-drained soil.

Comments: Like the sunflower, daffodils often face the sun. Therefore, consider where you want to plant them in the garden in relation to sun exposure. The foliage is narrow and long and can look messy once the flowers are spent and the foliage browns. If the long leaves are tied in a knot, they will look tidier in beds or borders. These worthwhile bulbs should be planted as early as possible in the fall, certainly before the ground freezes. They grow very well in containers and look spectacular when planted with bright red tulips. For these bulbs to multiply, the leaves must be left to turn brown and die down for a few weeks after blooming. This allows nutrients to be absorbed into the bulb. For more details on the care and planting of bulbs, refer to *Chapter 5*.

☐ OREGON GRAPE - SEE MAHONIA

☐ OXYDENDRUM   ERICACEAE

O. arboreum (**sourwood or sorrel tree**) ❺

A slow growing, upright, broadleaf, deciduous tree.

Feature: This tree displays eye-catching, 25 cm (10 in) long, arching clusters of whitish, bell-shaped blooms at the tips of branches, from mid-summer into the fall. Its narrow leaves turn brilliant orange-red before they drop in the autumn.

Size: Over 4.5 m (15 ft) tall / over 5 m (16 ft) spread.

Location: Sun or shade, in moist, well-drained acidic soil.

Comments: This is an outstanding small tree with many interesting features, as mentioned above. Its 15 cm (6 in) long leaves have a bronze tint in the spring. The spent flower clusters turn into greenish seed capsules that become silver-grey in winter. These complement the fabulous fall colour of the leaves. It grows well in a container. Avoid planting it where its roots will be cultivated or disturbed. For example, do not plant it in the lawn or in a flower bed. It is also an excellent tree for a patio due to its spreading canopy and interesting shape.

☐ PACHYSANDRA   BUXACEAE

P. terminalis (**Japanese spurge**) ❹

A medium growing, spreading, broadleaf evergreen perennial.

Feature: The lush, dense growth gives this ground cover a tropical appearance.

Size: 25 cm (10 in) tall / 30 cm (12 in) spread.

Location: Partial shade to shade (becomes yellowish in too much sun), in rich moist soil.

Comments: This is an extremely low maintenance plant for shady areas and is very hardy. Japanese spurge spreads underground and can be a great help in controlling soil erosion on slopes. It retains its rich, dark-green leaves year-round. *Pachysandra terminalis* 'Variegata' has creamy, variegated leaves, providing a striking contrast to green shrubs surrounding it.

☐ PAGODA DOGWOOD - SEE CORNUS

☐ PALM - SEE CORDYLINE OR DRACAENA OR TRACHYCARPUS

☐ PAMPAS GRASS - SEE CORTADERIA

☐ PANSY - SEE VIOLA

☐ PARTHENOCISSUS   VITACEAE

P. quinquefolia (**Virginia creeper**) ❸

A fast growing, broadleaf, deciduous, clinging vine.

Feature: Its medium green leaves are divided into five leaflets, each 15 cm (6 in) long, that turn brilliant red and orange in autumn.

Size: Over 6 m (20 ft) spread.

Location: Sun or shade, in moist well-drained soil.

Comments: The plant adheres to fences or walls by tendrils with sucker discs at the ends. Virginia creeper is often used for erosion control on slopes. *Parthenocissus tricuspidata* (Boston ivy) has the same features of colour and growth habit as the Virginia creeper, but the leaves are divided into only three leaflets (or sometimes just a single, three lobed leaf).

PELARGONIUM   GERANIACEAE

P. x *hortorum* (common, garden or zonal geranium)

A medium growing, upright, rounded, broadleaf annual.

Feature: Large, colourful single, double, or semi-double flower clusters bloom all summer.

Size: 30 cm (12 in) tall / 30 cm (12 in) spread.

Location: Sun or partial sun, in rich well-drained soil.

Comments: From year to year, the names of specific varieties change, depending on availability. The *Pelargonium x hortorum* is commonly known as the "geranium". *Pelargonium* (*domesticum*) refers to the Martha Washington (or Lady Washington) variety. Do not overwater geraniums and regularly remove the old blooms to encourage more flowers.

P. *peltatum* (ivy geranium or trailing geranium)

A medium growing, trailing or hanging, broadleaf annual.

Feature: This geranium has glossy, succulent, bright green, ivy-like foliage and produces masses of single or double, 2.5 cm (1 in) across, clusters of blooms throughout the summer.

Size: 20 cm (8 in) tall / 30 cm (12 in) spread.

Location: Sun or partial sun, in rich well-drained soil.

Comments: The flowers can be various shades, from dark maroon to soft pinks, lavender, white, and hot pink with a white stripe. Ivy geraniums combine well with other annuals in hanging baskets or containers.

PENNISETUM   GRAMINEAE

P. *alopecuroides* 'Hameln' (dwarf fountain grass) ❺

A medium growing, upright, broadleaf evergreen, ornamental grass.

Feature: Attractive fall colour.

Size: 60 cm (2 ft) tall / 60 cm (2 ft) spread.

Location: Best in a sunny spot, in well-drained soil.

Comments: Silvery brown flowers, resembling tapered bottle brushes, bloom in late summer into autumn, above narrow arching leaves. A good ornamental grass for use in dried arrangements. Purple fountain grass (*Pennisetum setaceum* 'Atropurpurea') is another interesting grass, with red plume-like blooms in late summer.

PERIWINKLE - SEE VINCA

PERNETTYA   ERICACEAE

P. *mucronata* (pernettya) ❼

A medium growing, spreading, broadleaf evergreen shrub.

Feature: This shrub has large berries, 1.5 cm (½ in) wide, from autumn through winter, and produces small, white blooms in spring.

Size: 75 cm (2½ ft) tall / 91 cm (3 ft) spread.

Location: Tolerates some shade, but is best in full sun, in moist, well-drained acidic soil.

Comments: Like blueberries, it is recommended to plant these in groups to ensure better pollination and encourage berry production. There are many varieties with berries in bright shades of white, red, pink, or purple. The narrow, pointed leaves are 2 cm (¾ in) long and the shrub responds well to pruning. It spreads by underground runners, the growth of which can be easily controlled. Just use a spade to prune the roots.

☐ **PETUNIA** SOLANACEAE
P. x *hybrida* (petunia or common garden petunia)
A rapidly growing, spreading or trailing annual.
Feature: These annuals produce slightly scented, single or double blooms, 5 cm (2 in) wide, from late spring into early autumn.
Size: 18 cm to 30 cm (7 in to 12 in) tall / 18 cm to 30 cm (7 in to 12 in) spread.
Location: Full sun, in rich well-drained soil.
Comments: Many shades are available, from white, pink, red, mauve, dark purple, yellow, peach, to some bicolour varieties. A popular bicolour is 'Blue Picotee', which has a smashing white margin to contrast with the dark mauve centre. The term "cascade" refers to a plant that trails or hangs down to a greater extent than the more common petunias. Petunias with larger blooms are known as "grandifloras", and those with many small flowers are called "multifloras". Petunias with single blooms withstand wet summers better than the double blooming types. All petunias are dazzling as border plants or in containers, especially the more compact "Supermagic" and "Ultra" series.

☐ **PHILADELPHUS** SAXIFRAGACEAE
P. x *virginalis* (virginal mock orange) ❹
A medium growing, upright, broadleaf, deciduous shrub.
Feature: It produces extremely aromatic, semi-double, white flowers in late spring.
Size: Over 1.8 m (6 ft) tall / 1.5 m (5 ft) spread.
Location: Best in sun, in regular soil.
Comments: This shrub is highly prized for its sweet fragrance and it should be planted where one can enjoy its scent. A dwarf variety is *Philadelphus x virginalis* 'Dwarf Snowflake', 1 m (3 ft) tall, with double, pure white flowers.

☐ **PHLOX** POLEMONIACEAE
P. *subulata* (creeping phlox or moss phlox) ❷
A medium growing, dense, spreading, evergreen perennial.
Feature: Forms a very low mat of tiny leaves covered with a profusion of white, pink, mauve or bluish flowers in April and May.
Size: 10 cm (4 in) tall / 60 cm (2 ft) spread.
Location: Full sun, in well-drained regular soil.
Comments: Shear it lightly after it has bloomed, just as you would an *Aubrieta* or *Arabis* plant. It is recommended to divide *Phlox* every two years to prevent it from becoming thin.

☐ **PHOTINIA** ROSACEAE
P. x *fraseri* (Fraser's photinia) ❼
A fast growing, rounded, small, upright, broadleaf evergreen tree.
Feature: Its bright scarlet, new foliage lasts through the year.
Size: Over 2.4 m (8 ft) tall / over 2.4 m (8 ft) spread.
Location: Best in sun, in well-drained soil.
Comments: The glossy dark green leaves are 10 cm (4 in) long and 5 cm (2 in) wide. It is often trained into a small tree. *Photinia* is fairly drought-tolerant and is frequently used as a tall hedge plant.

☐ PHYLLITIS   POLYPODIACEAE
P. scolopendrium (Hart's tongue fern) ❹
A slow growing, upright, broadleaf evergreen perennial.
Feature: Shiny bright green, wide, blade-like fronds characterize this fern.
Size: 30 cm (12 in) tall / 30 cm (12 in) spread.
Location: Partial sun or shade, in rich moist soil.
Comments: This fern grows well in a container and shows to advantage when planted with bedding plants or placed in a woodland setting or rock garden. Its unusual leaves are 15 cm to 30 cm (6 in to 12 in) long and 3.8 cm (1½ in) wide and bear a resemblance to those of an indoor plant called, bird's nest fern.

☐ PHYLLOSTACHYS   GRAMINEAE
P. aurea (goldstem or golden bamboo) ❼

A medium growing, upright, broadleaf evergreen shrub.
Feature: The delicate, narrow leaves of this plant form a dense, rustling screen.
Size: 1.8 m (6 ft) tall, if kept pruned, or over 3 m (10 ft) tall, if left un-controlled / 1.5 m (5 ft) spread (root pruning is necessary).
Location: Sun or part sun, in regular soil.
Comments: This tropical-looking shrub makes an excellent screen and is drought-tolerant. If you are concerned about the roots being invasive, sink a band of metal, 45 cm (18 in) deep, into the ground around the roots. Bamboo grows well in a large container, but keep it well watered and feed it monthly with a fertilizer with a high nitrogen content. The new shoots that appear in mid-spring are edible.

☐ PICEA   PINACEAE
P. omorika (Serbian spruce or omorika spruce) ❹

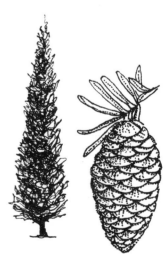

A slow growing, narrow, pyramidal, coniferous evergreen tree.
Feature: This tree has a narrow growing habit with short, stiff, ascending branches.
Size: Over 4 m (13 ft) tall / 1.5 m (5 ft) spread.
Location: Full sun, in well-drained acidic soil.
Comments: The branches of the *Picea omorika* are grey-blue underneath and dark green above. Their short needles have two distinguishing white bands on the underside. This dense, pyramidal tree is widely used in narrow ar-eas. Other evergreen plants for constricted spots are the emerald cedar, *Pyracantha* (if trained or espaliered), pyramid cedar (*Thuja*) and yew (*Taxus*). Another attribute of the omorika spruce is that it develops black-purple cones as it gets older. Unlike other spruces, the Serbian spruce is not as sus-ceptible to spider mite infestation. It is best to purchase it in early December when other live Christmas trees are sold.

☐ PIERIS   ERICACEAE
P. japonica 'Mountain Fire' (lily-of-the-valley shrub or 'Mountain Fire' an-dromeda) ❻
A medium growing, rounded, broadleaf evergreen shrub.
Feature: Clusters of small, white, bell-shaped flowers bloom in March or April, followed by fiery red new growth that lasts for weeks.
Size: 1.2 m (4 ft) tall / 1.2 m (4 ft) spread.

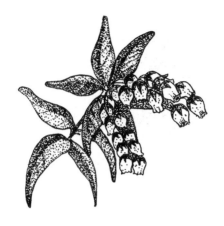

Location: Sun or part shade, in rich, well-drained acidic soil (ie. the same type of soil preferred by *Rhododendrons*).

Comments: *Pieris japonica* 'Mountain Fire' is very easy to care for. It tolerates some drought and needs little, if any, pruning to keep it looking its best. Another popular variety is *Pieris japonica* 'Forest Flame', which has the same, 5 cm (2 in) long, narrow leaf. Instead of the bronze-red leaf colour of the *Pieris j.* 'Mountain Fire', the *Pieris j.* 'Forest Flame' starts out bright red, changes to hot pink, fades to a lighter pink, then a soft yellow and, finally, turns light green, darkening to medium green. The *Pieris j.* 'Forest Flame' is also not quite as hardy and therefore should be planted in a more protected area of the garden. A variegated (creamy yellow and green) variety called *Pieris japonica* 'variegata' is also a valuable plant because it is slower growing and adds a bright contrast to other common green plants. Try planting the *Pieris j.* 'variegata' with a darker *Arctostaphylos uva-ursi* 'Vancouver Jade' underneath it. The newest, and the most difficult to find, is *Pieris japonica* 'Flaming Silver', which is an outstanding combination of *Pieris j.* 'variegata' and *Pieris j.* 'Forest Flame'.

☐ PINUS   PINACEAE

P. densiflora 'Pendula' (weeping Japanese red pine) ❺

A slow growing, drooping, coniferous evergreen shrub.

Feature: The horizontal branches of this pine arch over the ground and cascade over walls.

Size: 91 cm (3 ft) tall (depending on where it is grafted) / 1.8 m (6 ft) spread.

Location: Full sun, in regular well-drained soil.

Comments: This shrub truly makes an exceptional focal point in the garden. It can be difficult to find at local nurseries, but well worth the search. It is superb when draping over a raised planter or spilling over large rocks, resembling a waterfall of greenery. Another variety, *Pinus densiflora* 'Umbraculifera' (Japanese table top or Tanyosho pine), is a bit easier to find at nurseries. The Tanyosho pine grows over 1.5 m (5 ft) tall and has multiple branches that form a flat, umbrella-like top. Both these pines have attractive red-brown bark in youth. Most pines grow very well in containers.

P. mugo pumilio (dwarf pumilio mugho pine) ❸

A slow growing, spreading, coniferous evergreen shrub.

Feature: An extremely hardy shrub with short, 2.5 cm (1 in) long, dark green needles.

Size: 91 cm (3 ft) tall / 1.5 m (5 ft) spread.

Location: Sun or partial shade, in well-drained average soil.

Comments: The dwarf pumilio mugho pine is ideal for small gardens and, when combined with a Japanese maple and a pagoda, it lends an oriental flavour. A more common variety, *Pinus mugo mughus* (mugho pine), grows over twice as large as the dwarf pumilio. A pine that grows in a slightly rounder fashion than the mugho pine, is the *Pinus thunbergii* 'Yatsubusa' ('Yatsubusa' Japanese black pine), which has stiff, thick needles, 8 cm (3 in) long.

P. nigra (Austrian black pine) ❹

A medium growing, pyramidal, coniferous evergreen tree.

Feature: This tall pine provides a majestic accent in the background of a garden.

Size: Over 6 m (20 ft) tall / 3 m (10 ft) spread.

Location: Full sun, in well-drained soil (pines do not like having wet feet!).

Comments: The *Pinus nigra* makes a handsome, dense specimen tree or windbreak. It is widely used as the background or focal point in an oriental garden. These pines grow well near the ocean and even tolerate salt spray.

☐ POLYSTICHUM   POLYPODIACEAE

P. munitum (western sword fern) ❹

A medium growing, vase-shaped, upright, broadleaf evergreen perennial.

Feature: This fern has glossy, leathery fronds.

Size: 60 cm to 1.2 m (2 ft to 4 ft) tall / 1.2 m (4 ft) spread.

Location: Part to full shade, in rich damp soil.

Comments: Numerous long, sword-like fronds rising from the centre of the crown give this plant a tropical appearance. It lends a natural look to a garden when used in the right combination with other plants. This easy-to-grow fern makes an ideal "filler" plant near water features or among other acid-loving shrubs.

P. setiferum (Alaska fern) ❻

A slow growing, spreading, broadleaf evergreen perennial.

Feature: A very fine textured fern.

Size: 30 cm to 45 cm (12 in to 18 in) tall / 45 cm (18 in) spread.

Location: Shade to part sun, in an acidic soil rich in organic matter.

Comments: This relatively dwarf species of fern grows well in containers. Its lacy, finely cut fronds combine nicely with tuberous begonias.

☐ PORTUGAL LAUREL - SEE PRUNUS

☐ POTENTILLA   ROSACEAE

P. fruticosa 'Yellow Gem' ('Yellow Gem' cinquefoil) ❷

A medium growing, mounding, broadleaf, deciduous shrub.

Feature: Large yellow blooms resembling buttercups appear in May and last through October.

Size: 30 cm (12 in) tall / 60 cm (2 ft) spread.

Location: Sun or partial sun, in well-drained soil.

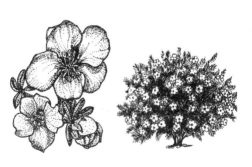

Comments: This outstanding cinquefoil is not widely known, but is becoming quite a noteworthy ground cover. It is also used in borders, in containers, and in larger groupings. This species was first introduced by the University of British Columbia Botanical Garden in Vancouver, British Columbia.

☐ PRIMULA   PRIMULACEAE

P. juliae 'Wanda' ('Wanda' primula) ❸

A rapidly growing, spreading, broadleaf perennial.

Feature: Magenta-purple flowers cover the bright green foliage, late in February through May.

Size: 15 cm (6 in) tall / 30 cm (12 in) spread.

Location: Part sun to shade, in rich, moist well-drained soil.

Comments: 'Wanda' primula is an old compact variety that remains popular among gardeners. These primulas are very good for naturalizing. Their eye-catching flowers are especially pleasing when daffodils are allowed to grow up through them. Use them in a woodland setting or in borders.

P. vulgaris or polyantha (primroses, English primrose or polyanthus primroses)

zones **4** to **9**

A medium growing, spreading, broadleaf perennial.

Feature: This outstanding, cool weather annual (or perennial) is available in a large variety of colours.

Size: 15 cm to 60 cm (6 in to 24 in) tall, depending on the variety / 20 cm to 30 cm spread.

Location: Sun to part sun, in rich, moist well-drained soil.

Comments: Primrose flowers are highly prized for their bright blooms, appearing in spring along with flowering bulbs, such as tulips and daffodils. They grow extremely well in cool, moist climates. The flowers of *Primula vulgaris* or *polyantha* have a glorious range of colours, in shades of pink, blue, mauve, red, yellow, orange and pure white (most with a yellow centre). They grow to only 15 cm to 20 cm (6 in to 8 in) tall. There are taller primroses, called *Primula x Bressingham Strain*, that have candelabra spikes of flowers, 60 cm to 70 cm (24 in to 28 in) high. These flowers, often prized as cut flowers, are orange, yellow, salmon and deep pink.

☐ PRUNUS   ROSACEAE

P. lusitanica (Portugal laurel) **7**

A fast growing, rounded, small, upright, broadleaf evergreen tree.

Feature: This tree has dark green leaves that resemble, when viewed from a distance, those of the indoor *Ficus benjamina* (Weeping Chinese Banyan).

Size: Over 2.4 m (8 ft) tall / 2.4 m (8 ft) spread.

Location: Sun or partial shade, in regular soil.

Comments: This hardy broadleaf evergreen makes an excellent hedge plant as well as a small tree. It is drought-tolerant and can withstand a windy location. Do not grow it in a container unless the container is large, and the plant is sure to be well fed. The Portugal laurel produces very small, fragrant, white flowers in late spring and dark red to purple cherry-like fruit in the summer.

P. serrulata 'Amanogawa' ('Amanogawa' flowering cherry) **5**

A medium growing, columnar, broadleaf, deciduous tree.

Feature: This tree has an extremely narrow growing habit. It produces soft, fragrant, semi-double, pink blossoms in late March to early April.

Size: 5.5 m (18 ft) tall / 1.5 m (5 ft) spread.

Location: Full sun, in regular well-drained soil.

Comments: This is one of few available tree species that are exceedingly narrow in growth habit. It is especially suitable as a screen for a very narrow or small garden area. Other types of ornamental flowering cherries, with unusual growing habits, include: *Prunus s.* 'Kwanzan', with its Y-shape, is widely used as a boulevard tree or as a specimen, and has pendulous, double pink blossoms in April; and *Prunus s.* 'Mount Fuji' ('Shirotae'), which has a more horizontal growing habit, and fragrant, semi-double, white blooms in April to May.

P. subhirtella 'Autumnalis' (autumn flowering cherry) **5**

A medium growing, rounded, broadleaf, deciduous tree.

Feature: Semi-double to double, white or pink blossoms appear in autumn (sometimes in winter) and in early spring.

Size: over 5 m (16 ft) tall / over 4.5 m (15 ft) spread.

Location: Sun to part shade, in average well-drained soil.

Comments: The autumn flowering cherry is one of few winter-blooming trees. Another highly sought after ornamental flowering cherry is the *Prunus subhirtella* 'Pendula', which has a pronounced weeping or drooping form, with single, light pink flowers appearing in early spring.

☐ PYRACANTHA   ROSACEAE

P. coccinea (firethorn) ❼

A fast growing, upright, broadleaf evergreen shrub.

Feature: Tiny white, clustered flowers appear in March or April, followed by berries that turn bright, orange-red in autumn.

Size: Over 1.8 m (6 ft) tall, unless pruned / 1.8 m (6 ft) spread.

Location: Best in full sun, in well-drained soil.

Comments: *Pyracantha* is best known for its use as an espalier on fences or walls. Different trained shapes, such as pillar, fan or diamond, of this plant are available at local nurseries. Two favoured varieties are, 'Mohave' (orange-red berries) and 'Orange Glow' (orange berries). All species of *Pyracantha* are drought-tolerant and their colourful berries attract birds.

☐ REDTWIG DOGWOOD - SEE CORNUS

☐ RHODODENDRON   ERICACEAE

As there are hundreds of Rhododendron varieties, too many to list, we have chosen to describe only the most popular dwarf, medium and tall growing varieties, proven to perform well in acidic soils. The *Rhododendrons* featured below are characterized by their attractive, compact growth habits and their showy blooms. They can be relied upon to retain a pleasing appearance in all seasons and can be generally described as follows:

Various zones (see the descriptions that follow, for zones of individual varieties)

Slow growing, rounded, broadleaf evergreen shrubs.

Feature: Rhododendrons produce eye-catching blooms in spring.

Size: Dwarf hybrids remain under 91 cm (3 ft) tall / 91 cm (3 ft) spread. Medium and tall hybrids range from 1.2 m (4 ft) to 1.8 m (6 ft) tall / 1.2 m (4 ft) to 1.8 m (6 ft) spread.

Location: Sun to partial sun, in well-drained acidic soil rich in humus.

Comments: To successfully grow plants in the ericacea family (eg. rhododendrons, heathers, *Pieris*, and evergreen hybrid azaleas), it is crucial to plant them at the correct depth and keep them well watered, especially during the first year.

Dwarf Hybrids

Recommended varieties include:

'Elizabeth Hobbie' - 60 cm (2 ft) tall and 91 cm (3 ft) wide, with bright, blood-red blooms in early spring. It is hardy to zone 5.

impeditum - 60 cm (2 ft) tall and 91 cm (3 ft) wide, with blue-mauve blooms in early spring. It is hardy to zone 4.

'Shamrock' - 40 cm (16 in) tall and 60 cm (2 ft) wide, with greenish-yellow blooms in early spring (usually near St. Patrick's Day) and very neat, clean-looking leaves throughout the year. It is hardy to zone 6.

Medium and Tall Hybrids

Recommended varieties include:

'Anah Kruschke' - 1.5 m (5 ft) tall and 1.8 m (6 ft) wide, with lavender blooms in late spring. It is a compact plant that tolerates sun, and has outstanding dark green leaves. It is hardy to zone 5.

'Anna Rose Whitney' - 1.8 m (6 ft) tall and wide, with large trusses of rose-pink blooms in late spring. It is hardy to zone 6.

'Elizabeth' - 1.2 m (4 ft) tall and 1.5 m (5 ft) wide, with rosy-red blooms in early spring and often in the fall, as well. It is hardy to zone 6.

'PJM' - 1.2 m (4 ft) tall and 60 cm (2 ft) wide, with lavender-pink blooms in early spring. It is a very narrow shrub that displays strong autumn colour and tolerates heat, cold, and sun. It is hardy to zone 4.

'Rosamundi' - 91 cm (3 ft) tall and 1.2 m (4 ft) wide, with clear pink blooms in very early spring. It is hardy to zone 7.

'Unique' - 1.2 m (4 ft) tall and wide. Its flowers appear in early spring, emerging as pink and fading to a creamy white. This plant is hardy to zone 6.

'Vulcan's Flame' - 1.2 m (4 ft) tall and 1.5 m (5 ft) wide, with bright red blooms in mid-spring. Fairly sun and heat tolerant. It is hardy to zone 5.

Evergreen Hybrid Azaleas (commonly known as Japanese Evergreen azaleas) ❻

A slow growing, rounded, broadleaf evergreen shrub.

Feature: A profusion of blooms blankets the leaves during April and May, for approximately three weeks.

Size: 30 cm to 1.2 m (12 in to 4 ft) tall / 30 cm to 1.2 m (12 in to 4 ft) spread, depending on the variety.

Location: Sun (if the roots can be kept moist) or semi-shade, in moist, well-drained, acidic soil.

Comments: Some popular varieties include, 'Buccaneer' (orange-red), 'Coral Bells' (soft pink), 'Everest' (white), 'Gumpo Pink' (rose-pink, and very dwarf), 'Hino-crimson' (bright pink or red, and is the most popular variety), 'Sherwood Orchid' (reddish-violet), and 'Vuyks Rosy Red' (which grows slightly taller than those previously mentioned). Evergreen azaleas are invaluable low growing landscape shrubs. They remain compact in growth, and are exceptional when paired with ferns and, especially, with *Euonymus fortunei* 'Emerald Gaiety'.

☐ RHUS   ANACARDIACEAE

R. typhina (sumac or stag's horn sumac) ❸

A medium growing, upright, broadleaf, deciduous tree.

Feature: Spectacular autumn colours of yellow-orange, scarlet and red, characterize this tree. It also produces tiny blooms, followed by grape-like clusters of fuzzy, reddish fruit that lasts through the winter.

Size: 4 m (13 ft) tall / 5 m (15 ft) spread.

Location: Sun or part shade, and tolerates poor well-drained soil, but not wet soil.

Comments: Sumacs are drought-tolerant and are often used for erosion control because of their underground suckers. Keep the suckers trimmed and under control or they will grow into new trees. Both the shape of the tree and its attractive 12.5 cm (5 in) long leaflets are splendid attributes, lending tropical ambience to a garden. The branches are covered with velvety, short, brown hairs.

Annuals provide continuous summer colour

LEFT: Fuchsia and lobelia in the shade

MIDDLE: Collection of annuals in a large moss basket

BOTTOM: Swan river daisy

Using white in the garden will enhance your other colours.

RIGHT: *White alyssum, red fibrous begonia, yucca*

ABOVE: *White candytuft, pink daphne, golden cedars*

RIGHT: *White candytuft, orange deciduous azalea, pink rock daphne and basket of gold alyssum*

olour for the shade

PER LEFT: Hosta, bergenia and primrose

PER RIGHT: Coleus and white polka-dot plant

OVE: Aucuba, lobelia, ferns, astilbe

GHT: 'Emerald Gaiety' euonymus, tuberous begonia, 'Wanda' primula

Fall and winter can also be colourful

LEFT: 'Autumn Joy' sedum, Hosta

MIDDLE: Harry Lauder's walking stick

BOTTOM: Dwarf nandina, yellow cedar, winter heather, ornamental grass

☐ RICCARTONI - SEE FUCHSIA

☐ ROBINIA   LEGUMINOSAE

R. pseudoacacia 'Frisia' (black locust or honeylocust) ❹

A rapidly growing, upright, broadleaf, deciduous tree.

Feature: Fragrant, white blossoms in spring, followed by dark, bean-like pods in the fall. The leaves are bright yellow from spring to autumn.

Size: Over 7.5 m (25 ft) tall / 4 m (13 ft) spread.

Location: Full sun, in average well-drained soil.

Comments: The *Robinia*, a rugged tree with thorny branches, tolerates heat and drought. Pruning and properly training it when it is young ensures that it will be, at maturity, an outstanding focal point in a large garden.

☐ ROSA   ROSACEAE

R. meidilandTM (meidilandTM rose)

zones ❹ to ❼

A medium growing, spreading, broadleaf, deciduous shrub.

Feature: This is a new variety of rose and it blooms from late spring until frost, in shades of peach, red, white and pink.

Size: .5 m to 1.5 m (1½ ft to 5 ft) tall / 1 m to 1.5 m (3 ft to 5 ft) spread.

Location: Full sun, in well-drained regular soil.

Comments: These roses are a new variety from France and are often used as a ground cover or low hedge. They are more pest and disease resistant than other roses and, consequently, need little or no spraying with chemicals. Two of the lower growing, mounding types used for ground covers, include: *Rosa* x 'Meiflopan' *Alba meidiland*TM (alba meidilandTM rose), with single, white blooms; and *Rosa* x 'Meineble' *red meidiland*TM (red meidilandTM rose), with single, red flowers. A good, double-flowering, pink rose is the *Rosa* x 'Meidomonac' *meidiland Bonica*TM (BonicaTM rose), which is often used in creating a low barrier.

☐ ROSE-OF-SHARON - SEE HIBISCUS

☐ SAGINA   CARYOPHYLLACEAE

S. subulata (Irish moss) ❹

A medium growing, spreading perennial.

Feature: Tiny, white, flowers appear in spring on a carpet of rich, emerald green foliage.

Size: 5 cm (2 in) tall / 30 cm (12 in) spread.

Location: Sun to part sun, in moist well-drained soil.

Comments: This moss-like plant is well suited to filling cracks between stones and for growing over rocks. It is often used in oriental gardens, beneath maple trees. A substitute is *Sagina subulata* 'Aurea' (Scotch moss), with a golden or lime green colour.

☐ SALAL - SEE GAULTHERIA

☐ SALVIA   LABIATAE

S. farinacea (Victoria blue salvia)

A rapidly growing, upright, broadleaf annual.

Feature: Violet-blue flower spikes stand high above grey-green leaves, 7.5 cm (3 in) long.

Size: 60 cm (2 ft) tall / 25 cm (10 in) spread.

Location: Full sun, in rich well-drained soil.

Comments: Try combining this interesting bedding plant with fibrous begonias or white petunias. Since the flower spikes of the Victoria blue salvia stand well above most other annuals, ensure that they do not crowd out or cover other plants. The more common variety of *Salvia* has bright scarlet flower spikes that are striking when combined with orange or yellow marigolds.

☐ SARCOCOCCA   BUXACEAE

S. hookeriana humilis (Himalayan sweet box) ❼

A slow growing, spreading, broadleaf evergreen shrub.

Feature: Extremely fragrant with white feathery flowers appearing in late winter, followed by bluish-black berries.

Size: 45 cm (18 in) tall / 45 cm (18 in) spread.

Location: Grows well in shade and part sun, in peat-rich soil.

Comments: This dense, compact, dwarf evergreen shrub is ideal for shady areas, or near an entryway. It is also suitable for planting underneath low-branching evergreen trees. It has glossy, deep green, narrow, pointed leaves, 5 cm (2 in) long. If planted in a protected area, the Himalayan sweet box will make an attractive low hedge. It spreads by underground suckers.

S. ruscifolia (fragrant sarcococca) ❼

A slow growing, rounded, broadleaf evergreen shrub.

Feature: Very fragrant white blooms appear in late winter, followed by dark red berries.

Size: 1.2 m (4 ft) tall / 1.2 m (4 ft) spread.

Location: Shade or part sun, in rich well-drained soil.

Comments: The fragrant sarcococca has a strong sweet scent and is one of few broadleaf evergreen plants that grow well in the shade. This shrub may be espaliered against a wall, or planted by itself, near a shady entrance or an outdoor sitting area. *Sarcococca confusa* is similar, except that its berries are black instead of red.

☐ SCIADOPITYS   TAXODIACEAE OR PINACEAE

S. verticillata (Japanese umbrella pine) ❼

A slow growing, pyramidal, small, coniferous evergreen tree.

Feature: This tree has unusual needles that are thick and 10 cm (4 in) long.

Size: Over 2 m (6½ ft) tall / 1.5 m (5 ft) spread.

Location: Part shade, in a protected area, in rich moist soil.

Comments: This tree is native to Japan and is easily incorporated into an oriental garden setting. It can also be used as a focal point in the garden. The needles are arranged in similar fashion to the spokes of an umbrella. Its bark and cones are also attractive. It can usually be found at nurseries in March or April.

☐ SEA THRIFT - SEE ARMERIA

☐ SEDUM   CRASSULACEAE

S. spurium 'Dragon's Blood' ('Dragon's Blood' sedum) ❹

A medium growing, spreading perennial.

Feature: Rose-red flowers bloom from mid-summer into autumn, rising above bronze-red fleshy leaves.

Size: 5 cm (2 in) tall / 30 cm (12 in) spread.

Location: Sun or part sun, in well-drained regular soil.

Comments: Its ability to creep over rocks and walls make this plant an asset in a rock garden. *Sedum spurium* 'Tricolour' is also used for this purpose in rock gardens, but its succulent leaves are a mixture of pink, yellow and green.

S. telephium 'Autumn Joy' ('Autumn Joy' sedum) ❸

A medium growing, upright, broadleaf perennial.

Feature: Pink to rose coloured flowers bloom in late summer until frost.

Size: 30 cm (12 in) tall / 45 cm (18 in) spread.

Location: Sun to part sun, in well-drained sandy soil.

Comments: Its succulent, light green leaves contrast well with its pink flower clusters. Its attractive autumn colour makes this an ideal plant for a border.

☐ SENECIO   COMPOSITAE

S. cineraria (dusty miller)

A rapidly growing, upright annual.

Feature: This plant has fuzzy, grey, blunt-tipped, lobed leaves year-round, and produces golden yellow, 1 cm (⅓ in) wide, flowers sporadically throughout the summer and autumn.

Size: 45 cm (18 in) tall / 30 cm (12 in) spread.

Location: Full sun, in well-drained average soil.

Comments: Most grey-leaved plants are drought-tolerant and require little watering. Dusty miller is no exception. To maintain its fresh grey-white appearance and prevent it from becoming woody, shear it lightly in the early spring and again in mid-summer. As with *Coleus*, pinch off the flowers to encourage bushier growth. Dusty miller is often combined with red annual salvia, in masses for a showy and low maintenance summer display. *Senecio cineraria* (dusty miller) generally becomes woody and less attractive after the second year, and should be replaced. Because of this, treat it as an annual.

☐ SEQUOIADENDRON   TAXODIACEAE

S. giganteum 'Pendulum' (weeping sequoia) ❻

A medium growing, columnar, coniferous evergreen tree.

Feature: This tree has a unique narrow, arching shape.

Size: Over 4.5 m (15 ft) tall / 91 cm (3 ft) spread.

Location: Sun or part shade, in well-drained acidic soil.

Comments: The weeping sequoia has a very distinctive arching form and is often used near the corner of a building to soften the look of the structure. It can also be planted by itself as a spectacular centre piece in a small garden. Stake the plant to encourage it to grow more vertically.

☐ SERBIAN SPRUCE - SEE PICEA

☐ SILK TREE - SEE ALBIZIA

☐ SKIMMIA   RUTACEAE

S. japonica (Japanese skimmia) ❼

A slow growing, rounded, broadleaf evergreen shrub.

Feature: Bright red clusters of berries last from autumn through winter. The shrub produces slightly fragrant blossoms in April or May.

Size: 1.2 m (4 ft) tall / 1.2 m (4 ft) spread.
Location: Part shade to shade, in acidic soil.
Comments: A male *Skimmia* should be located nearby if the female is to produce berries. It grows well as a seaside shrub. Its leaves are dark in colour and narrow, approximately 8 cm (3 in) long. The white flower clusters of male skimmias, are oval and 8 cm (3 in) long, while those of the female plants are smaller and tighter in form.

☐ SNOWBELL OR SNOWDROP TREE - SEE STYRAX

☐ SNOWDROP - SEE GALANTHUS

☐ SPRING BOUQUET VIBURNUM - SEE VIBURNUM

☐ SPRUCE - SEE PICEA

☐ ST. JOHN'S WORT - SEE HYPERICUM

☐ STAG'S HORN SUMAC - SEE RHUS

☐ STIPA　　GRAMINEAE
　　S. tenuissima (feather grass) ❻
　　A medium growing, upright, broadleaf evergreen, ornamental grass.
　　Feature: Wispy seed heads appear in July through January.
　　Size: 45 cm to 60 cm (18 in to 24 in) tall / 45 cm (18 in) spread.
　　Location: Best in full sun, in average well-drained soil.
　　Comments: Needle-fine leaves and seed heads resembling coarse hair, combine to make this a very finely textured ornamental grass. The gracefully arching, clump-forming grass is used for dried arrangements.

☐ STYRAX　　STYRACACEAE
　　S. japonica (Japanese snowbell or snowdrop tree) ❺
　　A slow growing, rounded, broadleaf, deciduous tree.
　　Feature: This tree features scented, pendulous, white flowers in May or June.
　　Size: 4.5 m (15 ft) tall / 3 m (10 ft) spread.
　　Location: Sun or partial sun, in moist, fairly good, well-drained soil.
　　Comments: This unusual small tree is disease and pest free. It is an exotic tree and is best viewed when looking up into the branches when it is in bloom. Consequently, it is best to plant it in a raised container or situate it part of the way up a slope. It is available at most nurseries in March or April. The *Styrax* is native to Japan and Korea.

☐ SUMAC - SEE RHUS

☐ SWAN RIVER DAISY - SEE BRACHYCOME

☐ SWEETGUM - SEE LIQUIDAMBAR

☐ SWORD FERN - SEE POLYSTICHUM

☐ SYRINGA   OLEACEAE

S. *patula* 'Miss Kim' ('Miss Kim' lilac or dwarf Korean lilac) ❹

A slow growing, rounded, broadleaf, deciduous shrub.

Feature: This shrub produces fragrant lavender-blue to deep lilac flowers in May or early June.

Size: 1.2 m (4 ft) tall / 1.2 m (4 ft) spread.

Location: Sun or part sun, in well-drained, slightly alkaline soil.

Comments: Due to the wet climate of the Pacific coastal region, most common lilacs have severe problems with bacterial blight and leaf spot, causing them to drop their leaves. However, the 'Miss Kim' variety is not subject to such problems and is easily maintained as well. Another problem-free plant is *Syringa meyeri palibin*, also a dense and compact lilac, but with darker, violet-purple flowers. It grows taller than the 'Miss Kim' variety.

☐ TAGETES   ASTERACEAE OR COMPOSITAE

T. *patula* (marigolds)

A medium growing, rounded annual.

Feature: The flowers are dazzlingly bright yellow, golden-yellow, or orange, or a bicolour mixture of maroon and orange. They bloom from late May until frost.

Size: 20 cm to 30 cm (8 in to 12 in) tall / 20 cm to 25 cm (8 in to 10 in) spread.

Location: Full sun, in average, well-drained sandy soil.

Comments: The dwarf French marigolds are most popular. Some common varieties to look for, include: 'Queen Sophia', which is a broad-petalled type, 25 cm to 30 cm (10 in to 12 in) tall, with flowers that have a red throat bleeding into an orange margin; and the 'Orange Boy' and 'Yellow Boy', crested types, measuring 20 cm to 25 cm (8 in to 10 in) tall, with orange or yellow petals. All are used in borders or for creating large floral patterns or designs in beds.

☐ TAXUS   TAXACEAE

T. *baccata* 'Melford' ('Melford' yew) ❻

A medium growing, columnar, coniferous evergreen shrub.

Feature: This shrub forms an extremely narrow hedge and responds well to pruning. In autumn, it produces large red berries that contrast well with its dark green, 1.25 cm (½ in) long needles.

Size: 1.5 m (5 ft) tall / 30 cm (12 in) spread.

Location: Sun or part shade, in regular well-drained soil.

Comments: 'Melford' yew is ideal for use in narrow spaces where a plant of only medium height is required. An excellent, although scarce yew, is the *Taxus baccata* 'Fastigiata Aurea', which is a golden colour most of the year and is especially bright in the spring. There are more common, larger growing varieties, but the two mentioned here are the most notable. Ask for them at your local nursery in March or April.

T. x *media* 'Hicksii' (Hick's yew) ❺

A medium growing, upright, coniferous evergreen shrub.

Feature: A narrow, dark green shrub.

Size: Over 1.8 m (6 ft) tall / 91 cm (3 ft) spread.

Location: Sun or shade, in well-drained average soil.

Comments: The shape of this variety is wider in the middle than at the base, and is more often used as a hedge than are the dwarf varieties mentioned above. Its fleshy berries and foliage are considered poisonous when consumed.

☐ THUJA   CUPRESSACEAE

T. occidentalis 'Smaragd' (Danish, emerald or 'Smaragd' cedar) ❸

A slow growing, pyramidal, coniferous evergreen shrub.

Feature: A hedging shrub with a narrow growing habit, and rich emerald foliage.

Size: Over 2 m (6½ ft) tall / 60 cm (2 ft) spread, depending on the size of the plant at purchase and how quickly the hedge needs to be filled in.

Location: Sun or part sun, in well-drained soil.

Comments: This hedging cedar is more ornamental and narrower than most, and requires little or no pruning. Another popular variety, *Thuja o.* 'Fastigiata' (pyramid cedar), is a duller green and produces many small round cones, especially when under stress (possibly due to excessive or insufficient watering, or from being planted too deeply). The pyramid, or pyramidalis, cedar grows approximately 30 cm (12 in) per year, slightly faster than the emerald cedar. Light trimming can be performed any time of the year.

T. plicata 'Excelsa' ('Excelsa' cedar) ❺

A fast growing, pyramidal, coniferous evergreen tree.

Feature: These trees can be easily trimmed to form a tall, dense hedge.

Size: Over 3 m (10 ft) tall / 91 cm (3 ft) spread, if kept trimmed.

Location: Sun or part shade, in well-drained acidic soil.

Comments: Once established, the 'Excelsa' cedars grow 60 cm to 91 cm (2 ft to 3 ft) per year. For use as background trees, they can be spaced over 3 m (10 ft) apart. Hard pruning is usually done in March, before the new growth appears. However, mid-summer is also an acceptable time of the year to do this. Light trimming can be attempted any time of year. All cedars benefit from an application of hedging fertilizer high in nitrogen, in spring and early summer. The best quality cedars can be purchased in the spring and in late fall (after the autumn rains begin and after the plants have become dormant).

☐ THYMUS   LABIATAE

T. serpyllum 'Coccineus' (red mother of thyme) ❺

A rapidly growing, creeping perennial.

Feature: Fragrant, small, rose-red flowers cover the plant in June through July. Its extremely tiny leaves are aromatic.

Size: 7.5 cm (3 in) tall / 30 cm (12 in) spread.

Location: Full sun, in well-drained regular soil.

Comments: This thyme is a carpet-forming plant with fragrant leaves, like woolly thyme (*Thymus pseudolanuginosus*). It is often used as a ground cover or to fill crevices. It is a wonderful addition to an oriental landscape and presents the appearance of grass or turf, without the maintenance.

☐ TILIA   TILIACEAE

T. cordata (little leaf linden) ❹

A medium growing, pyramidal, broadleaf, deciduous tree.

Feature: Fragrant, creamy white flowers bloom on this tree in mid-summer.

Size: Over 10 m (26 ft) tall / 4.5 m (15 ft) spread.

Location: Full sun, in moist regular soil.

Comments: The *Tilia* is wonderfully suited for use as a street or garden tree, with its 5 cm (2 in) long, heart-shaped leaves, green above and silvery underneath.

☐ TRACHYCARPUS   PALMAE

T. fortunei (windmill palm) **8**b

A slow growing, upright, broadleaf evergreen tree.

Feature: Fan-shaped leaves, measuring over 45 cm (18 in) across, and a trunk covered with thick, hairy fibre are the noteworthy features of this tree.

Size: Over 2 m (6½ ft) tall / 1.8 m (6 ft) spread.

Location: Sun or partial sun, in a protected area, in rich well-drained soil.

Comments: The windmill palm is a hardy palm, ideal for coastal gardens. It grows very well near heated pools and hot tubs and prefers a southern exposure. In windy areas, the older foliage becomes bent and droops at the tips. An addition of mushroom manure benefits this plant. It is recommended to wrap the plant for protection during a severe winter.

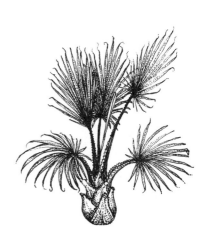

☐ TSUGA   PINACEAE

T. canadensis 'Pendula' (Sargent's weeping hemlock) **4**

A slow growing, spreading, coniferous evergreen shrub.

Feature: This shrub features long, overlapping, drooping branches with needle-like leaves.

Size: Over 1.5 m (5 ft) tall, especially if it is staked / 1.5 m (5 ft) spread.

Location: Sun or part shade, in moist alkaline or acidic soil.

Comments: A spectacular specimen for cascading over rocks and walls. A valued dwarf hemlock is *Tsuga c.* 'Jeddeloh', which grows only 30 cm (12 in) tall and 60 cm (2 ft) wide. The 'Jeddeloh' is highly sought after for rockeries, and is usually available in March and April at retail nurseries.

T. mertensiana (mountain hemlock) **6**

A slow growing, upright, coniferous evergreen tree.

Feature: Short, blue-grey needles and an interesting irregular growth habit characterize this tree.

Size: Over 1.8 m (6 ft) / 1.2 m (4 ft) spread.

Location: Sun or partial shade, in regular soil.

Comments: The mountain hemlock makes a good bonsai subject and grows well in containers. Place this small tree among dwarf broadleaf evergreen shrubs for an exceptional effect.

☐ TULIP - SEE TULIPA

☐ TULIPA   LILIACEAE

T. hybrids (tulips)

all zones

A slow growing, upright bulb.

Feature: Lovely, stately flowers that bloom in early spring to late spring, in a wide range of colours.

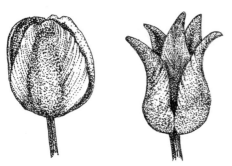

Size: 15 cm to 60 cm (6 in to 24 in) tall / 15 cm (6 in) spread.

Location: Full sun, in well-drained, almost sandy soil.

Comments: Most bulbs (discussed in *Chapter 5*) should be planted in groups of five to twelve bulbs per square foot, rather than in a straight line. Tulips are particularly effective when combined with low growing, early blooming perennials, such as forget-me-nots, pansies (*Viola*) or *Primula*. In windy locations, plant shorter tulips, such as 'Red Riding Hood' (in a container, perhaps). The wind could cause the stems of taller varieties to bend and lean, or even to break.

☐ **UMBRELLA PINE** - see Sciadopitys

☐ **VACCINIUM**   Ericaceae

V. corymbosum (blueberry) ❺

A medium growing, upright, broadleaf, deciduous shrub.

Feature: Clusters of pink to white, urn-shaped flowers bloom in spring, followed by edible, sweet, blue berries that ripen by August. The fall foliage is brilliant scarlet.

Size: 1.5 m to 1.8 m (5 ft to 6 ft) tall / 1.2 m (4 ft) spread.

Location: Full sun, in moist well-drained soil (it is recommended to add hemlock sawdust and peat to the soil).

Comments: The pointy-leaved foliage is rusty-bronze to start, changes to medium green, and finally, turns vivid scarlet in the fall. Plant at least two cultivars of blueberries for better pollination. If you and your family enjoy eating the berries, plant at least one bush per family member. This will ensure that you have enough berries come harvest time. There are 'early', 'mid-season' and 'late' varieties that ripen in mid-June through late August. Some noteworthy cultivars include: 'Bluecrop', with large berries ripening in mid-season; 'Concord', with large tart berries ripening in mid-season; and 'Dixi', with a more open growth habit and tasty, large berries ripening later in the season.

V. vitis-idaea minus (lingonberry or mountain cranberry) ❻

A slow growing, spreading or upright, broadleaf evergreen shrub.

Feature: Urn-shaped, pink-white flowers bloom from late spring into the summer, followed by edible, bright red berries (used for syrups and preserves).

Size: 30 cm (12 in) tall / 45 cm (18 in) spread.

Location: Sun or partial shade, in moist regular soil.

Comments: Lingonberry spreads by underground runners and is therefore an ideal ground cover for slopes, to control erosion. This is also an excellent broadleaf evergreen for use as a small-scale ground cover or as a border plant, in slightly wetter areas.

☐ **VIBURNUM**   Tcaprifoliaceae

V. davidii (David's viburnum) ❼

A slow growing, spreading, broadleaf evergreen shrub.

Feature: Clusters of white blooms appear in June, followed by cobalt blue berries in autumn, lasting through winter.

Size: 60 cm (2 ft) tall / 1.5 m (5 ft) spread.

Location: Sun or partial sun, in soil rich in humus (it will grow in the same type of soil as that of *Rhododendrons*).

Comments: Not only does this broadleaf evergreen feature flowers and berries, it also has bold, attractive leaves. The 10 cm (4 in) long, leathery, rich dark green leaves are conspicuously veined. This shrub is often used as a filler plant between evergreens, such as the golden thread cypress (*Chamaecyparis pisifera* 'Filifera Aurea Nana').

V. plicatum 'Summer Snowflake' ('Summer Snowflake' viburnum) ❺

A medium growing, rounded or upright, broadleaf, deciduous shrub.

Feature: White flowers from May until frost, with lovely red to purple leaf colour in the fall, characterize this shrub.

Size: Over 1.8 m (6 ft) tall / 1.5 m (5 ft) spread.

Location: Sun to partial shade, in well-drained average soil.

Comments: The flowers measure 6 cm (2¼ in) across, a combination of large, sterile blooms surrounded by a tight cluster of smaller flowers. This is an outstanding, long-blooming shrub for the garden. It is an introduction from the University of British Columbia Botanical Garden in Vancouver, British Columbia.

V. tinus 'Spring Bouquet' (laurustinus 'Spring Bouquet') ❼

A medium growing, rounded, broadleaf evergreen shrub.

Feature: Clusters of white flowers bloom from winter to early spring, followed by metallic blue berries, lasting into summer.

Size: 1.2 m (4 ft) tall / 1.2 m (4 ft) spread.

Location: Sun or part shade, in rich well-drained soil.

Comments: This plant is one of a few broadleaf evergreens that bloom in the winter. Try using it as a background plant behind evergreen Japanese azaleas or blue star junipers.

☐ VINCA   APOCYNACEAE

V. minor (periwinkle) ❸

A rapidly growing, spreading, broadleaf evergreen perennial.

Feature: Lavender-blue flowers, 2.5 cm (1 in) across, bloom from May through June, and again sporadically until autumn.

Size: 15 cm (6 in) tall / 45 cm (18 in) spread.

Location: Part sun to full shade, in good, moist, well-drained soil.

Comments: This is a fast growing ground cover, especially suited for covering shady areas on slopes. Other forms are available in maroon, white, blue, and one with variegated foliage.

☐ VINE MAPLE - SEE ACER

☐ VIOLA   VIOLACEAE

V. hortensis (pansy)

A medium growing, spreading, broadleaf annual.

Feature: Depending on the cultivar, these flowers usually measure 5 cm (2 in) across and are classified as either "summer" or "winter" pansies.

Size: 20 cm (8 in) tall / 20 cm (8 in) spread.

Location: Sun or part sun, in cool, moist, rich soil.

Comments: Most gardeners are familiar with regular pansies (*Viola hortensis*), with their large flowers and foliage. "Summer pansies" are characterized by large blooms in shades of yellow, orange, blue, lavender, white, and red, measuring 5 cm to 10 cm (2 in to 4 in) across. Many have blotches or "faces" in the centre of each flower. They are available in early spring and are more heat-tolerant than other varieties. These bloom from mid-spring into the summer, becoming somewhat leggy after that. When they reach this state, replace them with other, more showy annuals. "Winter pansies", available from late September onwards, bloom sporadically throughout the winter and peak in the spring. The "winter pansies" are extremely cold-tolerant, and thrive much better in the ground than in a container. Occasionally, remove the spent flowers to encourage more flower production. They will eventually, however, bloom themselves out and become long and leggy in the heat of summer. When this occurs, remove the entire plant to tidy the area and prevent disease.

V. tricolor (Johnny-jump-up or European wild pansy)
A slow growing, tufted, broadleaf annual.
Feature: This annual produces small flowers, 1.25 cm (½ in) across, in spring in a variety of colours.
Size: 15 cm (6 in) tall / 15 cm (6 in) spread.
Location: Sun or part sun, in rich, cool, moist, well-drained soil.
Comments: Johnny-jump-ups are like miniature pansies, with flowers in solid or mixed colours of yellow, purple and white.

☐ VIRGINIA CREEPER - SEE PARTHENOCISSUS

☐ WEEPING MULBERRY - SEE MORUS

☐ WEIGELA   CAPRIFOLIACEAE
W. 'Bristol Ruby' (weigela 'Bristol Ruby') ❺
A medium growing, upright, broadleaf, deciduous shrub.
Feature: Brilliant ruby-red, tubular flowers bloom in late spring into the summer.
Size: 1.5 m (5 ft) tall / 1.5 m (5 ft) spread.
Location: Sun or part shade, in regular soil.
Comments: This plant is not particularly good-looking when the flowers have finished blooming. Nevertheless, it is often effectively used as a background or summer screen. A more outstanding variety is *Weigela florida* 'Variegata', with attractive cream and green leaves and pink flowers.

☐ WESTERN RED CEDAR - SEE THUJA

☐ WESTERN SWORD FERN - SEE POLYSTICHUM

☐ WILD LILAC - SEE CEANOTHUS

☐ WINDFLOWER ANEMONE - SEE ANEMONE

☐ WINDMILL PALM - SEE TRACHYCARPUS

☐ WINTERGREEN - SEE GAULTHERIA

☐ WISTERIA   LEGUMINOSAE
W. floribunda (Japanese wisteria) ❺
A fast growing, broadleaf, deciduous, twining vine.
Feature: Fragrant trusses of flowers, 45 cm (18 in) long, hang like clusters

of grapes in late spring. The wisteria leaf has fifteen to nineteen leaflets.

Size: Over 7 m (23 ft) spread.

Location: Best in full sun, in moist, well-drained average soil.

Comments: It may be of interest to know that the stems of the Japanese wisteria twine in a clockwise direction whereas the Chinese wisteria (mentioned below) twines in an anti-clockwise direction. The flowers of the Japanese wisteria are lilac-blue, but there is also a pink variety. If you wish to avoid having to wait years for the wisteria to bloom, purchase a grafted variety. Wisteria plants are usually available in the spring at most garden centres.

W. sinensis (Chinese wisteria) ❺

A fast growing, broadleaf, deciduous, twining vine.

Feature: Clusters of fragrant, violet-blue flowers, 30 cm (12 in) long, appear before the leaves open in late spring. The leaves have seven to thirteen leaflets.

Size: Over 8 m (26 ft) spread.

Location: Full sun, in moist, well-drained regular soil.

Comments: It is important to prevent the branches and new shoots of the wisteria from growing into the eaves and under the shingles of the house. It must not be allowed to infiltrate cracks. Proper pruning is also vital to keep the plant contained in size. It can be shaped by rubbing off the buds or pruning off the side shoots in early spring.

☐ **WITCH HAZEL** - SEE HAMAMELIS

☐ **WOOLLY YARROW** - SEE ACHILLEA

☐ **WORMWOOD** - SEE ARTEMISIA

☐ **YEW** - SEE TAXUS

☐ **YUCCA**   AGAVACEAE

Y. recurvifolia or Yucca pendula (weeping yucca) ❼

A medium growing, upright, broadleaf evergreen shrub.

Feature: This tropical-looking shrub has narrow, sword-like foliage, and produces a spike of clustered white flowers in early summer.

Size: 1.5 m (5 ft) tall / 1.5 m (5 ft) spread.

Location: Sun or part shade, in well-drained soil.

Comments: The *Yucca* tolerates pollution and is often used in boulevard plantings, and in areas that receive little water. Another use for this unusual shrub is around pools, or just to add a bold texture to the garden. The pointed leaf tips are sharp and you may wish to clip them off to avoid injury (especially if the plant is located near a walkway or close to a child's play area).

Glossary of Gardening Terms

Acidic soil

This refers to the pH level of the soil. Soil with a pH level registering below 7.0 is called acidic, the opposite of alkaline. Plants such as *Rhododendron* grow best in a slightly acidic soil with a pH level of approximately 4.5 to 5.5. In order to raise the pH level of soil (making it more alkaline), lime can be added.

Aeration

To loosen up the soil to enable air to mix into the soil, allowing for better drainage.

Alkaline soil

If soil is alkaline, then its pH level is above 7.0. Most plants grow well at a pH level registering between 6.5 and 7.5, although many field crops will do well between pH 5.5 and pH 8.0. In order to lower the pH level of soil (making it more acidic), sulphur and aluminum or iron sulphate can be added.

Annual

A plant that completes its life cycle in a single growing season, growing from a seed into an adult plant and then producing seed once again.

Balled and Burlapped (B&B)

A tree or shrub with its root ball wrapped and tied in burlap is called Balled and Burlapped (B&B). The plant is first grown in the ground, rather than in a pot, and when it is removed from the soil it is wrapped in this fashion before being sold.

Bare root

Some plants, especially roses, can be purchased bare root. This means that a dormant plant is packaged, with its roots bare of soil, in a bag or carton.

Bedding plant

A plant used for single seasonal display in the garden. It can be an annual, a biennial or a tender perennial.

Berry

A type of fruit produced by a plant. Unlike a seed pod, berries do not open in order to disperse their seed cargo.

Biennial

A plant that completes its life cycle within a two year period. Usually, foliage is grown in the first year and flowers and seeds follow in the second.

Botanical name (or scientific name)

The universally accepted name of a plant, often in Latin, as defined by the *International Code of Botanical Nomenclature*. While a plant can be known by more than one "common name", it has a single botanical name.

Bracts

Modified leaves that grow just below the flower of a plant. While bracts are usually green, they sometimes resemble a flower, eg. dogwood and poinsettia.

Broadleaf evergreen

A tree or shrub that retains its green foliage year round, but is not an evergreen conifer.

Bud

A tightly closed shoot, blossom or leaf of a plant, before it starts to grow. Deciduous trees provide a good example, their buds emerging in autumn or early spring and growing into leaves or new shoots in spring and summer.

Bulb

A bulb is a storage organ, usually underground. Each bulb contains a whole, small plant.

Calliper

The diameter of the trunk of a tree.

Chlorosis

Chlorosis is evident when the green colour of a plant (usually the leaves) decreases leaving a yellow or white appearance. This often occurs when nutrients are lacking, but may also be caused by a virus. If left unattended, browning of the foliage and death of the plant will likely follow.

Climate

The weather conditions and environment of a region, including temperature, precipitation, wind and sun exposure.

Common name

A popularly known name of a plant. A plant can be known by several common names, as opposed to only one botanical name.

Compost

1. (*The process*) The careful layering of biodegradable materials to produce a growing medium. Decomposition results in a mixture of ingredients full of nutrients that can be used to augment existing soil, can be spread as a mulch, or be used as a growing medium in pots or containers.

2. (*The substance*) An organic growing medium.

Cone

The fruit of a coniferous tree.

Conifer

A tree or shrub that is usually evergreen, with needle-like or scale-like foliage. It often produces seed within a cone. *Ginkgo*, an exception, is a conifer with deciduous leaves. The larch (*Larix*) is another tree that does not conform to the rule as it is a conifer that loses its needles.

Corm

A thickened underground stem that acts as a plant storage organ. The *Crocus* provides an example.

Crown

1. The spot where the stem and the roots join on a perennial, tree or shrub. It is from this point that the roots grow.

2. It can also refer to the entire branch structure of a tree, including foliage.

Cultivar

A specific plant variety created through cultivation. In the *Plant Encyclopaedia*, cultivars are indicated with single quotation marks.

Cutting

A small section removed from a plant, usually taken for the purpose of propagation.

Dead-heading

The removal of dead flowers from a plant. This prevents the plant from manufacturing seed and encourages the production of more flowers.

Deciduous

The term refers mainly to trees and shrubs that drop their leaves at the end of the growing season.

Dieback

This usually refers to the dead tips or ends of a plant. An example is a tree with a virus. Branch tips will die before the rest of the tree. Winter conditions can also cause dieback.

Dormant

The resting period between growing seasons, usually during the autumn and winter. A dormant plant appears as though it has stopped growing.

Dust (insecticidal)

Insecticidal dust is used to kill certain insects on plants. The dust comes in a soft plastic container that is aimed at a plant and squeezed gently so that the dust will puff out in a cloud and cover the targeted plant or leaf area.

Espalier

A style of pruning and training a tree against a wall or fence, characterized by the horizontal growth pattern of the branches.

Essential nutrients

Nutritional elements required by plants in order for them to complete their life cycles. There are three categories of essential nutrients:

Major Nutrients:	Nitrogen (N)
	Phosphorus (P)
	Potassium (K)
Secondary Nutrients:	Calcium (C)
	Magnesium (Mg)
	Sulphur (S)
Micronutrients:	Boron (B)
	Chlorine (Cl)
	Cobalt (Co)
	Copper (Cu)
	Iron (Fe)
	Manganese (Mn)
	Molybdenum (Mo)
	Zinc (Zn)

Evergreen

A tree or shrub that retains most of its foliage throughout the year or, at least, never loses all of it at one time, as do deciduous plants.

Eye

1. An immature growth bud.
2. The centre of a flower.

Falls

The outer petals of an iris, that bend downwards.

Family name

The name given to a group of related plants (genus). The family name generally ends in *aceae*, eg. the family name, or genus, of maple trees is *Aceraceae*.

Fertilization

The joining of pollen and undeveloped seed, resulting in the formation of a mature seed.

Fertilizers

Material added to the soil, containing specific nutrients that add to the soil composition. Fertilizer can be organic or inorganic.

Flats

The trays or multi-packs that contain the bedding plants for sale at nurseries.

Flower

The specialized part of a plant, often colourful, that contains the sexual organs of the plant.

Flowers attract insects that serve to pollinate the plant and ensure its reproduction.

Forcing

The hastening of a plant into bloom, by controlling growing conditions, usually by simulating the passing of the seasons in an accelerated manner.

Fruit

The mature ovary of a plant, containing ripe seeds. Fruit can take the form of dry pods, capsules or soft members.

Fungicide

A chemical used to kill fungal disease, often containing copper or sulphur.

Gall

An abnormal growth on a plant.

Genus

A botanical name given to a group or family of plants that are similar in appearance.

Germination

The first stage of development of a plant grown from a seed.

Grafting

A method of propagation where a stem or bud is united with a root or trunk, often used with regard to ornamental and fruit trees.

Ground cover

Plants grown to cover the soil, often forming a dense blanket of growth that weeds cannot penetrate. Ground covers are often planted under large trees or hedges, or on slopes to control erosion.

Half-hardy

This term refers to a plant that will survive an average winter in a specified zone, but is likely to die during an unusually severe winter or if it is planted in a cold, unsheltered spot.

Harden off

To harden off means to slowly introduce a plant to a new location, especially if the new plant has been in a greenhouse environment before being planted outside. This is done to avoid subjecting the plant to shock.

Heeling in

The temporary planting of a plant or covering of its roots with soil to maintain moisture until such a time as the plant can be permanently planted. Usually, the plant is just laid in a hollow and the roots covered with soil.

Herbaceous

A plant that does not form a woody stem or trunk.

Honeydew

A sticky excretion from insects that suck the juice from plants. Aphids are well known for the honeydew they leave behind.

Humus

The material obtained when vegetable matter, like leaves and grass clippings, has been broken down. It is the substance resulting from the last stage of decomposition.

Hybrid

A plant resulting from the joining or deliberate crossing of two specific varieties of a given species or even between two plants of different botanical families. Generally, each parent plant has distinctive favourable characteristics and hybridizing them will result in a plant exhibiting the positive characteristics of both. Plants grown from seeds produced by a hybrid will not necessarily exactly resemble the hybrid. The characteristics of one parent plant may dominate. For this reason, hybrids are best propagated by taking cuttings.

Inorganic matter

Matter that is not now and never was living. Examples in the garden are rocks and sand.

Insecticide

A chemical used to kill insects. Many forms are available.

Larva

The caterpillar or grub stage of an insect that will ultimately turn into a butterfly or moth (pl. larvae).

Leader

The main stem of a shrub or tree that extends beyond all others.

Leaching

When water drains through the soil it removes or "leaches" soluble nutrients from it.

Lime

Calcium used to bring the pH level of soil closer to a neutral state.

Manure

Organic matter added to the soil in order to increase its fertility. Manure can be obtained from animal matter or dead plant matter.

Microclimate

The environment immediately surrounding a specific plant in the garden, ie. sun and wind exposure and moisture.

Micronutrients

Essential elements in the soil, present in relatively low quantities. See *Essential nutrients*.

Moth

The mature stage of a caterpillar's life cycle. Moths do not harm plants, but caterpillars do, by consuming foliage.

Mulch

Mulch is organic matter spread on the surface of the soil in a layer. Common mulches include peat moss, well-rotted steer manure, compost, mushroom manure, cedar chips, or straw. The use of mulch retards weed growth and reduces soil compaction and moisture evaporation.

Mushroom Manure

A mixture of well-rotted manures (usually horse manure) that has had mushrooms growing in it. The manure mixture is usually free of weeds.

Naturalizing

The spacing of plants, often bulbs, in a random fashion simulating nature.

Neutral

Refers to a soil that is neither acid nor alkaline, with a pH level between 6.5 and 7.0.

Organic matter

Part of a living or once living plant or animal. Examples in the garden are leaves, peat moss and steer manure. As it decomposes it can add nutrients to the soil.

Panicles

Many tiny individual flowers that together form one large flower cluster.

Peat

Organic matter that is partly decomposed. The decomposition has halted, for whatever reason, often because the organic matter is water logged. Peat has little nutrient value, but when added to soil it resumes the decomposition process once more and, consequently, benefits the soil.

Perennial

A plant that lives for an indefinite length of time. The term usually refers to herbaceous plants.

Perlite

A lightweight material, often used instead of sand or grit in soil composition for potted plants. It weighs less than sand and improves drainage.

Petal

A modified leaf, often brightly coloured, that is part of the anatomy of a flower. Petals attract pollinating insects.

pH

A pH scale measures acidity or alkalinity in the soil.

Pinching back

This refers to the removal of the growing tips of plants, often annuals, in order to encourage more branching and produce bushier plants.

Pollen

The male cells of a plant.

Pollination

The transfer of pollen from the stamens to the pistils of a flower results in pollination, necessary for seed formation. Pollination is accomplished through the agency of gravity, wind, insects, animals, birds or even humans.

Potting

Planting a plant into a container filled with soil.

Propagation

This refers to increasing plant numbers from a single plant. It can be done by collecting and sowing seeds or through vegetative means, such as taking cuttings.

Pruning

The controlled cutting and shaping of plants, usually those with woody stems.

Rhizome

An underground stem that acts as a storage organ.

Rootstock

The root of a plant onto which another plant is grafted.

Runner

A type of stem, growing on the surface, that creeps along the ground. Under normal conditions, it roots as it grows along.

Seedling

A young plant after germination.

Shrub

A perennial with woody stems, branching in a natural shape.

Species

The classification name given to a group of specific or closely related plants.

Specimen plant

Usually a tree or shrub that is purposely grown in a spot where it can be viewed from all sides.

Staking

To support a plant by securing it with a stretchy fabric or soft ties, to sticks or canes driven into the ground.

Stress

Any condition, whether environmental, climatic, chemical or organic in nature, that is less than ideal for a plant. A lack of water can be a major stress on a plant. If a plant is under stress, it is more susceptible to disease and insect infestation.

Subgrade

The soil layer immediately below the topsoil. Topsoil is spread overtop.

Succulent

A plant with thick, fleshy leaves containing water that allow the plant to live under particularly dry conditions. Cactus is a succulent.

Sucker

1. A shoot that grows out of the ground, usually from the roots of a tree or shrub, eg. roses.

2. A sucker growing straight up from a branch may also appear if a plant has been pruned excessively, for example, in the case of fruit trees.

Systemic

Chemicals referred to as systemic are chemicals that can be absorbed by any part of a plant and transported throughout its tissues. It is much like taking medication that travels throughout the body. Because of this, when spraying with a systemic, it is not necessary to cover the entire plant with the chemical. Systemic insecticides are used for sucking or chewing insects which feed on juices in plant tissues.

Taproot

The main, anchoring root of a plant.

Tender

Any plant that is susceptible to frost damage.

Tendril

A modified stem or leaf that twines around available support, allowing a plant to climb.

Terminal

The topmost shoot or branch or flower of a plant.

Topdressing

To apply a thin layer of soil or compost over a specific area. It is often used on lawns, in areas that have suffered damage.

Transpiration

The loss of water from plants. This occurs naturally and continually, even in winter.

Transplant

To move plants from one place to another. It is best accomplished during the period when plants are dormant.

Tree

A woody plant with a notable trunk that grows in a vertical fashion.

Trunk

The main stem of a tree, emerging at ground level and soaring up to the point where the first set of branches grows.

Tuber

A thickened fleshy root, like that of a *Dahlia*, or an underground stem, such as a potato, which acts as a storage organ.

Underplant

To plant a smaller plant beneath a larger one, eg. a ground cover.

Variegated

Refers to leaves that display more than one colour. Variegation often takes the form of spotted or blotchy patterns on the surface of leaves.

Variety

A variety is a distinct subspecies of a species of plant. In the *Plant Encyclopaedia*, the variety is represented by the third word in the succession of botanical names.

Vector

A means of transmitting disease from one plant to another. Insects often serve as vectors.

Weed

Any plant growing spontaneously where you do not want it to grow.

Weeping

The term given to the shape of a tree or shrub having pendulous branches.

Xeroscaping

To plan a garden that can survive long periods of drought. Very specific plants are used.

Bibliography

A Gardener's Guide to Pest Prevention and Control in the Home and Garden. Victoria: Province of BC, Ministry of Agriculture and Food, 1986.

Commercial grower catalogue. Adera Nurseries Ltd., Sidney, BC., 1994.

Commercial grower catalogue. Hines Nurseries Ltd., Santa Ana, CA., l994.

Commercial grower catalogue. Monrovia Nurseries Co., Oregon, 1994.

Eggens, Jack. *Qualified Plantsman.* Ministry of Agriculture and Food of Ontario, Ontario, 1990.

Frankton, Clarence and Milligan, Gerald A. *Weeds of Canada.* Canada Department of Agriculture, Ottawa, Ontario, 1977

Garden Pests and Diseases. Simon and Shuster, New York, 1980.

Gault, S. Mollar. *The Color Dictionary of Shrubs.* Crown Publisher Inc., New York, 1976

Goodwin-Wilson, Ralph. *Soils for Horticultural Crops.* University of Guelph, Guelph, Ontario , 1993.

Hauger, J. and Saulbury, D. *Gardenware Computer Software.* Cannon Beach, Oregon, 1992.

Hellyer, Arthur. *The Collingridge Illustrated Encyclopaedia of Gardening.* Collingridge Books, Rushden, Northants, England, 1982.

Hortus Third. Edited by the staff of the Liberty Hyde Bailey Hortorium, Macmillan Publishing Company, New York, 1976.

Integrated Pest Management in British Columbia. Victoria: Pesticide Management Branch, Ministry of Environment, Lands and Parks, May 1992.

Jones, Carolyn. *Bedding Plants.* Whitecap Books, Vancouver/Toronto, 1989.

Perennial Garden Guide. Heritage Perennials, Abbotsford, BC, 1994

Reader's Digest Encyclopaedia of Garden Plants and Flowers. Reader's Digest Association Limited, London New York, 1989.

Sunset Western Garden Book. By the Editors of Sunset Books and Sunset Magazine, Sunset Publishing Corporation, Menlo Park, California, March 1992.

Taylor, Norman. *Shrubs.* Houghton Mifflin Company, Boston, Massachusetts, 1987.

Taylor, Norman. *Trees.* Houghton Mifflin Company, Boston, Massachusetts, 1988.

Taylor, T.M.C. *The Ferns and Fern-allies.* K.M. MacDonald, British Columbia, Canada, 1973.

The Complete Book of Gardening. Michael Wright, ed., Chestergate House, London, 1978.

The Hillier Manual of Trees & Shrubs. By Hillier Nurseries Limited, Redwood Press Ltd., Great Britain, Melksham, Wiltshire, l993.

UBC Guide to Gardening in British Columbia. The Botanical Garden, The Faculty of Agricultural Sciences, The University or British Columbia, Vancouver, 1990.

Photo Credits for Colour Pages

Backyard photographs of scale drawing in Chapter 1

Upper left: Colleen Adam
Middle: Colleen Adam
Bottom: Colleen Adam

Using white in the garden will enhance your other colours

Upper right: Kathy Van Vliet
Middle: Bill Rivard Photography
Bottom: Bill Rivard Photography

Specimen trees can be underplanted with a variety of plant material

Left: Colleen Adam
Middle: Kathy Van Vliet
Bottom: Kathy Van Vliet

Colour for the shade

Above left: Kathy Van Vliet
Above right: Colleen Adam
Above: Colleen Adam
Right: Kathy Van Vliet

Annuals provide continuous summer colour

Left: Colleen Adam
Middle: Colleen Adam
Bottom: Colleen Adam

Plant textures vary

Upper left: Colleen Adam
Middle: Colleen Adam
Left: Colleen Adam

Fall and winter can also be colourful

Upper left: Colleen Adam
Middle: Bill Rivard Photography
Bottom: Calen Darnel © Terra Images

Hard landscape materials

Right: Calen Darnel © Terra Images
Middle: Colleen Adam
Bottom: Colleen Adam

Index

199